First Things First

FIRST THINGS FIRST

*For Inquiring Minds
and Yearning Hearts*

Khalid Baig

open mind press
STANTON • CALIFORNIA

Copyright ©2004 Khalid Baig.
First Edition Jamad-ul-Awwal 1425/July 2004.

All rights reserved. Aside from fair use, meaning a few pages or less for educational purposes, review, or scholarly citation, no part of this publication may be reproduced, stored in a retrieval system or transmitted in any form or by any means electronic, mechanical, photocopying, recording or otherwise, without the prior written permission of the copyright holder.

Published by:
Open Mind Press
P. O. Box 1241
Stanton, CA 90680
www.openmindpress.com

Printed in the United States of America

Library of Congress Control Number: 2004105650

ISBN 0-9755157-0-5

Published in arrangement with Jamiatul Ulama, South Africa.
Exclusive distributor in South Africa:
    Jamiatul Ulama
    P.O. Box 42863, Fordsburg 2033
    South Africa
    www.jamiat.co.za

This book is printed on acid-free paper.

Cover: The inscription on the cover is Arabic calligraphy for *La ilaha illa Allah, Muhammad ur rasool-ulllah*. (There is no god except Allah, Muhammad is the Messenger of Allah.)

To Abbajan and Ammijan who inculcated in me the love for reading and writing.

$$رَبِّ ارْحَمْهُمَا كَمَا رَبَّيَانِي صَغِيرًا$$

To my wife. My partner and supporter whom Allah ﷻ made a means of bringing so many blessings in our lives.

A million gripes against the darkness will not make a dent in it. But a little candle will.

This book is about lighting that little candle.

Contents

Preface — 1
Foreword — 4

BASICS — 7

Reason and Revelation — 9
Belief and Superstition — 13
Allahu Akbar — 18
Kenosis: A Christian Response to Allahu Akbar — 23
Prophets and Books — 31
Joy Forever, Grief Forever — 35
A Look at Hadith Rejecters' Claims — 39

QUR'AN — 51

Qur'an: Witness the Miracle — 53
The Miracle of the Qur'an — 57
Relating to the Qur'an — 62

LOVING THE PROPHET ﷺ — 67

Sall-Allahu Alayhi Wa Sallam ﷺ — 69
Loving the Prophet ﷺ — 73
Be Careful with Muhammad ﷺ — 77

CONTENTS

ACTS OF WORSHIP — 83

The Purpose of Prayer (Du'a)	85
The Key to Paradise	90
The Meaning of Ramadan	94
Zakat	98
The Road from Makkah	103
The Power of Du'a	107

ISLAM IS THE SOLUTION — 111

Better, Try to See the Light	113
Islam is the Solution	117
What Does Islam Teach About Justice?	121
The Message of Mercy	126
On Religious Tolerance	130
On Extremism	134
Whose Islam?	138

THE CHOICE IS YOURS — 143

Lowest of the Low	145
The Choice is Yours	149
The Road to Paradise	154

SELF REFORM — 159

Reward Only from Allah	161
On Intentions and Actions	166
Virtues, Real and Apparent	170
Istighfar: Seeking Forgiveness from Allah	174
Humility in Knowledge and Arrogance in Ignorance	179
Do We Mind Our Language?	183
The Value of Words	187
Good Muslim, Good Human Being	191
No Haya, No Life	195

Taqwa is for Everyone	199
Dhikr: Remembering Allah ﷻ	204
On Arrogance, Ignorance, and Inferiority Complex	209
Time is Life	213
Preparing for Death	217
Natural Disasters: Test, Punishment, or Blessing?	221
Seeking Halal Earning	225
Sunnah and Bid'ah	229
On the Dress Code	233
All Virtues, Big or Small	238
Amr-bil-Maroof	242
What is Tasawwuf?	246

WOMEN AND FAMILY   251

Fair Ladies for the Altar	253
Home, Sweet Home	257
Gold and Glitter	261
For Ever After...	266
Motherhood	270
Your Heaven, Your Hell	274
Parenting Goals and Ideas	279
Bonds of Kinship	283
Educated, Ignorant, and Feminist	287
The Crusade Against Hijab: Then and Now	296
Women's Rights: An Islamic Declaration	300

EDUCATION   305

Seeking Knowledge	307
The Real Purpose of Education	311
What is Wrong with Our Education System?	315

CONTENTS

Unity — 319

Muslim Unity — 321
Islamic Brotherhood — 328
Religious Wars — 333
Kosova: Where Were the Muslims? — 337

Staying the Course — 343

Surviving the Melting Pot — 345
"Not Fearing the Blame…" — 350
Valentine Day, Birthdays, and Other Daze — 354

History — 359

Baghdad — 361
Jerusalem — 364
Christmas — 368

A Second Look — 373

The News Protocol - Toward an Islamic Framework — 375
Islamic Ummah vs the Nation-State — 384
Beyond Elected Government. Just Government — 390
Secularism in France — 394
The Fundraising Dinner — 402
The Myth of Population Crisis — 406
Islamic Renaissance? — 411

Index — 415

Preface

THIS IS A COLLECTION of articles that were originally published in the "First Thing First" column of monthly *Impact International* beginning in December 1995. The idea has been to present Islamic beliefs and practices as well as to highlight Islamic values in the context of current social, cultural, and political discussions. The broad range of topics includes beliefs, acts of worship, self-reform, women, family, unity, democracy, education, and the media. They aim at providing reflection, exposition, inspiration, and intellectual stimulation.

The magazine's format and focus preclude parochial subjects, scholarly treatises, or plain lectures. This has been fortunate for I have no interest in the first, no capability for the second, and no eligibility for the third. However I have benefited from the written and spoken words of many great scholars and tried to make their knowledge and wisdom accessible to the English-speaking world. A couple of articles were condensed directly from Urdu and have been noted as such. Some others were inspired by the works of such luminaries as Maulana Ashraf Ali Thanvi, Maulana Abul Hasan Ali Nadwi, Maulana Manzoor Naumani, Mufti Muhammad Shafi, Mufti Taqi Usmani, and others.

It was Allah's blessing that the articles were received very well. My original assignment was to contribute four articles for this column. But those articles generated interest and the assignment was continued. People liked to share them by

Preface

making photocopies for distribution. Then, as the Internet became the new global wallpaper, people started posting them on their websites too. Some also took the trouble of translating them in other languages. I am aware of translations in Malaysian, Spanish, French, Bosnian, Chinese, and Urdu languages. Some articles have also been reproduced in the Muslim world press like *The News* (Pakistan) and the *Saudi Gazette*. Students and their teachers at high schools, universities, and Islamic religious schools in the English-speaking world have at times found some of the articles helpful in their studies and class discussions.

In preparing the articles for the present book, extensive changes were made. Articles were arranged in sections according to common themes. Original Arabic text and references of quoted Qur'anic verses and ahadith[1] were provided. References for other quotes were also provided in most cases. Footnotes were added. Some articles had references to then recent news items. They were either entirely rewritten or an update was provided. The article on Kenosis was written especially for this book. There are some other articles that were not written for the First Thing First column but have been included here because of their appropriateness.

The sections used to group articles are self-explanatory, with the possible exception of the last one. The common thread in the articles in that section is that they invite the reader to break the mold and take a second look at some commonly held views and practices.

The entire collection was edited to follow a consistent style for spelling and punctuation. In style I have generally followed the Chicago Manual but have also purposely violated it on occasion. For example Chicago suggests writing Mecca instead of Makkah; I enthusiastically disregard that

---

[1] Throughout this book, hadith numbering for the ahadith from the *Sihah Sittah*, *Musnad Ahmed*, and *Muwatta Imam Malik* is according to the Al-Alamiah enumeration.

2

Preface

suggestion. English will have to become more polite and learn to pronounce Islamic names and terms correctly.

My deepest thanks go to Hashir Farooqi sahib, the editor of *Impact*, who started it all in the first place by inviting me to write for the important column in this unique Islamic news and views magazine and graciously tolerated my chronic failure to meet deadlines.

I was asked many times to compile these articles in the form of a book. But it was the persistence and deep interest of Maulana Ebrahim I. Bham of Jamiatul Ulama, Johannesburg, South Africa that made it possible. The Jamiat's help has been invaluable in getting this book published. I am grateful to them for this.

The hard work of typesetting and producing the camera-ready copy from the original articles was carried out by my children, especially by Muneeb and Areeba. They inserted Qur'anic verses, searched for and added Arabic text of ahadith, produced the index, designed the cover, and offered me every assistance I needed in editing the book. Without their youthful energy and enthusiasm this book could not have seen the light of day.

And I am most indebted to my wife who gave up a promising medical career to take care of the home. In addition to managing a home where this book was possible, she also directly helped with it by proposing ideas, searching for background material, and offering feedback.

Finally, a request to the reader: If you find something beneficial here, please remember me in your prayers. And if you find an error please inform me so it can be corrected.

May Allah ﷻ accept this humble effort and richly reward all those who helped in its compilation and publication.

Khalid Baig

Jamad-ul-Awwal 1425
June 2004

Foreword

THE GREAT MASTER of Urdu ghazal poetry, Mirza Asadullah Khan Ghalib (1797-1869), famously said that even if the discourse was about God, to know Him, and to relate with Him, it is hard to avoid mundane metaphors, liquor and glass. Such is the power of metaphor.

What Khalid Baig has done is to turn around the metaphor itself. You may be talking about anything but God, not excluding the mundane, but there is no way to avoid or escape His powerful and comforting omnipresence. Where would one be if there was no God?

This is not a textbook on Islam; it is a text that tries to take a look at some contemporary Muslim concerns, from culture and history to family and population, politics and international relations, as well as beliefs and values that inform or ought to inform all our thoughts and endeavors. The idea is to put the metaphor of Islam back into life.

The Islamic discourse is premised on the inborn goodness of human nature, *fitra*, and although the FTF's[2] primary readership is naturally Muslim, its message is universal and inclusive. One doesn't have to be a Muslim, let alone an eager and earnest Muslim, to be able to read and reflect on the simple and day to day truisms of life we tend to pass by rather unthinkingly. FTF encourages readers to think straight and to think for themselves.

---

[2] FTF: "First Thing First".

Foreword

I am, therefore, little surprised and indeed gratified that FTF is the most popular and must-read feature article of *Impact*. The reward is Khalid Baig's, though the gift is there to be shared by everyone. *Allahumma zid fazid* اللهم زد فزد - May Allah ﷻ enhance him in knowledge.

Muhammad Hashir Farooqi
Editor, *Impact International*

Basics

In this section:

- Reason and Revelation
- Belief and Superstition
- Allahu Akbar
- Kenosis: A Christian Response to Allahu Akbar
- Prophets and Books
- Joy Forever, Grief Forever
- A Look at Hadith Rejecters' Claims

Reason and Revelation

AMERICAN ECONOMIST Robert Samuelson once made an interesting observation about the American society in his *Newsweek* column: "America's glories and evils are tightly fused together."[3] Quoting sociologist Seymour Lipset, he asserted that America's economic vitality and progress came from the same source as did crime, family breakdown, inequality, and vulgarity. Freedom and individualism had fired economic advance, yet had also inhibited social control. But why the qualities that bring the best in a nation also should bring the worst in it? Is humanity doomed by having its vices and virtues so intricately mixed?

Samuelson does not probe the issue. Instead he seems to be happily resigned to it. "We are burdened as well as blessed by our beliefs," he says. Economics, we may be reminded, is the dismal science.

Actually the world is not doomed by design. Samuelson comes very close to the truth but he confuses approaches or tools with attributes. A tool that works great in one area is also being used in another for which it was never designed. The problem lies with the user who keeps on insisting on its use in the second area citing its success in the first. To put

---

[3]Robert Samuelson, "The Vices of Our Virtues," *Newsweek*, 11 March 1996

matters simply, it's the free use of reason and intellect that is behind most of America's (and the West's in general) phenomenal scientific and material progress. It's the use of the same tool in moral and religious life that has caused its equally phenomenal moral degeneration!

Every tool has a designated area of application. Outside, it will fail to work. A 4 bit computer is good for some elementary math involving whole numbers. It may multiply 2 by 20 and give the correct answer instantly. But burdened with complex calculations involving several decimal digits, it will give the *wrong* answers. A weighing scale meant for gold will not work for iron and vice versa. Their resolution and capacity are inappropriate for those applications.

Same with the tools we use for learning about the world. Our senses and intellect are wonderful things. Science and technology are all about their use. Certainly it was free inquiry driven by reason that led to so many of the discoveries of science. It happened at an accelerated pace during the past four centuries and the results are everywhere around us to be seen.

But a tool that is so great in one area may be totally useless, even dangerous, in another. Pure reason, uninformed by Divine guidance, is a defective tool for deciding the purpose of life or suggesting its values. What is Right and what is Wrong? These questions require knowledge beyond what we can acquire by using our senses and reasoned analysis. As a direct result, everyone's reasoning is different. That is why philosophers have never been able to agree upon what should be the goal of life. Happiness? Survival? Pleasure? Love? Self-fulfillment? You name it. In addition, it is impossible for us to separate our reasoning in these matters from our feelings. Pure or uninformed reason becomes just a tool to justify what we desire.

Today the West's problem is that it has accepted the wrong tool for developing its moral compass. Probably the majority of its people abhor homosexuality. They may know that it is an abomination and evil. Yet today same-sex marriages are getting legal sanction in the West. And they are helpless in trying to stop its advances. Why? Because they cannot argue that it is wrong based on pure reason. It is easier to make a case against smoking in public places, then against the worst forms of immorality. Such is the result when pure reason becomes the accepted arbiter of right and wrong.

There is nothing modern about this either. Several centuries ago, Obaidullah Hasan Qirwani, a leader of the renegade *Batani* cult declared it foolish for a brother to marry away his beautiful sister to a total stranger, while trying to be content with a less qualified wife—another stranger. She would be much more suited to be wife of her own brother, with whom she may be a lot more compatible, he argued. His argument is, no doubt, sickening. But is there a counter argument based on pure reason?

Certainly mankind needs a superior tool for determining the values and purpose of life. A source of guidance that is based on certain knowledge, not conjecture. One that can inform our desires rather than being subservient to them. This is what Prophets, *alayhim-us-salam*[4] عليهم السلام, came with. They claimed to have access to the higher source of knowledge, the Divine Revelation. Those who accepted them used reason and observation to verify their authenticity and character. But they accepted Divine Revelation as a *superior* source of knowledge! That is why a son[5] can tell his father:

$$\text{يَٰٓأَبَتِ إِنِّى قَدْ جَآءَنِى مِنَ ٱلْعِلْمِ مَا لَمْ يَأْتِكَ فَٱتَّبِعْنِىٓ أَهْدِكَ صِرَٰطًا سَوِيًّا ۝}$$

"O my father! To me has come knowledge that had not reached you. So follow me. I will guide you to a Way that is even and straight." [Maryam, 19:43]

---

[4] Upon them be peace.
[5] Prophet Ibrahim (Abraham) عليه السلام

11

BASICS

All this is obvious, except in implications. We accept this is right and that is wrong because the Revelation *told* us, not because it *proved* it to us. What is wrong with *riba*? Gambling? Pork? Alcohol? Revelation told us that they were wrong. Why is *hijab* necessary? Allah ﷻ[6] and His Prophet ﷺ[7] ordered that. What are the rights of men and women? Those given to them by Allah ﷻ and His Prophet ﷺ. The attribute of Muslims is that they "listened and followed."[8] It is not that they listened and questioned, and argued, and investigated and then if they felt like it, they followed. That is also the message of Prophet Ibrahim's ﷺ[9] sacrifice, a defining event for Islam. For the Qur'an describes the moment when the father and son were ready for the ultimate sacrifice, by saying, "When they surrendered."[10] Literally it can also be translated, "When they accepted Islam." For pure reason could have raised a million questions about the command for that sacrifice.

Normally it is difficult for us to say, "I don't know." It is even more difficult for nations to admit a weakness in their celebrated tools of inquiry. That is the dilemma of the modern world, which sees so much wrong with itself but cannot bring itself to admitting the problem with its basic approach. But a Muslim is the person who has both the wisdom and the courage to surrender before the higher source of knowledge and guidance. For him Revelation informs his reason and his reason controls his emotions. Such is the person who is blessed, but not burdened, by his beliefs.

---

[6] *Subhanahu wa ta'la:* Glory to Him, and He is the Most High.
[7] *Sall-Allahu alayhi wa sallam*: Allah's blessings and peace upon him.
[8] Al-Baqarah, 2:285
[9] *Alayhi salam:* upon him be peace.
[10] As-Saffat, 37:103

Belief and Superstition

وَمَا تَدْرِى نَفْسٌ مَّاذَا تَكْسِبُ غَدًا

"No soul knows what it will earn tomorrow." [Luqman, 31:34]

مَنْ أَتَى كَاهِنًا أَوْ عَرَّافًا فَصَدَّقَهُ بِمَا يَقُولُ فَقَدْ كَفَرَ بِمَا أُنْزِلَ عَلَى مُحَمَّدٍ صَلَّى اللَّهُ عَلَيْهِ وَسَلَّمَ

"The person who goes to a diviner or fortune-teller and believes in him has rejected that which was revealed to Muhammad ﷺ." [*Musnad Ahmed*, Hadith 9171]

THE PRESIDENT OF an American company informs his anxious employees that they are about to get a big contract that will ensure jobs for coming years. Then he adds, "Knock on wood." If things are more uncertain, he will say, "Keep your fingers crossed." Keeping fingers crossed is expected to ward off evil. Knocking on wood is meant to bring good luck by enlisting the support of spirits that according to the ancient pagan Druids lived in trees. There are US Air Force crews who insist on touching or knocking on trees before taking off.

The fear of the number thirteen is so pervasive in the United States and Europe that there is a term for it: triskaidekaphobia. American presidents Herbert Hoover and Franklin Roosevelt avoided eating at tables where 13 people were present. Many tall buildings avoid having a 13th floor or room number 13. According to one report published in 1990, this fear costs America more than a billion dollars a year in absenteeism, travel cancellations, and drop in trade on the 13th of the month. Of course, it is the horror of horrors if the 13th of a month were to fall on a Friday. (This has a Christian root; thirteen is reportedly the number of people who sat at the Last Supper on the night Judas betrayed Jesus and it was a Friday!)

Welcome to the postmodern, post-enlightenment, neo-pagan civilization. Superstition is alive and well here. In a big city like Los Angeles or New York, one can find thousands of palm-readers, tarot-card readers, and astrologers who even have professional associations and certification programs. Daily horoscopes are an indispensable part of even the most prestigious newspapers. Every year as the year ends, big names in the prediction business make big headlines—and millions of dollars—telling the world what will happen in the coming year.

Superstitions are as old as darkness itself. Fear of the unknown and inability to control or predict our own future have led people to all kinds of irrational acts and beliefs. But that was during the Dark Ages. In the age of science and technology that was supposed to end. The *Britannica* notes, "Being irrational, it [superstition] should recede before education, and especially Science." That did not happen.

So the experts have chosen to do the second best thing: put a happy face on their defeat by giving "scholarly" explanations. The *Americana* recognizes superstitions as part of being human. It calls it folklore. "Plainly, despite supposed sophistications, human beings are all the folk and thus are—the source of folklore." It goes on to quote American anthropologist Melville Herskovits as saying: "All human custom is meaningful; nothing without some living value survives in any culture."

Such fancy rationalization cannot hide the fact that belief in the irrational is a direct result of lack of belief in the All Knowledgeable, All-Powerful God who controls everything. He created this vast universe and it is running according to His plan. Not a leaf falls from a tree or a droplet of water from the sky except through His Will.

We do not know what will happen to us tomorrow, but He does. We put our trust in Him, seek His protection and help, and accept His Will. The person lacking this awareness will endlessly take omens from cats, birds, and mice; sticks and greasy stones; the sun and stars; or itching in one's body.

The Arabs were as superstitious as anyone before Islam. They would not undertake a journey or do anything important without first "determining" that it would be safe to do so—by looking at birds and beasts. If a bird flew from right to left in front of them, that was a bad omen; flight in the other direction was a good omen. During travel, if a deer crossed going from right to left, the trip was cancelled. When they reached a destination, they would seek protection of jinn by supplicating to them. Yet, such deeply held beliefs and practices were uprooted completely by Islam in a very short period.

Much later, weakening of faith in segments of Muslim societies did lead to superstitious practices seeping in from other societies. Weakening of our understanding of—and belief in—the articles of faith inevitably leads to superstitions of one form or another. That, unfortunately, is the situation of large segments of our *Ummah* today.

The illiterate masses may go to a soothsayer who tells the future with the help of a bird. The western educated elite of their country laugh at their ignorant ways, yet depend on horoscopes, sayings of Nostradamus, and predictions of Jane Dixon. Both are equally ignorant and equally involved in unbelief!

There is no doubt that a believer faces the same uncertainties in life as a non-believer, but he faces them with the help of Allah ﷻ. When announcing a plan, he does not knock on wood; he says *Insha-Allah* (if Allah wills), putting his trust in his Creator. When embarking on a journey, he makes supplication to Allah ﷻ for his safety. When he is unsure about a plan, he seeks Allah's help in making up his mind. Here is the hadith teaching the beautiful *du'a* of *Istikharah* for this purpose:

عَنْ جَابِرِ بْنِ عَبْدِ اللهِ قَالَ كَانَ رَسُولُ اللهِ صَلَّى اللهُ عَلَيْهِ وَسَلَّمَ يُعَلِّمُنَا الإِسْتِخَارَةَ فِي الأُمُورِ كُلِّهَا كَمَا يُعَلِّمُنَا السُّورَةَ مِنَ الْقُرْآنِ يَقُولُ إِذَا هَمَّ أَحَدُكُمْ بِالأَمْرِ فَلْيَرْكَعْ رَكْعَتَيْنِ مِنْ غَيْرِ الْفَرِيضَةِ ثُمَّ لِيَقُلْ اللَّهُمَّ إِنِّي أَسْتَخِيرُكَ بِعِلْمِكَ وَأَسْتَقْدِرُكَ بِقُدْرَتِكَ وَأَسْأَلُكَ مِنْ فَضْلِكَ الْعَظِيمِ فَإِنَّكَ تَقْدِرُ وَلَا أَقْدِرُ وَتَعْلَمُ وَلَا أَعْلَمُ وَأَنْتَ عَلَّامُ الْغُيُوبِ اللَّهُمَّ إِنْ كُنْتَ تَعْلَمُ أَنَّ هَذَا الأَمْرَ خَيْرٌ لِي فِي دِينِي وَمَعِيشَتِي وَعَاقِبَةِ أَمْرِي أَوْ قَالَ فِي عَاجِلِ أَمْرِي وَآجِلِهِ فَيَسِّرْهُ لِي ثُمَّ بَارِكْ لِي فِيهِ وَإِنْ كُنْتَ تَعْلَمُ أَنَّ هَذَا الأَمْرَ شَرٌّ لِي فِي دِينِي وَمَعِيشَتِي وَعَاقِبَةِ أَمْرِي أَوْ قَالَ فِي عَاجِلِ أَمْرِي وَآجِلِهِ فَاصْرِفْهُ عَنِّي وَاصْرِفْنِي عَنْهُ وَاقْدُرْ لِي الْخَيْرَ حَيْثُ كَانَ ثُمَّ أَرْضِنِي بِهِ قَالَ وَيُسَمِّي حَاجَتَهُ

Sayyidna Jabir bin Abdullah ؓ reports: "The Messenger ﷺ used to teach us *Istikharah* the same way he taught us chapters from the Qur'an. He said: 'When one of you faces a major decision, he should offer two units of voluntary salat and then he should say: O Allah! I seek Your guidance (in making a choice) by virtue of Your knowledge, and I seek ability by virtue of Your power, and I ask You of Your great bounty. You have power, I have none. And You know, I know not. You are the Knower of hidden things.

'O Allah! If in Your knowledge, this matter is good for my religion, my livelihood, and my affairs; immediate and in the distant future, then ordain it for me, make it easy for me, and bless it for me. And if in Your knowledge, this matter is bad for my religion, my livelihood, and my affairs; immediate and in the distant future, then turn it away from me, and turn me away from it. And ordain for me the good wherever it be and make me pleased with it.'" (He should mention his need.) [*Tirmidhi*, Hadith 442]

Each word of this du'a invites reflection. It shows how uncertainties in our life bring us closer to Allah ﷻ. In Allah ﷻ we put all our hopes, not in the cryptic words of an ignorant astrologer or soothsayer.

It is not the human destiny to be afflicted with superstitions; it is just an evil consequence of unbelief. The light of Islam can cure it.

Allahu Akbar

ALLAHU AKBAR. ALLAH is the Greatest. These are the first words a Muslim child hears after entering this world. The father makes the call to prayer in his or her ears as the welcome-to-this-world message. The same call is heard wherever there are Muslims, five times a day. The prayers (salat) also begin with this pronouncement. Certainly this is the symbol, the cornerstone, as it were, of Islam. There is no power in the world equal to the power of the One God. Allah is the Greatest.

This has been the Islamic message right from the beginning. The very first *surah* (chapter) to be revealed to Prophet Muhammad ﷺ was Surah Mudathir. And it contains the command: "And thy Lord, do thou magnify."[11] The Arabic word is *kabbir*. Declare Allahu Akbar. Announce that Allah is the Greatest.

The pagans of Arabia did not like it. The Jews and Christians were not happy with it either. The irony is that at the same time all of them professed belief in the statement. The pagans believed in many gods, but did believe in the Supreme God too. They claimed authority for their smaller gods, but did not claim them to be bigger than Allah ﷻ. Jews

---

[11] Al-Muddathir, 74:3

and Christians clearly believed in God, the Creator and Lord of the universe. With the exception of a small group of atheists, that remains valid until today, as the US dollar bill announces to the whole world: "In God we trust." The question is, then, why should anyone have a problem with Allahu Akbar? Why feel uneasy with it or feel threatened by it? Is it not saying the same thing that they already agree with? The answer lies in the Islamic concept of God.

In the western literature, God is presented as a wise man. (To the feminists He is increasingly a She.) To the mathematician-philosopher, He may be a super mathematician or even a differential equation. To the scientist, He is the First cause that jumpstarted this universe, which is now running on its own. To all of them, He is a good subject for a hobby but is irrelevant to our day-to-day affairs. As one scientist puts it, "I subscribe to Einstein's religion. It's an oceanic feeling; there's that great big thing out there that's pretty marvelous." Thing?

Einstein, who reportedly considered himself spiritual but not religious, said, "I want to know how God created this world." The implication is that He did it once. I am studying and conquering His universe now. But for intellectual curiosity it will be good to learn a little more about Him. "He may have created the laws of nature but since creation He has left them pretty much alone. He does not come in and tweak them any more."

A people's concept of God is the first place to look for to get an idea of the corruption that their religion has gone through. Now let us compare the above confusions with Islam's declaration of an All Knowing, All Powerful God who created the Universe and who is running it every second. His attributes are best described in the well-known *ayatul-kursi*. Look at this marvelously profound declaration that is beyond any human's capacity to compose but within everyone's ability to feel:

BASICS

$$\text{اللَّهُ لَا إِلَٰهَ إِلَّا هُوَ الْحَيُّ الْقَيُّومُ ۚ لَا تَأْخُذُهُ سِنَةٌ وَلَا نَوْمٌ ۚ لَّهُ مَا فِي السَّمَاوَاتِ وَمَا فِي الْأَرْضِ ۗ مَن ذَا الَّذِي يَشْفَعُ عِندَهُ إِلَّا بِإِذْنِهِ ۚ يَعْلَمُ مَا بَيْنَ أَيْدِيهِمْ وَمَا خَلْفَهُمْ ۖ وَلَا يُحِيطُونَ بِشَيْءٍ مِّنْ عِلْمِهِ إِلَّا بِمَا شَاءَ ۚ وَسِعَ كُرْسِيُّهُ السَّمَاوَاتِ وَالْأَرْضَ ۖ وَلَا يَئُودُهُ حِفْظُهُمَا ۚ وَهُوَ الْعَلِيُّ الْعَظِيمُ}$$

"Allah! There is no god but He, the Living, the Eternal, Supporter of all. Neither slumber nor sleep can seize Him. His are all things in the heavens and on earth. Who is he that intercedes with Him except by His leave? He knows that which is in front of them and that which is behind them, while they encompass nothing of His knowledge except what He wills. His throne extends over the heavens and the earth and He is never weary of preserving them. He is the Most High, the Supreme." [Al-Baqarah, 2:255]

What a tremendously empowering creed! From the smallest to the largest, everything in the universe depends on Him. He depends on none. All other powers are illusory. His is the only real Power. When He is on our side, we need not fear anyone. If He is not pleased with us, the support of the whole world for us will be for naught. Worldly powers try to manipulate people by telling them what they can do *for* them and what they can do *to* them. But a person informed by Allahu Akbar will not be tempted by the first or intimidated by the second. The power of "world powers" evaporates before the shouts of Allahu Akbar. In fact there is no empowerment outside this belief, and no enslavement to other humans with it! We can see why the claimants to power in this world may be threatened by it.

What a tremendously liberating creed! It liberates us from slavery to our own desires also. His knowledge is unlimited. Ours is extremely limited. What can we do except follow His commands? He is watching us all the time. We cannot get away with disobedience because of His oversight. He will judge us and no one will be able to intercede on our behalf except with His permission. We can see why those who are afraid of accountability may be threatened by it.

What a tremendously humbling creed! It reminds us of our humble station in life with respect to God. As the Qur'an says at another place,

$$\text{إِنَّ ٱلَّذِينَ يُجَٰدِلُونَ فِىٓ ءَايَٰتِ ٱللَّهِ بِغَيْرِ سُلْطَٰنٍ أَتَىٰهُمْ إِن فِى صُدُورِهِمْ إِلَّا كِبْرٌ مَّا هُم بِبَٰلِغِيهِ}$$

"Those who dispute about the Signs of Allah without any authority bestowed on them, there is nothing in their hearts except the quest of greatness, which they will never attain." [Ghafir, 40:56]

We can see why those with arrogance may be threatened by it.

This includes the arrogance of science. We see it in the scientist who declares that there is no need to invoke a spiritual hand of God since everything has a rational basis. Or the medical doctor who thinks that he can control the biological processes. (Remember the genetic engineering pundits, euthanasia advocates, and population control gurus?) On the other hand, a scientist free of such sickness looks at the workings of this universe, the great design in it, and the tremendous purpose in every creation. And he finds himself compelled to say: Subhan-Allah. Allahu Akbar. Glory be to Allah. Allah is the Greatest. Similarly a medical doctor constantly finds the Hand of God in the life and death struggles of his patients; some succumb to minor problems, others survive major ones. Allahu Akbar!

BASICS

Allahu Akbar is the weapon that gives us the courage to challenge all subjugation, political or intellectual. It makes us turn our attention to the Creator and ignore other creations like ourselves. In the battlefields of jihad, the power of this weapon has been felt by people on both sides of the conflict. In every conflict the shouts of Allahu Akbar instilled fear in the hearts of the oppressors. It boasted the morale of the mujahideen with new levels of hope and courage. And that is the way it should be. Because Allah is the Greatest.

Kenosis: A Christian Response to Allahu Akbar

THE ARTICLE "ALLAHU AKBAR" (which was originally published in the October 1996 issue of *Impact*) evoked an interesting response from a well-known Christian authority. The *Pontificio Istituto di Studi Arabi e d'Islamistica* in Italy devoted the February 2001 issue of its monthly newsletter *Encounter* to an article by Christian Troll containing that response.

Christian Troll, a member of the Society of Jesus, has lived and worked for many years in the Indian subcontinent as well as in Turkey. He is also author of many books on Islam and recent Muslim history. The *Encounter* editor published the article in the hope that it would "raise points of discussion and dialogue between Christians and Muslims." It did, and here is a Muslim perspective on his response.

After summarizing my article Christian Troll raises the question: "Would one think that it would be possible and advantageous for Christians to formulate a phrase based on a specific concept in Christianity, specifying the real essence of the Christian Message (*den Inbegriff des Christlichen*), as, *mutatis mutandis*, the *shahada* or the invocation Allahu Akbar of Islam?" Or as the editor put it in a sidebar: "Does there exist the possibility, the need, and the desirability or non-desirability for a Christian key exclamation comparable to Allahu Akbar?"

Christian Troll notes that the Christian theology lacks such a formula and sees the desirability of offering one. He then mentions *Kenosis* as a key phrase of Christian faith and proceeds to give a new account of it. Before discussing it a brief background note is in order. *Kenosis* is derived from the Greek word "*kenoo*" which means "to empty." It is used in Phil. 2:7. "Have this attitude in yourselves which was also in Christ Jesus, who, although He existed in the form of God, did not regard equality with God a thing to be grasped, but emptied Himself, taking the form of a bond servant, and being made in the likeness of men. And being found in appearance as a man, He humbled Himself by becoming obedient to the point of death, even death on a cross."[12]

The *kenosis* theory, first introduced in 1860s in Germany by Gottfried Thomasius (1802-75), a Lutheran theologian, was an attempt to solve one of the problems in the incomprehensible idea of Trinity: was Jesus, peace be upon him, man or God? The Catholic claim is that he was both. But how can a person be both man and God? Just like the idea of Trinity[13] itself, this idea (One Person. 100% man, 100% God) also defies logic or comprehension. Here is, for example, contemporary Christian theologian John Knox on the subject: "How can two 'natures' ('each presumably involving consciousness and will') belong to one person inconfusedly, unchangeably, indivisibly, and inseparably…

---

[12] Phil. 2:5-8
[13] "The Father is God, the Son is God, and the Holy Spirit is God, and yet there are not three Gods but one God." Since each is considered an eternal, immutable and sovereign divine person, that clearly adds up to three Gods.

Of no normal human being could such things be truly said."[14]

There are other problems with this belief about the nature of Jesus, peace be upon him. The picture of Jesus, peace be upon him, in the Bible—despite all the distortions in it—is that of a man not of an Omniscient, Omnipotent, Omnipresent, and Immortal God. For example he said, "But of that day or hour no one knows, not even the angels in heaven, nor the son, but the Father alone."[15] Is that the Omniscient God speaking? Further, Jesus, peace be upon him, worshiped and prayed to the Father, even calling Him "The Only True God." There are numerous examples where Jesus, peace be upon him, is subservient to God on earth and in heaven. How could then he be not only God but co-equal with God?

Christian ministers sometimes relate the story of Daniel Webster, a 19th-century American statesman. He was asked, "Can you comprehend how Jesus Christ could be both God and Man?" "No, sir, I cannot understand it," replied Webster, "and I would be ashamed to acknowledge Christ as my Savior if I could comprehend it. He could be no greater than myself, and such is my conviction of accountability to God, my sense of sinfulness before Him, and my knowledge of my own incapacity to recover myself, that I feel I need a superhuman Savior." This is the talk one expects from a politician. But any serious person would be amazed that an idea should be accepted as a tenet of faith precisely because it makes no sense!

So there have been constant efforts to make sense out of it. In fact to a large extent the history of Christian theology is a history of attempts to explain the mysteries of trinity and the nature of Jesus, peace be upon him. It seems that each new attempt has led to the birth of a new denomination. And the answers keep coming—a clear indication that the

---

[14] John Knox. *The Humanity And Divinity Of Christ.* Cambridge: University Press, 1967.
[15] Mark 13:32

previous attempts failed to resolve the issue. Anyway, the answer according to kenosis is that Jesus voluntarily gave up (emptied himself of) some of his divine attributes while he was a man here on earth. These attributes were omniscience, omnipresence, and omnipotence. He did it so that he could function as a man in order to fulfill the work of redemption! The *Kenosis* theory does not resolve the problem, though, because if it were true then it would mean that Jesus was not fully divine, after all. If Jesus was not fully divine, then his atoning work would not be sufficient to atone for the sins of the world. No wonder many Christian authorities have declared kenotic theology to be heresy.

Here Christian Troll resorts to an interesting twist—the idea developed by H-J Lauter, of *kenosis* not of the "Son" but of the "Triune God." This is complex philosophy, and it does not make the incomprehensible any less so. He talks of the "self-giving into each other of the Divine Persons" and comes up with seven modes of divine *kenosis*: "(1) the *Ur-Kenose* in God, which is the generation of the Son and the breathing of the Holy Spirit; (2) the *kenosis* of God in creation which I could detect in relation to the incarnation; (3) towards which it is ordered; (4) the *kenosis* of Christ on the cross; (5) which is sacramentaly continued in the Eucharist; (6) the *kenosis* of the Holy Spirit in the minds and hearts of human beings; (7) the participation of Christians, in spirit and life, in the *kenosis* of Christ."

He then proposes that kenosis means self-sacrificing love and therefore all this can be summarized in an Arabic expression: Allahu mahabbah ("God is Love"?), which "would definitely appear to be a most appropriate phrase to echo from the perspective of Christian faith." Presto! There is a Christian response to Allahu Akbar. Needless to say, it is superior to Allahu Akbar: "When Christian believers again and again hear the call Allahu Akbar from the minaret, they are reminded of the love of God—Allahu mahabbah—revealed in Jesus Christ, the Risen Lord, a love that far exceeds any imaginable greatness."

Kenosis: A Christian Response to Allahu Akbar

It is interesting to see our friend struggle with the response to a simple question: "How do you summarize your creed?" He reminds us of the person who claims that he has the Message of God for you. You are skeptical, seeing that he carries so many conflicting drafts all labeled "Message of God." But he insists that he indeed has nothing but the true Message of God in God's own Words. To end the long argument you finally ask, "Okay, so what it is." And that catches him by surprise. "Hmmm. Now let me think how *I* want to say it."

It is not news that the Muslim proclamation of belief or its key expressions like "Allahu Akbar" are not the result of the efforts by religious leaders, scholars, saints, or intellectuals. They were not formulated in the councils of elders or on the orders of kings. Islam is the Last Message of Allah for the entire humanity, sent through His Last Messenger ﷺ. He sent the Book that remains the only Revealed Book that exists in the original language of its revelation. He sent the Messenger ﷺ whose entire life remains visible to us in all its historic details. And all the tenets of faith and key expressions describing the Message of Islam came to us directly from Allah ﷻ and His Prophet ﷺ. Islam is *not* a man-made religion. Allahu Akbar.

For the Muslim the process of coming up with the theological positions in Christianity is also very interesting. None of the components of the *kenotic* theory can be found in the verses that it is claimed to be based on. Phil. 2:5-8 does not say that Jesus gave up the divine attributes of omniscience, omnipresence, and omnipotence; that he did so temporarily while he was a man here on earth; that he did it so that he could function as a man in order to fulfill the work of redemption. All of that (and a lot more, as there are so many varying and conflicting accounts of what *kenosis* means) has been supplied by the theologians!

Contrast this with Islam's simple, unambiguous, and extremely powerful declaration: "There is no god but Allah, Muhammad ﷺ is the Prophet of Allah." There is no mystery here nor any complex philosophy. God is One, the Eternal. He is the Creator and the entire universe and everything in it is His Creation. The Qur'an makes this very clear at numerous places. Listen to this for example:

$$\text{وَقُلِ ٱلْحَمْدُ لِلَّهِ ٱلَّذِى لَمْ يَتَّخِذْ وَلَدًا وَلَمْ يَكُن لَّهُۥ شَرِيكٌ فِى ٱلْمُلْكِ وَلَمْ يَكُن لَّهُۥ وَلِىٌّ مِّنَ ٱلذُّلِّ ۖ وَكَبِّرْهُ تَكْبِيرًا}$$

"And say: Praise be to Allah, Who has not taken unto Himself a son, and Who has no partner in the Sovereignty, nor has He any protecting friend through dependence. And magnify Him with all magnificence." [Al-Israa, 17:111]

A man may logically seek help from his juniors, equals, or seniors. This verse rejects all three possibilities for Allah ﷻ. Man is weak and needs help from children. To attribute a son to Allah ﷻ is to attribute a weakness to Him that no amount of philosophizing will hide. But Allah ﷻ is above such dependence. And He has no partners and equals. It is also absurd to talk about God humiliating himself before any other person as some Christian explanations of Christ's alleged sacrifice suggest. The response to the command at the end of the verse is that Allah ﷻ is the Greatest.[16] Allahu Akbar.

Allah ﷻ has many, many attributes as His ninety-nine names mentioned in the Qur'an reveal. He is the Most

---

[16] *Encounter* notes that Allahu Akbar literally translates into Allah is Greater. That is incorrect. In Arabic the same word is used for the superlative and the comparative forms and its usage and context determine which one is meant. Normally an explicit 'min' (than) is used when comparative form is intended. For example in "Ithmuhuma akbaru min nafihima" (their sin is greater than their benefit). Here the reference is absolute. In other words Allahu Akbar means Allahu Akbaru min kulli shai. Allah is Greater than everything. Or in simple English, Allah is the Greatest.

Beneficent, the Most Merciful, Kind, All-Knowing, All Powerful, The Wise, The Creator and the Provider for all His creations. He is the Lord and Master of the Universe. He loves the believers and they love Him. He forgives the sins and accepts repentance. Who are we to decide which of His attributes is more important than the others? There is only one way of summarizing His total Supremacy: by admitting that He is the Greatest. Allahu Akbar is not the negation of any of the other attributes of Allah ﷻ, as Troll incorrectly assumes, but a simultaneous affirmation of all of them.

We also invite everyone to ponder over these verses, which follow the verse quoted above.

$$\text{ٱلْحَمْدُ لِلَّهِ ٱلَّذِى أَنزَلَ عَلَىٰ عَبْدِهِ ٱلْكِتَٰبَ وَلَمْ يَجْعَل لَّهُۥ عِوَجَا ۜ ۝ قَيِّمًا لِّيُنذِرَ بَأْسًا شَدِيدًا مِّن لَّدُنْهُ وَيُبَشِّرَ ٱلْمُؤْمِنِينَ ٱلَّذِينَ يَعْمَلُونَ ٱلصَّٰلِحَٰتِ أَنَّ لَهُمْ أَجْرًا حَسَنًا ۝ مَّٰكِثِينَ فِيهِ أَبَدًا ۝ وَيُنذِرَ ٱلَّذِينَ قَالُوا۟ ٱتَّخَذَ ٱللَّهُ وَلَدًا ۝ مَّا لَهُم بِهِۦ مِنْ عِلْمٍ وَلَا لِءَابَآئِهِمْ ۚ كَبُرَتْ كَلِمَةً تَخْرُجُ مِنْ أَفْوَٰهِهِمْ ۚ إِن يَقُولُونَ إِلَّا كَذِبًا ۝}$$

"Praise be to Allah, Who has sent to His Servant the Book, and has allowed therein no Crookedness. (He has made it) Straight (and Clear) in order that He may warn (the godless) of a terrible Punishment from Him, and that He may give Glad Tidings to the Believers who work righteous deeds, that they shall have a goodly Reward. Wherein they shall remain forever. Further, that He may warn those (also) who say, 'Allah has begotten a son.' They have no knowledge of it, nor had their fathers; a grievous word it is that comes out of their mouths; they speak nothing but a lie." [Al-Kahf, 18:1-5]

BASICS

Jesus (Sayyidna Isa ﷺ) was a great prophet of Allah ﷻ. His miraculous birth without a father became a test for both Jews and Christians. The Jews denied the miracle, declared him to be a criminal, and tried to kill him. The Christians, on the other hand, elevated him to the rank of God, thereby creating a theological mess that only grows with each attempt to clear it. This, despite the fact that they had been clearly commanded to believe in One God only, Who has no partners. In between the two extremes, stand the clear teachings of Islam showing the Straight Path.

Whether the question is about the nature of God or that of Jesus, peace be upon him, or about the requirements for our salvation, anyone who studies the Christian discourses on the subject, with their mysteries and infinite complexities, will immediately find enlightenment in the simple but profound teachings of Islam. He will find the Qur'anic verses speaking to him directly, removing all mysteries, resolving the apparently unsolvable issues, and moving him from darkness into light. And he will find himself saying out of deep gratitude and awe: Alhamdulillah. Allahu Akbar.

Prophets and Books

ACCORDING TO A REPORT in the *Musnad Ahmed* collection of hadith, Prophet Muhammad ﷺ said: "From Adam to me, Allah ﷻ sent a hundred and twenty-four thousand Prophets, of whom three hundred and fifteen were Messengers (i.e. were entrusted with a Book)."[17] The question is why were there so many more Prophets than Books? To reflect on this is to gain an understanding about the very institution of Prophethood. If the role of a Prophet were simply to deliver the Book, as some misguided people in our time try to argue, there should have been as many Books as Prophets. But the very fact that there have been many Prophets without a new Book, firmly establishes the need for the Prophethood as a source of guidance in its own right.

It had to be so because life emulates life. We need live human beings to inspire us, to show right from wrong in everyday struggles of life, to confront us and pose questions, to answer questions, to clarify misconceptions, to hold our hand, to be the model. We certainly need principles to guide our thoughts and actions. But we also need real-life examples to relate the principles to real-life situations. For most of our living experience involves judgment calls. Politeness is a

---

[17] *Musnad Ahmed*, Hadith 21257

desirable moral value. But when does politeness turn into weakness? Firmness is also a desirable attribute. But when does it turn into arrogance? How do we balance our duties towards Allah ﷻ with those towards other human beings? How do we balance both with duties towards ourselves? We are constantly faced with conflicting claims on our resources, energies, and attention. How do we resolve those conflicts without doing any injustice? These are real-life questions that require real-life answers.

This point is beautifully established in the Opening Chapter (Surah Fatiha) of the Qur'an. It is a short surah, consisting of only seven verses, and it consists of a prayer for guidance: "O Allah! Show us the Straight Path." Yet two of the seven verses are used to describe the Straight Path in terms of people. "The path of those on whom You have bestowed Your Grace. Not the path of those who earn Your wrath nor of those who go astray." It would have been simpler to just refer to the Straight Path as the Path of the Qur'an. But the longer description has been used to emphasize the fact that human beings need a human model to provide complete guidance.

Of course Prophets were sent to provide the needed guidance. It is also obvious that whatever a Prophet declares is binding on all his followers. "To accept a person as a Prophet of God and then to refuse to accept his commands, is so ridiculous that I would not have believed any sensible person would ever offer this proposition," says prominent Hadith scholar Maulana Manzoor Naumani. But this most irrational of ideas has been promulgated by a segment of western educated Muslims. They say, without a sense of irony, that we accept the Qur'an but not the Hadith.

Anyone who says that he accepts the Qur'an but rejects the Hadith cannot be serious. Or he has not read the Qur'an either. For the Qur'an says:

Prophets and Books

$$\text{وَأَنزَلْنَآ إِلَيْكَ ٱلذِّكْرَ لِتُبَيِّنَ لِلنَّاسِ مَا نُزِّلَ إِلَيْهِمْ وَلَعَلَّهُمْ يَتَفَكَّرُونَ}$$

"And We have sent down unto you the Message so that you may explain clearly to the people what is sent for them and so that they may give thought." [An-Nahl, 16:44]

It also declares:

$$\text{لَقَدْ مَنَّ ٱللَّهُ عَلَى ٱلْمُؤْمِنِينَ إِذْ بَعَثَ فِيهِمْ رَسُولًا مِّنْ أَنفُسِهِمْ يَتْلُواْ عَلَيْهِمْ ءَايَـٰتِهِۦ وَيُزَكِّيهِمْ وَيُعَلِّمُهُمُ ٱلْكِتَـٰبَ وَٱلْحِكْمَةَ وَإِن كَانُواْ مِن قَبْلُ لَفِى ضَلَـٰلٍ مُّبِينٍ}$$

"Allah did confer a great favor on the believers when He sent among them a Messenger from among themselves, reciting unto them His Verses (i.e. the Qur'an), purifying them, and instructing them in Scripture and Wisdom, while before that they had been in manifest error." [Al-i-'Imran, 3:164]

So it is the job of the Prophet ﷺ to explain the Qur'an. And it is the job of the believers to obey him.

$$\text{مَّن يُطِعِ ٱلرَّسُولَ فَقَدْ أَطَاعَ ٱللَّهَ}$$

"He who obeys the Messenger has indeed obeyed Allah." [An-Nisa, 4:80]

And even more emphatically it says:

$$\text{وَأَطِيعُواْ ٱللَّهَ وَأَطِيعُواْ ٱلرَّسُولَ}$$

BASICS

"And obey Allah and obey His Messenger." [At-Taghabun, 64:12]

It is to be noted that here the Qur'an did not say "Obey Allah and His Messenger." By using the command "obey" independently, the fact has been firmly established that the status of an order given by the Prophet ﷺ is the same as that given by Allah ﷻ.

Even a casual reader of the Qur'an can notice that it gives commands without giving many details. For example it refers to salat (ritual prayers) sixty-seven times. But it never explains how the salat has to be performed. The question is not just how a follower of the Qur'an is to follow that command, but the bigger question is, why the omission in the first place? Is it an oversight, in which case one cannot consider it to be the Book of Allah, or is it simply because another source for those details had been provided? Similarly the Qur'an approvingly mentions many other practices, like the call to prayer (*adhan*) and the Friday prayer, but never gives commands about them. Again, why? Is there any other explanation possible except for the obvious one that there is a parallel source of instruction in the person of the Prophet ﷺ?

Actually in the form of Hadith, Muslims have an unprecedented branch of knowledge. Just a list of all the books written on the subject would take several thousand pages. "Hadith is a branch of knowledge whose equivalent is not to be found in other religions," says Dr. Hamidullah.

For the design-your-own-religion crowd, that may be a problem, but for the sincere follower, it is a great favor and blessing of Allah ﷻ. We have been entrusted with a unique treasure trove of guidance. An appreciation of that favor is the first step towards benefiting from that treasure.

Joy Forever, Grief Forever

ALL THROUGH THE CENTURIES Allah ﷻ sent down thousands of messengers, dozens of books, and *one* Message. This central Message has three components. 1) Allah is the Creator and the Master of the universe. He is the One we must worship and obey. 2) He sent down guidance through messengers and books. 3) Just as death is certain in this world, so is resurrection in the Hereafter. Then everyone will face everlasting consequences of their response to Allah's commands: joy forever or grief forever.

It is this last part that can bring immediate clarity and concentration to our minds and change the call of the messengers from "interesting" to immensely serious and urgent. The messengers do not do philosophy or present theories. They have News for us and it is extremely urgent. That is why the Qur'an refers to the messengers as *nadhir* (warners) and describes this as their primary mission:

BASICS

$$\text{وَمَا نُرْسِلُ ٱلْمُرْسَلِينَ إِلَّا مُبَشِّرِينَ وَمُنذِرِينَ ۚ وَيُجَٰدِلُ ٱلَّذِينَ كَفَرُوا۟ بِٱلْبَٰطِلِ لِيُدْحِضُوا۟ بِهِ ٱلْحَقَّ ۖ وَٱتَّخَذُوٓا۟ ءَايَٰتِى وَمَآ أُنذِرُوا۟ هُزُوًا ۝}$$

"We have sent emissaries only as heralds and warners while those who disbelieve idly argue away so they may refute the Truth by means of it. They treat My signs and what they are warned of as a joke!" [Al-Kahf, 18:56]

An unimaginably huge catastrophe is about to befall humanity. Let it be warned, so it can ward it off. You must drop everything and listen to the Messenger ﷺ with all seriousness. Now.

This is a life-altering message. Anyone who understands and accepts it can no longer remain the same old person who did not understand or accept it. It says that this world is not what it appears to be. This is not our destination; what happens to us here is not our ultimate destiny. Any life lived here on the assumption that this life is all there is to it will be entirely wasted.

We know there are problems in this world. The strong can get away with murder. The weak are oppressed. We yearn for justice and don't find it. The joys of this life are also both short-lived and mixed with sorrows. We yearn for pure bliss and don't find it. This message tells us that our desires for justice and unmixed happiness are not in vain. We will get them in the eternal Afterlife. What seems to be an imperfect world is actually a perfect testing ground. The joys and sufferings here are meant to test how we behave under different circumstances in life. Those who lead a life of righteousness and obedience to Allah will taste real joy in the Hereafter. Those who lead a life of disobedience, sin, and corruption will taste real punishment.

This message gives us hope when there is no hope. It gives us the strength to be steadfast in the face of the forces of evil. It liberates us from the bondage to here and now. It changes our outlook and consequently our entire life.

It is impossible for our thoughts and actions to be right and righteous in the absence of belief in the Hereafter. How many people will resist temptations if there are no consequences to be feared for not doing so? And for how long? How many will engage in good even though it costs and avoid evil even though it seems to pay? Human beings are driven by rewards and punishments. But the only perfect system of reward and punishment is offered by the Hereafter. Therefore it is impossible to fix this world by ignoring the Hereafter.

There is more. The Qur'an says:

$$\text{إِنَّ ٱلَّذِينَ لَا يُؤْمِنُونَ بِٱلْآخِرَةِ لَيُسَمُّونَ ٱلْمَلَٰٓئِكَةَ تَسْمِيَةَ ٱلْأُنثَىٰ}$$

"Those who do not believe in the Hereafter, call the angels by the names of females." [An-Najm, 53:27]

What has the disbelief in the Hereafter to do with this act? They engage in this conjecture about the angels whom they have not seen and have no sure way of knowing about, because they are not serious. And they are not serious because of their disbelief in the Hereafter. Frivolity and vanity are a side effect of this disbelief. And when they take control of life, the entire life is destined to ruin.

While the disbelief in the Hereafter has no legs to stand on, this world does have the charm that can overcome that disadvantage! The result may be that we continue to profess belief in the Hereafter, yet live as if it does not matter. Or that we even change our beliefs too. It has happened before. Rabbi Dr. Louis Jacobs, rabbi of the New London Synagogue, writes, "Among many contemporary Jewish theologians there is a marked tendency to leave the whole question of eschatology without discussion, either because they do not believe in the Hereafter at all or because they believe that the finite mind of man is incapable of piercing the veil and it is best to leave the subject severely alone."[18] And while Orthodox Jews still believe in resurrection, it is with a twist. They believe that when the Messiah (who they think will be a person from the family of King David) comes, the righteous dead will be brought back to life to enjoy life here again. The wicked will not be resurrected. So the Hereafter will be *here* and there will be no real punishment for the wicked.

We can now appreciate the emphasis Islam places on remembering death and resurrection. As a Muslim wakes up, he says: "Praise be to Allah Who gave us life after death and unto Him is the Resurrection." When he goes to bed his prayer is: "O Allah, in Your name do I die and live." When he begins eating he says: "O Allah, bless us in what You have provided for us and protect us from the Fire." When he rides he says: "Glory be to Him Who has subjected these to our (use), for we could have never accomplished this (by ourselves). And to our Lord shall we be sent back."[19] So our sleep reminds us of our death and all through the waking hours we keep on refreshing that remembrance. In regular prayers and while reading the Qur'an it is impossible to continue for any length of time without being reminded that this life is temporary and our permanent abode is in the Hereafter. A beautiful du'a (supplication) further highlights a Muslim's concerns: "O Allah, do not make this world our greatest worry, the sum total of our knowledge, and the object of our desires."

The person who always remembers the Hereafter is like the driver who constantly keeps his eyes on the destination. He is the only one likely to successfully get there.

---

[18] Louis Jacobs, *The Jewish Religion: A Companion*. (Oxford University Press, 1995).
[19] Az-Zukhruf, 43:13-14

A Look at Hadith Rejecters' Claims

وَمَن يَعْصِ ٱللَّهَ وَرَسُولَهُۥ فَقَدْ ضَلَّ ضَلَـٰلًا مُّبِينًا ﴿٣٦﴾

"Anyone who disobeys Allah and His Messenger has wandered off into manifest error." [Al-Ahzab, 33:36]

وَمَن يُطِعِ ٱللَّهَ وَرَسُولَهُۥ فَقَدْ فَازَ فَوْزًا عَظِيمًا ﴿٧١﴾

"He who obeys Allah and His Messenger has already achieved a splendid Triumph." [Al-Ahzab, 33:71]

FOR THE PAST fourteen centuries Qur'an and Sunnah have been the twin undisputed sources of Guidance for Muslims. In every generation, Muslims devoted the best of their minds and talents to their study. They learned both the words and meanings of the Qur'an through the Prophet ﷺ and made an unprecedented effort in preserving them for the next generation. The result: the development of the marvelous—and unparalleled—science of Hadith, one of the brightest aspects of Muslim history.

What does it mean to believe in a Prophet except to pledge to follow him? And so the teachings of the Prophet ﷺ have always guided this Ummah. Nobody, in his right mind, could or did question this practice. Then something happened. During the colonial period, when most of the Muslim world came under the subjugation of the West, some "scholars" arose in places like Egypt (Taha Hussein), India (Abdullah Chakralawi and Ghulam Ahmed Pervaiz), and Turkey (Zia Gokalp), who began questioning the authenticity and relevance of Hadith. It was not that some genius had found flaws in the Hadith study that had eluded the entire Ummah for thirteen centuries. It was simply that the pressures from the dominant western civilization to conform were too strong for them to withstand. They buckled. Prophetic teachings and life example—Hadith—was the obstacle in this process and so it became the target.

Another factor helped them. Today most Muslims, including the vast majority of the western educated Muslims, have meager knowledge of Hadith, having spent no time in studying even the fundamentals of this vast subject. How many know the difference between *sahih* and *hasan*, or between *maudau* and *dhaif*? The certification process used in hadith transmission? Names of any Hadith book produced in the first century of Hijrah, or the number of such books? A majority probably would not be able to name even the six principal Hadith books (*Sihah Sitta*) or know anything about the history of their compilation. Obviously such atmosphere provides a fertile ground for sowing suspicions and doubts.

They sometimes call themselves as Ahle-Qur'an or Qur'anists. This is misleading. For their distinction is not in affirming the Qur'an, but in rejecting the Hadith. The ideas of *munkareen-e-hadith* evolve into three mutually contradictory strains. The first holds that the job of the Prophet ﷺ was only to deliver the Qur'an. We are to follow only the Qur'an and nothing else, as were the Companions. Further, Hadith is not needed to understand the Qur'an, which is sufficient for providing guidance. The second group holds that the Companions were required to follow the Prophet ﷺ but we are not. The third holds that, in theory, we also have to follow the Hadith but we did not receive Hadith through authentic sources and therefore we have to reject all Hadith collections!

Internal contradictions are a hallmark of false ideologies. How can anyone hold the first position yet profess belief in the Qur'an while it says:

$$وَأَنزَلْنَآ إِلَيْكَ ٱلذِّكْرَ لِتُبَيِّنَ لِلنَّاسِ مَا نُزِّلَ إِلَيْهِمْ وَلَعَلَّهُمْ يَتَفَكَّرُونَ ﴿٤٤﴾$$

"And We have sent down unto You the Message so that you may explain clearly to mankind what was sent down to them, and so that they may give thought." [An-Nahl, 16:44]

And this:

$$لَقَدْ مَنَّ ٱللَّهُ عَلَى ٱلْمُؤْمِنِينَ إِذْ بَعَثَ فِيهِمْ رَسُولًا مِّنْ أَنفُسِهِمْ يَتْلُواْ عَلَيْهِمْ ءَايَٰتِهِۦ وَيُزَكِّيهِمْ وَيُعَلِّمُهُمُ ٱلْكِتَٰبَ وَٱلْحِكْمَةَ وَإِن كَانُواْ مِن قَبْلُ لَفِى ضَلَٰلٍ مُّبِينٍ ﴿١٦٤﴾$$

"Allah did confer a great favor on the Believers when He sent among them a Messenger from among themselves, who rehearses unto them the Signs (Verses) of Allah, purifies them, instructs them in Scripture, and teaches them Wisdom, whereas previously they had been in plain error." [Al-i-'Imran, 3:164]

How can anyone hold the second position (limiting the Prophethood to 23 years) yet profess belief in the Qur'an, while it says:

BASICS

$$\text{وَمَآ أَرْسَلْنَٰكَ إِلَّا رَحْمَةً لِّلْعَٰلَمِينَ}$$

"We did not send you except as Mercy for everybody in the universe." [Al-Anbiyaa, 21:107]

And,

$$\text{وَمَآ أَرْسَلْنَٰكَ إِلَّا كَآفَّةً لِّلنَّاسِ بَشِيرًا وَنَذِيرًا}$$

"And We have not sent you (O Muhammad) except as a giver of glad tidings and a warner to all mankind." [Saba, 34:28]

The third position seems to have avoided these obvious pitfalls, yet in reality it is no different. It agrees that we need Hadith, but then goes on to claim that Allah did not provide what we need for our guidance.

The following are some of the statements normally made by Hadith rejecters.

THE RELIABILITY OF RESOURCES

> "We accept Allah's Word that He has protected the Qur'an from corruption, but why should we accept the words of the Hadith collectors? Are they as infallible as Allah ﷻ?"

This makes you wonder whether the Hadith rejecters realize how we received the Qur'an. For we have received both the Qur'an and the Hadith through exactly the same channels. The same people transmitted this as the Word of Allah ﷻ and that as the word of the Prophet ﷺ. Even the verse claiming that the Qur'an will be protected came to us through the same people. Through what logic can anyone declare that the channels are reliable for the Qur'an and unreliable for Hadith? On the contrary the Qur'anic promise of protection must apply to Hadith as well for there is no point in protecting the words but not the meanings of the Qur'an.

WERE AHADITH WRITTEN DOWN FOR THE FIRST TIME IN THE THIRD CENTURY OF HIJRA?

The very existence of a huge library of Hadith, the only one of its kind among the religions of the world, assures us that our expectation that Hadith—the embodiment of Prophetic explanation of the Qur'an—must have been protected is not in vain. To dismiss all that as later day fabrication requires lots of guts—and equal parts ignorance.

Were ahadith written down for the first time in the third century of Hijra? Not at all. Actually hadith recording and collection started at the time of the Prophet ﷺ.

Abdullah ibn Amr ibn al-'As ؓ[20] sought and was given the permission to write everything he heard from the Prophet ﷺ:

عَنْ عَبْدِ اللَّهِ بْنِ عَمْروٍ قَالَ كُنْتُ أَكْتُبُ كُلَّ شَيْءٍ أَسْمَعُهُ مِنْ رَسُولِ اللَّهِ صَلَّى اللَّهُ عَلَيْهِ وَسَلَّمَ أُرِيدُ حِفْظَهُ فَنَهَتْنِي قُرَيْشٌ وَقَالُوا أَتَكْتُبُ كُلَّ شَيْءٍ تَسْمَعُهُ وَرَسُولُ اللَّهِ صَلَّى اللَّهُ عَلَيْهِ وَسَلَّمَ بَشَرٌ يَتَكَلَّمُ فِي الْغَضَبِ وَالرِّضَا فَأَمْسَكْتُ عَنْ الْكِتَابِ فَذَكَرْتُ ذَلِكَ لِرَسُولِ اللَّهِ صَلَّى اللَّهُ عَلَيْهِ وَسَلَّمَ فَأَوْمَأَ بِأُصْبُعِهِ إِلَى فِيهِ فَقَالَ اكْتُبْ فَوَالَّذِي نَفْسِي بِيَدِهِ مَا يَخْرُجُ مِنْهُ إِلَّا حَقٌّ

Sayyidna Abdullah ibn Amr ؓ reports: "I used to write everything I heard from the Messenger ﷺ as I wanted to preserve it. The Quraish forbade me, saying: 'Do you write everything that you hear [from him] and the Messenger is a human being who sometimes speaks in anger and joy?' [i.e., he may say something under the influence of emotions that may not be worth writing.] So

---

[20] *Radi-Allahu anhu:* May Allah be pleased with him.

I stopped. Then I mentioned this to the Messenger ﷺ. He pointed with his fingers to his mouth and said: 'Write! By the One in Whose Hands is my life! Nothing proceeds from here except the truth.'" [*Abu Dawood*, Hadith 3161]

He produced *Sahifa Sadiqa*, which contained more than six thousand ahadith. Anas ibn Malik ؓ, who spent ten years in Prophet's household, not only recorded the ahadith but also presented them to the Prophet ﷺ and got corrections. Abu Hurairah ؓ had many volumes of his collections and even produced smaller compilations for his students. Prominent Hadith scholar Dr. Mustafa Azami has shown in his doctoral thesis that in the first century of Hijra many hundred booklets of hadith were in circulation. By the end of the second century, "by the most conservative estimate there were many thousands."

Of course most of these books do not exist today. They were simply absorbed into the encyclopedic collections that emerged in the third century. One manuscript from the first century was discovered in this century and published by Dr. Hamidullah. It is *Sahifa Hammam ibn Munabbah*, who was a disciple of Abu Hurairah ؓ. It contains 138 ahadith. Muhaddithin knew that the ahadith of this *Sahifa* had been absorbed into *Musnad Ahmed* and *Muslim* collections, which have been published continuously since their third century debut. After the discovery of the original manuscript it was naturally compared with the ahadith in *Muslim* and *Musnad Ahmed* that were thought to have come from that *Sahifa*. And what did they find? There was not an iota of difference between the two. Similarly *Mussanaf* of Abd al-Razzaq is extant and has been published. As has been Mu'ammar ibn Rashid's *al-Jami*. The recent appearance of these original manuscripts should bring the most skeptical into the fold of believers.

SALAT AND HADITH REJECTERS

"The Messenger ﷺ may have elaborated on items like mode of salat. Such hadith is probably from the Messenger ﷺ and should be obeyed. But we cannot believe the rest of the ahadith."

The Hadith rejecters have a particularly difficult time explaining how to offer salat if we are to throw away the Hadith. So they offer concessions like the one quoted above. But we don't need a favor for Hadith about salat (coming from the same books and the same narrators who are declared as unreliable). We need an answer to this question: If the Qur'an is the only authentic source of Guidance, why did it never explain how to offer salat, although it repeatedly talks about its importance, associating it with eternal success and failure? What would we think of a communication that repeatedly emphasizes a certain act but never explains how to perform it? There are only two possibilities. Either it is a terrible omission (and in that case it cannot be from God) or another source for the how-to information is provided and it is a terrible mistake for any recipient to ignore that.

Some Hadith rejecters have realized the difficulty of their position on salat. But they have made a claim that is even more ludicrous, namely that the Qur'an gives details on how to offer salat. "A careful reading of the Koran reveals that we are to get our salat from *the Masjid-al Haraam [the continuous practice at Makkah since the time of Abraham]*," says one proponent, "specifically the place of Abraham (*Muqam-e-Ibrahim*)." Let us leave aside all the practical questions about such a fluid answer. Whose salat? When? Are we to follow anyone and everyone we find praying at *Muqam-e-Ibrahim*? How are those offering salat there to determine the proper way of offering it? How do you resolve their differences? In his enthusiasm in proposing this innovative solution, this proponent even forgot that the Qur'an says the following about the salat of *mushrikeen* (polytheists) at the Masjid-al-Haraam:

BASICS

$$\text{وَمَا كَانَ صَلَاتُهُمْ عِندَ ٱلْبَيْتِ إِلَّا مُكَاءً وَتَصْدِيَةً فَذُوقُوا۟ ٱلْعَذَابَ بِمَا كُنتُمْ تَكْفُرُونَ ﴿٣٥﴾}$$

"Their prayer at the House of Allah is nothing but whistling and clapping of hands. (Its only answer can be), 'Taste the chastisement because you blasphemed.'" [Al-Anfal, 8:35]

THE SAHIH AND THE GOSPELS

"Hadith is the same as the Gospels of Christianity. Indeed the time span between death of Messenger Muhammad ﷺ and the compilation of *Sahihs* was almost the same as that between the departure of Jesus عليه السلام and compilation of the Bible. How can Muslims reject one but accept the other?"

Regarding comparison of the *Sahih* with the Gospels, let's listen to Dr. Hamidullah. "The compilation of the Gospels, their preservation and transmission from one generation to the other, has not taken place in the way which governed the books of Hadith...We do not know who wrote them, who translated them, and who transmitted them. How were they transferred from the original Aramaic to Greek? Did the scribes make arrangements for a faithful reproduction of the original? The four Gospels are mentioned, for the first time, three hundred years after Christ. Should we rely on such an unauthentic book in preference to that of Bukhari who prefaces every statement of two lines with three to nine references?"

PROTECTION OF THE QUR'AN

"Allah ﷻ has protected only the Qur'an—not Islam—from corruption."

To say that Allah ﷻ promised to protect only the Qur'an but not Islam is being as ridiculous as one can get. Let's ignore the obvious question regarding the point of this Heavenly act. The question is if Islam has been corrupted and its true teachings have been lost, how can anyone claim to be its follower? Moreover, the Qur'an says:

$$\text{وَمَن يَبْتَغِ غَيْرَ ٱلْإِسْلَٰمِ دِينًا فَلَن يُقْبَلَ مِنْهُ وَهُوَ فِى ٱلْءَاخِرَةِ مِنَ ٱلْخَٰسِرِينَ ۝}$$

"Anyone who desires something other than Islam as a religion will never have it accepted from him, and in the Hereafter he will be among the losers." [Al-i-'Imran, 3:85]

How are we to follow the religion acceptable to Allah ﷻ if it was not to be protected?

THE COMMENTS OF DR. MAURICE BUCAILLE

"Dr. Maurice Bucaille finds that *Sahih Bukhari* is as unscientific as the Bible."

Dr. Maurice Bucaille earned the admiration of many Muslims because of his study of some scientific phenomena mentioned in the Qur'an and his testimony based on that study that the Qur'an must be the Book of Allah. However he is not a Hadith scholar and it is unfair to drag him into this discussion. His account of history of hadith compilation contains many errors, for example the claim that the first gathering of hadith was performed roughly forty years after Hijra or that no instructions were given regarding hadith collection. He questions about a dozen or so entries in *Bukhari* that he thinks deal with scientific matters. Even if all that criticism were valid, would it be sufficient ground to throw away the 9082 total entries (2602 unique ahadith) in *Bukhari*? He himself does not think so, for he writes, "The truth of Hadith, from a religious point of view, is beyond question."

THE HADITH REGARDING THE SUN

But even his criticism is of questionable value. Consider the hadith about the sun: "At sunset the sun prostrates itself underneath the Throne and takes permission to rise again, and it is permitted and then a time will come when it will be about to prostrate itself...it will seek permission to go on its course...it will be ordered to return whence it has come and so it will rise in the west."[21] His criticism: "This implies the notion of a course the sun runs in relation to the earth." Bucaille fails to understand the real message of this hadith. It was not meant to teach astronomy. Its clear message is that the sun is a slave of Allah, moving always through His Will. The hadith brings out that message very powerfully so that even the most illiterate bedouin would understand it fully.

Even today astronomers, when calculating the time of sunrise and sunset, use a mathematical model in which the sun revolves around the earth. If that is acceptable for scientific work as it makes calculations easier, why is it questionable when it makes communication easier?

Also there are other ahadith which clearly demonstrate a scientific fact beyond the knowledge of the times but Bucaille has failed to take notice. For example the hadith about solar eclipse:

إِنَّ الشَّمْسَ وَالْقَمَرَ آيَتَانِ مِنْ آيَاتِ اللَّهِ لَا يَنْكَسِفَانِ لِمَوْتِ أَحَدٍ وَلَا لِحَيَاتِهِ وَلَكِنَّ اللَّهَ تَعَالَى يُخَوِّفُ بِهِمَا عِبَادَهُ

"The sun and moon are two signs from the Signs of Allah. They are not eclipsed on account of anyone's death or on account of anyone's birth, but Allah sends them to strike fear in the hearts of His servants." [*Bukhari*, Hadith 990]

---

[21] *Bukhari*, Hadith 2960

The eclipse had coincided with the death of the Prophet's son. A false prophet would have tried to exploit the occasion. A fabricated hadith would require scientific knowledge on the part of the fabricator that did not exist then.

To reject Hadith is to reject the Qur'an for all practical purposes. The idea was concocted as a means of undermining the Qur'an while on the surface affirming faith in it. It is time those who were misled by it out of ignorance threw away this relic of our colonial past into the trash bin of history where it belongs.

Qur'an

In this section:
- Qur'an: Witness the Miracle
- The Miracle of the Qur'an
- Relating to the Qur'an

Qur'an: Witness the Miracle

NIGHT AFTER NIGHT in Ramadan, the believers witness a unique spectacle at masajid[22] around the world. They stand in special *Taraweeh* prayers in which the prayer leader will recite the entire Qur'an from memory. Those who have accomplished this extraordinary feat of memorizing all of the 6236 verses are not a handful of devotees but there are hundreds of thousands of them. Most, just like most Muslims in the world today, do not speak Arabic. Yet they have painstakingly learned to pronounce each and every word of the Qur'an correctly. The phenomenon is not a result of some religious resurgence that would pass. From the very first day that the Qur'an was revealed, it was memorized. And the number of those who have memorized it has been increasing ever since. Memorization of the Qur'an has been going on all through the centuries, all over the globe wherever Muslims are.

There are other religions that claim to possess the Word of God. There is none that can show a book that has

---

[22] Masajid: plural of masjid, which has been corrupted into "mosque" in French and English.

commanded anything even remotely comparable to this level of devotion. The Qur'an is the most read and the only completely memorized book in the whole world. It is also the most studied book in the world. It has stimulated development of entire disciplines of knowledge dealing with its reading, writing, and interpretation.

Miraculous as it is, this is not the only unique aspect of the Qur'an.

The Qur'an was the first book in the Arabic language. Yet fourteen centuries later, its language is as alive as it was when it was revealed. And there is no other example when the very first book in a language became any masterpiece let alone the eternal masterpiece that the Qur'an is.

This Book is meant to command and guide humanity until the end of time. That the passage of fourteen centuries has not made the slightest dent in its language or literary beauty is just one evidence of that unique role; its contents have also been unassailable by the passage of time. It makes statements of scientific facts that science would discover centuries later but none that science could ever refute. It tells about ancient history, like the civilization of the 'Aad people in the Empty Quarter of the Arabian desert that no other historical sources, then or since, contain any information about. Yet, its veracity has only recently been verified by scientific discoveries. Above all, it provides a system of beliefs and a code of conduct for life that is as relevant, illuminating, and true today, as it was fourteen centuries earlier and during all the centuries in between.

The believers know that this Book had to be above space and time because this is the Word of the Creator of space and time. And He has promised that it will always be above space and time. But those who are looking from the outside and are just curious may consider these additional facts:

Prophet Muhammad ﷺ did not go to any school, study from any teacher, or even learn how to read and write. He even had no interest in poetry, which was one of the most

Qur'an: Witness the Miracle

prized disciplines of his time. Yet suddenly at age forty, he began to recite this marvelous revelation.

The style of the Qur'an is very distinct from the words of the Prophet ﷺ himself, which also have been preserved in Hadith collections. His own sayings are embodiments of eloquence, but they have a different style. Moreover, they clearly are the words of a human being. Although never deviating from the truth, they do show human emotions and the effects of the circumstances in which they were said. The Qur'an, on the other hand, never shows the slightest trace of these effects. It always speaks from above.

It was revealed over a twenty-three year period and covers a very wide range of subjects yet it shows neither a gradual development of style nor any self-contradictions in the voluminous text.

The twenty-three years of Prophetic life was not a period spent in isolation. He did not retire to a cave to produce this miraculous work. The Prophet ﷺ did spend long periods of time in quiet meditation in Cave Hira before becoming a Prophet. But after Prophethood was conferred upon him, his life was one of constant struggle with the pagans, and later the Jews, of Arabia who spared no effort to stop and persecute him. It was during this period of persecution, wars, campaigns, and solving problems associated with the bringing about of the greatest civilizational revolution of all times—an extremely busy and challenging period—that the Qur'anic Revelation was also received and compiled.

The Prophet ﷺ himself was most deeply moved by the Book. He used to stand for hours in solitary midnight prayers reciting from the Book until his feet would get swollen. How preposterous that one should attempt to attribute the Book to him. Has there ever been another example of somebody getting so moved by his own words?

This is not meant to be an exhaustive list of all the evidence that proves the Qur'an to be the Word of God. Scholars have written books expounding the miracle of miracles that the Qur'an is. But even this small sampler may propel an inquiring mind to go and read the Book himself.

To read this Book with an open mind is to believe in it. Those who sincerely seek guidance will find their questions answered, their confusions removed, and their problems solved in its pages. From the beginning until the end, every word in the Qur'an tells the reader that it is the Word of Allah. And those who ignore it do so at their own peril.

وَإِن كُنتُمْ فِى رَيْبٍ مِّمَّا نَزَّلْنَا عَلَىٰ عَبْدِنَا فَأْتُوا۟ بِسُورَةٍ مِّن مِّثْلِهِۦ وَٱدْعُوا۟ شُهَدَآءَكُم مِّن دُونِ ٱللَّهِ إِنْ كُنتُمْ صَٰدِقِينَ ۝ فَإِن لَّمْ تَفْعَلُوا۟ وَلَن تَفْعَلُوا۟ فَٱتَّقُوا۟ ٱلنَّارَ ٱلَّتِى وَقُودُهَا ٱلنَّاسُ وَٱلْحِجَارَةُ ۖ أُعِدَّتْ لِلْكَٰفِرِينَ ۝

"And if you are in doubt as to what We have revealed to Our servant, then produce a surah (chapter) like thereof; and call your witnesses or helpers (if there are any) besides Allah, if your (doubts) are true. But if you cannot—and of a surety you cannot—then fear the Fire whose fuel is men and stones, which is prepared for those who reject Faith."
[Al-Baqarah, 2:23-24]

The Miracle of the Qur'an

IT HAPPENED AT an international interfaith conference. The organizers decided to end the conference with readings from the scriptures of major religions, done by followers of other religions. As it happened, an Arab Christian read a passage from the Qur'an. He was a good reciter. Everyone seemed to be moved by his heart-rending reading, including the reciter himself. Immediately afterward, prominent Muslim thinker and writer, Maulana Waheeduddin Khan, who narrated this story, asked him, "Do you think the Qur'an is the Word of God?" In a moment of truth he said yes. But, then, he had second thoughts. So he added, "But only for the Arabs."

Actually not only the Qur'anic message keeps attracting people all over the world, its words also move people who may not know a word of Arabic. Famous Egyptian reciter Qari Abdul Basit reportedly once accompanied then President Gamal Abdul Nasir to a meeting with the Soviet leaders. During a break in the meeting, Nasir asked him to recite the Qur'an before the top Soviet leaders. When he finished the recitation, Qari Abdul Basit saw four of them shedding tears. "We don't know what it was," they later explained. But there was something touching in those words!

QUR'AN

Ironically at that time the Qur'an was the forbidden tree for the Muslims in the Soviet Union. Reading, teaching, or even possessing a copy of the Qur'an resulted in the most severe punishments. The KGB was always on the lookout. Its agents could enter any house, any time, if they suspected anyone inside of reading the Qur'an or offering prayers. Religious leaders were drafted for compulsory labor. Masajid and Islamic schools were closed down and turned into cinema houses, factories, and offices. One could not find a copy of the Qur'an anywhere. The ruthless state machinery did everything within its power to extinguish the flame of the Qur'an from the empire. Yet during those seventy dark years Muslims kept the flame burning. They developed elaborate camouflage mechanisms, at tremendous risks, to teach the Qur'an to their children. Little children had to stay away from their parents for months at a time as they retired to secret *hujras* (rooms) where they memorized the Qur'an and received religious instructions without ever having looked at a printed page. Their stories remain a neglected but extremely bright part of our recent history.

What kind of book can command such devotion and sacrifices? Only the Book that begins by asserting:

$$ذَٰلِكَ ٱلْكِتَٰبُ لَا رَيْبَ ۛ فِيهِ ۛ هُدًى لِّلْمُتَّقِينَ ۝$$

"This is the Book whereof there is no doubt; in it is guidance to those who fear Allah." [Al-Baqarah, 2:2]

And then each and every line of it attests to that assertion. It declares:

$$ٱلرَّحْمَٰنُ ۝ عَلَّمَ ٱلْقُرْءَانَ ۝$$

"The Most Gracious! It is He Who has taught the Qur'an." [Ar-Rahman, 55:1-2]

It challenges:

The Miracle of the Qur'an

$$قُل لَّئِنِ ٱجْتَمَعَتِ ٱلْإِنسُ وَٱلْجِنُّ عَلَىٰٓ أَن يَأْتُواْ بِمِثْلِ هَـٰذَا ٱلْقُرْءَانِ لَا يَأْتُونَ بِمِثْلِهِۦ وَلَوْ كَانَ بَعْضُهُمْ لِبَعْضٍ ظَهِيرًا ۝$$

"Say: If the whole of mankind and Jinn were to gather together to produce the like of this Qur'an, they could not produce the like thereof, even if they supported each other." [Al-Israa, 17:88]

It claims:

$$إِنَّا نَحْنُ نَزَّلْنَا ٱلذِّكْرَ وَإِنَّا لَهُۥ لَحَـٰفِظُونَ ۝$$

"Verily it is We Who revealed the Remembrance (i.e. The Qur'an) and verily We are its Guardians." [Al-Hijr, 15:9]

The Qur'an is the first document in the Arabic language. There is no other language of the world that has withstood the passage of fourteen centuries. Over the centuries, rivers change courses, civilizations rise and fall, and languages become extinct and new ones develop. Consider the expression "faeder ure on heofonum" from Lord's Prayer in Matthew 6 from a Bible of 900 CE. We are told it means "our father in heaven." It also means that any writing from that time cannot be read by an English speaker today. But any Arabic speaker can open the Qur'an today and understand its message. As did all the people in the intervening centuries!

Prominent scholar Dr. Hamidullah tells of an effort in Germany by the Christian scholars to gather all the Greek manuscripts of Bible as the original Bible in Aramaic is extinct. They gathered all manuscripts in the world and after examining them reported: "Some two hundred thousand contradictory narrations have been found...of these one-eighth are of an important nature." When the report was published, some people established an Institute for Qur'anic Research in Munich with the goal of examining the Qur'an the same way. A gigantic research project was started that continued for three generations. By 1933, 43,000 photocopies of Qur'anic manuscripts had been collected. A report published shortly before World War II showed the results of the examination of these manuscripts. While some minor mistakes of calligraphy were found, not a single discrepancy in the text had been discovered!

Of course the love, devotion, and care that Muslims showed toward the Qur'an, and that became the immediate cause of its miraculous preservation, was inspired by the Prophet Muhammad ﷺ. On one occasion he asked the Companions in *Suffa*: "Which of you would like to go out every morning to *Buthan* or *Al-Aqiq* (two markets near *Madinah*) and bring two large she-camels without being guilty of sin or without severing the ties of kinship?" Camels were the valuable commodity of the time, she-camels even more so. Its equivalent today may be a brand new automobile. As they showed interest, Prophet Muhammad ﷺ explained: "To teach or recite two verses of the Qur'an is better than getting two she-camels. And three verses are better than three she-camels."[23]

And so, for centuries this ummah displayed an unprecedented love and devotion for the Book of Allah. It began the education of its children by teaching them how to read the Qur'an. It began its day by reciting from the Qur'an. The Qur'an was divided into seven parts, each called a *manzil*, so it could be read completely every week. It was divided into thirty parts, each called a *juz*, so it could be read completely every month. The Qur'an is the most read and memorized book in the world!

Today, though, we see a change. Thanks to the twin scourges of a colonial education system and the television, today we find millions of Muslim children for whom learning

---

[23] *Muslim*, Hadith 1336

to read the Qur'an is not part of their education. We find millions of Muslim homes where Qur'an is read only on special occasions; when someone dies, for example. This despite the fact that in most parts of the world today, unlike the Soviet Union of yesterday, reading the Qur'an is no longer a high-risk proposition. How unfortunate is the person who should die of thirst while holding the refreshing glass of water in his hands! How unfortunate the person who should die of disease while holding the perfect medicine in his hands!

Of course we must read it, understand it, and put it into practice. But we must also remember that reading with full deference and proper etiquettes is a prerequisite for understanding the Qur'an, just as understanding its message is a prerequisite for practicing it. Our goal must be to live by the Qur'an. For only then we truly live. Otherwise we only pretend to live.

Relating to the Qur'an

THE QUR'AN IS the living miracle of Prophet Muhammad ﷺ. It contains nothing but the Word of Allah as revealed to Prophet Muhammad ﷺ, through angel Jibreel (Gabriel) ﷺ. It tells us where we are coming from and where we are going. It tells us what will happen after death. It shows the Straight Path that will lead to the place of eternal bliss called Paradise. And it warns us about following the crooked paths that lead to the place of eternal doom called Hell. It gives moral code for individuals as well as states. It gives the Shariah (Islamic Sacred Law) for them as well. It addresses both the heart and the intellect. It educates; it inspires; it heals. It shows the Path and it gives us the energy and motivation to follow it. No one can go wrong who makes it his guide. No one can succeed who ignores its guidance.

The Companions were the first group of people who followed it as it must be followed. They were transformed from being the lowest of the low to being the highest of the high. They established personal standards of piety and virtue that no other group of people since then can match. They established a society based on justice, fairness, and goodness that no other society can match.

"Then came their successors who deserted this Qur'an," says Shaikh Yusuf Qardawi in his book *Kaifa nata'amal ma'al*

Qur'an-il-Azeem (How Should We Interact With the Great Qur'an?). "They preserved its words but lost its injunctions. They understood it poorly. They did not put first what this Book puts first. They did not put last what this Book puts last. They did not give eminence to what this Book gives eminence to. They did not belittle what this Book belittles…There is no way for deliverance of this ummah from its loss, backwardness, and ruin except by turning back to this Qur'an. We must make this Qur'an as the guide and the leader."

This turning back to the Qur'an requires many steps. We must learn to read it in its original Arabic and we must teach our children to do the same. This learning to read is part of the knowledge referred to in the oft-quoted hadith that specifies that seeking knowledge is a duty of every Muslim male and female. We should memorize it as much as possible. We must recite it regularly. Not a day should go by in our life in which we forget to read the Qur'an. We must understand its message and ponder over its teachings. We must mold our life based on its commands. We must invite the entire humanity to the Path of the Qur'an.

The Qur'an is guidance for all humanity, but not everyone who reads it will get guidance from it. The Qur'an reserves its guidance for those who sincerely seek it and approach it in the proper way and with the right attitude. Many who have ignored these basic requirements have gone astray in their study of the Qur'an.

Interpreting the Qur'an requires expertise in several areas. First, one must have a firm command over classical Arabic language including its vocabulary, grammar, metaphors, and idioms.

Second, one must know the history of the Qur'an including where and when a verse was revealed; what other verses deal with the same subject; which of those, if any, supercede others. We must remember that the Qur'an is the first resource for its own interpretation.

Third, one must have good command over the Hadith literature, as it was the Prophet's job to explain the Qur'an to us and no other interpretation of a Qur'anic verse is acceptable in the presence of an authentic hadith that explains it.

Fourth, one must have knowledge of the comments of the Companions and their successors. After the Qur'an and Hadith, they are the third most important resource in interpreting the Qur'an.

Fifth, one must have knowledge of the rich *tafsir* (exegesis) literature produced by the most reputed scholars of this ummah.

Sixth, one must have sound knowledge of Shariah since no interpretation of the Qur'an is acceptable that violates accepted Shariah principles.

Seventh, one must be leading a life of *taqwa* and piety, as a sincere and serious effort at following it is a prerequisite for developing a proper understanding of the Qur'an.

We cannot just open the Qur'an and start interpreting it as if we are starting on ground zero. Anyone taking this road must be reminded of this grave warning: Sayyidna Abdullah ibn Abbas reported that Prophet Muhammad said,

مَنْ قَالَ فِي الْقُرآنِ بِغَيْرِ عِلْمٍ فَلْيَتَبَوَّأْ مَقْعَدَهُ مِنْ النَّارِ

"Whoever says something in interpreting the Qur'an without knowledge should find his place in the Fire."
[*Tirmidhi*, Hadith 2874]

Unfortunately, today a lot of well-meaning people are doing just this. They start, say, a Qur'anic study group, and start giving lectures on the Qur'an. If the person is a good speaker, he might also get warm reception from an audience that confuses eloquence with scholarship. Soon, they start giving expert opinions about the Shariah and the Qur'an without having even the minimum qualification for it. Many a time, the audience participates equally excitedly, discussing the Words of Allah and delicate issues of Shariah with the same assumed expertise that is normally reserved for discussion of current affairs.

This casual attitude must be contrasted with that of the Companions. Not only did they know the language of the Qur'an better than anyone else, they were also witnesses to its very revelation. Yet, they did not dare interpret it without first learning it, verse by verse, from Prophet Muhammad ﷺ himself. And even then they exercised extreme caution in making comments about the Qur'an. Sayyidna Abu Bakr ؓ said: "Which land will give me protection and which sky will give me cover if I say something in interpreting the Qur'an without knowledge." Similarly, Yazid bin Yazid reports: "We used to ask Sayyidna Saeed ibn Al-Musayeb ؓ regarding *halal* and *haram*. And he was the most knowledgeable person regarding it. But whenever we asked him to give *tafsir* for a verse he would keep quiet as if he had not heard us."

They knew that the Qur'an declares that it has been made easy for remembrance, but they did not misinterpret it as a license to give personal opinions in areas of belief or law. Their caution stemmed from their realization that to say that a verse means such and such is to attribute a statement to Allah ﷻ!

It is our duty to study the Qur'an. But the only proper way of doing it is by seeking a reliable *tafsir* and a qualified teacher.

Loving the Prophet ﷺ

In this section:

- ❁ Sall-Allahu Alayhi Wa Sallam ﷺ
- ❁ Loving the Prophet ﷺ
- ❁ Be Careful with Muhammad ﷺ

Sall-Allahu Alayhi Wa Sallam ﷺ

THEY WERE CIRCUMAMBULATING the Ka'ba, when Ka'ab bin Ujrah ؓ asked Abdul Rahman ibn Abi Lailah: "Shall I not give you a precious gift?" A gift in the middle of that act of intense devotion? Abdul Rahman was a prominent Successor (*tabi'i*), i.e. from the generation that came after the generation of the Companions. Ka'ab ؓ was one of the 1400 Companions who were part of the Covenant of al Ridwan, a covenant to live or fall together to avenge the blood of Uthman ibn Affan ؓ who had been feared to have been murdered by the Quraish. To know this background is to get a clue to the special gift.

While Muslims were stationed at Hudaybiyah, where the Covenant took place, many delegations of Quraish had visited them. Among them was Urwah ibn Mas'ud al Thaqafi. It was he who reported the extraordinary relationship of the Companions with the Prophet ﷺ: "I have seen Caesar and Chosroes in their pomp, but never have I seen a man honored as Muhammad ﷺ is honored by his comrades."

LOVING THE PROPHET ﷺ

The gift that Ka'ab ؓ gave to ibn Abi Lailah was the hadith that gives us the *salat-alan-nabi* that we use in regular prayers. The Companions asked the proper way of sending the blessings when the verse requiring them to do so was revealed.

إِنَّ ٱللَّهَ وَمَلَٰٓئِكَتَهُۥ يُصَلُّونَ عَلَى ٱلنَّبِيِّ ۚ يَٰٓأَيُّهَا ٱلَّذِينَ ءَامَنُوا۟ صَلُّوا۟ عَلَيْهِ وَسَلِّمُوا۟ تَسْلِيمًا ۝

"Indeed Allah and His angels shower blessings on the Prophet. O you who believe! Ask blessings on him and greet him with a worthy greeting." [Al-Ahzab, 33:56]

Then the Prophet ﷺ taught them the exact words, as revealed by Allah ﷻ.

A prophet of God is a unique person. He acts as the link between the people and their Creator. He is a human being, yet he speaks for God. The most difficult task for followers of a prophet has always been that of dealing with the prophet as a prophet. It is so easy to go to extremes. Make him divine, God-incarnate, Son of God. Or make him just another man, attributing all human weaknesses and sins to him. Religious literature of major religions in the world is testimony to these tendencies. It is a story of abject human failure in this matter.

One must contrast that with the beautiful and delicate balance presented by Islam. Here the Prophet ﷺ is the perfect human being, but he is not divine. He speaks for God but he is not God. He is the object of our gratitude, ardent love, devotion, unswerving allegiance, and deference. But he is not the object of our worship. We ask Allah ﷻ to send His blessings on him, which at once makes two very important statements. First, he needs Allah's blessings. Second, we cannot bless him, only Allah ﷻ can. It is not possible for those who always invoke Allah's blessings for the Prophet ﷺ to degrade him to the level of other human beings, or to elevate him to the level of divinity. The *salat-alan-nabi* is a powerful formula that fights both tendencies equally effectively. It also strikes at the roots of *shirk*, the tendency to associate partners with Allah ﷻ. For we have met the perfect human being, the example to follow. And we found him to be a servant of Allah. Sall-Allahu alayhi wa sallam.

For centuries Muslims lovingly added the *salat-alan-nabi*, whenever they mentioned the name of the Prophet ﷺ. The hadith literature is a good example of this labor of love. For here the name of the Prophet ﷺ is mentioned repeatedly. Yet the Hadith scholars never tired of writing the *salat-alan-nabi*. That was at a time when every book was written by hand, and all its copies were also made by hand. It was never considered a burden or an unnecessary interruption. A brief statement from a professor of Hadith at one Islamic religious school captures the spirit. "The merits of studying Hadith are innumerable and those interested can read Ibn Abdul Bar's book on the subject," he said. "But it is sufficient to note that through this study we get plenty of opportunities for saying the *salat-alan-nabi*."

And so for centuries this practice has continued throughout the Muslim world. Also, realizing the importance of a "worthy *salat-alan-nabi*" Muslims always used the Arabic expression in other languages, be they Urdu, Farsi, Bangla, Sindhi, Pushto, Baluchi, Malay, or others. For the first time in history we find a break from this practice—and this spirit—when reviewing the Islamic literature in English and other European languages.

Initially probably the Orientalists substituted "peace be upon him" for "Sall-Allahu alayhi wa sallam" but it is not even a proper translation. Then it was abbreviated to pbuh. It, of course, did not improve the translation or the readability. Others had other ideas. One Islamic textbook notes: "After using the name of the Prophet Muhammad, Muslims should write or say the honorific phrase, Sall-Allahu alayhi wa sallam...Due to limited space this honorific phrase has been omitted...but should be inserted when reading the book." Another book acknowledges the "long established and cherished tradition," but then announces bluntly that the practice is not being followed: "To avoid interrupting the flow of ideas, especially for non-Muslim readers." A large number of books published in the West by Muslims, though, do not feel the need for any excuse or explanation. They simply mention the Prophet ﷺ as they would any ordinary person.

It is time we moved beyond our hesitations, confusions, or inferiority complexes. This is the Ummah of the Last Prophet ﷺ. In every language of the world, our Prophet is Muhammad, Sall-Allahu alayhi wa sallam ﷺ. 🕋

Loving the Prophet ﷺ

ON THE TWELFTH of Rabi-ul-Awwal, Muslims all over the world hold special gatherings to commemorate and celebrate the birthday of Prophet Muhammad ﷺ. The special programs attract huge numbers of Muslims. There can be no two opinions among the believers that remembering the Prophet ﷺ and learning about his life example are highly meritorious acts. The *milad* celebrations show the deep love and devotion that all the believers have for the Messenger of Allah, Muhammad ibn Abdullah ﷺ. This love and devotion remains a distinct characteristic of Muslims throughout the centuries.

However, while the fact of this love has not changed, its nature has. It has taken different forms than what we find in the early generations. The Companions were the special people who came in direct contact with Allah's Messenger ﷺ, learned from him, joined his struggle, gave the most sacrifices for it, devoted their lives for his mission, and earned the credentials for being the model disciples, followers, and devotees.

Among them was Sayyidna Mus'ab ibn Umayr ﷺ. As a young pagan in Makkah, he was the best dressed, the best cared for youth. Clad in the most expensive silk and wearing the best perfumes, he would leave a trail of fragrance wherever he passed by. Then something happened. He met the Prophet ﷺ, and his message penetrated the depth of his heart. Life changed drastically. His pagan mother, who used to love him before, now despised him and began to punish him severely. His was a transformation from riches to rags. Once the Prophet ﷺ saw him covering his body with a patched up old hide and showing signs of the rough life he had embraced. He said, "I saw this young man some years ago in Makkah. There was none at that time who was more handsome, was living a more luxurious life, or was better dressed than him. But today he has sacrificed all the comforts of this life for the love of Allah and His Prophet." He was the first teacher of the Ansar in Madinah and the standard bearer of the Muhajireen in Badr. When he was martyred in Uhud, there was not enough cloth to cover his body completely; grass was used to supplement the small burial cloth. According to some reports, the Prophet ﷺ stood by his body and recited the verse:

$$\text{مِنَ ٱلْمُؤْمِنِينَ رِجَالٌ صَدَقُواْ مَا عَـٰهَدُواْ ٱللَّهَ عَلَيْهِ}$$

"From among the believers there are some men who fulfilled their pledge with Allah." [Al-Ahzab 33:23]

Among them was Sayyidna Sa'd ibn Mu'az ﷺ, the leader of the Ansar. The Ansar had provided hospitality and protection to the Prophet ﷺ and the Makkan Muslims, but soon they faced a bigger challenge. Would they be ready to fight against the much larger and better equipped Makkan army? His powerful words in the meeting before Badr captured the spirit of their commitment. "O Rasulullah ﷺ, we have believed in you, affirmed your Prophethood, and pledged obedience. By Allah, Who has sent you as a Messenger, if you were to command us to jump into the ocean we would do that. Not one soul among us would remain behind…Maybe Allah will show you from us what will bring pleasure to your eyes."

Among them was Sayyidna Jareer ibn Abdullah ﷺ. Once he sent his servant to buy a horse. The servant made a deal for three hundred dirhams and brought the seller with him so he could be paid. Sayyidna Jareer ibn Abdullah ﷺ looked at the horse and realized that the seller had undervalued it. "Would you sell it for four hundred?" he asked. The seller agreed. "How about five hundred?" He continued his unusual "bargaining" and finally bought the horse for eight hundred dirhams. He was later asked why he did so. "The seller was not aware of the true value of this horse," he explained. "I have simply given him a fair price because I had promised to Prophet Muhammad ﷺ to always be sincere and a well-wisher for every Muslim."

Among them was the unnamed person who was wearing a gold ring. It is prohibited for Muslim men to wear gold. The Prophet ﷺ took his ring and threw it on the ground, saying it was like wearing burning charcoal from Hell. Later on people suggested to him to pick up the ring as it could be used for other legitimate purposes. But he refused saying, "No, by Allah, I will never take it when it has been thrown away by the Messenger of Allah."

These are just some random glimpses into the lives and minds of the great Companions. Their life accounts are full of such examples. They accepted his Prophethood from the bottom of their hearts, knowing fully what that meant. From that point on, their lives revolved entirely around this belief. They loved the Prophet ﷺ more than anybody else in the world. They intently observed his actions and listened to his words. They remembered him all the time. They obeyed each and every one of his commands. They never said, "This is only a sunnah," meaning it can be ignored. They never asked why a command was given. They never sought excuses. Within the home and outside it, in business or on the battlefield, in their private gatherings or in the courts of kings and emperors, everywhere they were the most obedient servants of Allah ﷻ and the most obedient followers of the Prophet ﷺ.

None of them ever celebrated the Prophet's birthday. They did not need to have a day or a month devoted to the Prophet ﷺ, because they had devoted their entire lives to him.

Today our lives and our outlooks bear little resemblance to theirs. We praise but do not listen to him; we claim to love, but refuse to follow; we claim to believe but lead lives like those who don't. We emphasize what the Companions ignored and ignore what they emphasized.

They loved the Prophet ﷺ and had their lives to show for it. And we? Can we honestly say that we love the Prophet ﷺ as he should be loved?

Be Careful with Muhammad

THE CROWD WAS growing in size by the minute. They were beating drums, singing, dancing, and shouting with joy. Pagan Makkah was about to kill Khubaib ibn Adi Ansari ﷺ who had been captured through a sinister and treacherous plot, then sold in the slave market so the buyers could exact their vengeance.

It started when some tribesmen from Uthul and Qara went to Madinah and requested the Prophet ﷺ to send some teachers with them who could educate their fellow tribesmen about Islam. The request was granted and about ten Companions were sent with them. When the group reached Raji' two hundred armed men were lying in wait for them. Khubaib ﷺ and Zaid ibn Adathna ﷺ were captured alive, while the others were martyred. Then they were sold in exchange for a hundred heads of camel. Both had fought in the battle of Badr and their swords had killed some pagan soldiers. Now the relatives of those killed in war wanted to get even. Of course, Arab traditions did not allow revenge for war like this. But their opponents were Muslims. Then, as

LOVING THE PROPHET ﷺ

now, the pagan world was ready to violate its own rules and traditions when the victims were Muslims.

While facing death, Khubaib ﷺ said a poem that has been recorded by history. It includes these lines: "They say if I renounce Islam, my life will be spared. But it is better to die with belief than to live with unbelief."

At the last minute, the pagans asked him: "Don't you wish that you were spared and Muhammad ﷺ got this punishment? Would not you like that you were resting comfortably in your home, while he was killed in your place?" From the man who was about to die because he had accepted the Message brought by Muhammad ﷺ came this reply: "By Allah, I cannot even imagine that a thorn should prick the foot of Muhammad ﷺ while I rest in my home."

Abu Sufyan, an unbeliever at the time, remarked to his associates: "See, the love of the Companions for Muhammad ﷺ is unparalleled and unprecedented." At another time, a similar observation was made by another Quraish leader Urwah ibn Mas'ud al Thaqafi. "I have seen Ceasar and Chosroes in their pomp, but never have I seen a man honored, as Muhammad is honored by his comrades."

The biographies of the Companions are full of stories that show their extraordinary love and devotion for the Prophet ﷺ. The Qur'an itself attests to this.

$$ ٱلنَّبِىُّ أَوْلَىٰ بِٱلْمُؤْمِنِينَ مِنْ أَنفُسِهِمْ $$

"The Prophet is closer to the believers than even they themselves are." [Al-Ahzab, 33:6]

It is a statement of fact as well as a command. The following two ahadith, from among the many on the subject, clarify this point further.

$$ لَا يُؤْمِنُ أَحَدُكُمْ حَتَّى أَكُونَ أَحَبَّ إِلَيْهِ مِنْ وَالِدِهِ وَوَلَدِهِ وَالنَّاسِ أَجْمَعِينَ $$

Be Careful with Muhammad ﷺ

"None of you can be a believer until I become dearer to him than his parents, his children, and all the people." [*Bukhari*, Hadith 14]

ثَلَاثٌ مَنْ كُنَّ فِيهِ وَجَدَ بِهِنَّ حَلَاوَةَ الْإِيمَانِ مَنْ كَانَ اللَّهُ وَرَسُولُهُ أَحَبَّ إِلَيْهِ مِمَّا سِوَاهُمَا وَأَنْ يُحِبَّ الْمَرْءَ لَا يُحِبُّهُ إِلاَّ لِلَّهِ وَأَنْ يَكْرَهَ أَنْ يَعُودَ فِي الْكُفْرِ بَعْدَ أَنْ أَنْقَذَهُ اللَّهُ مِنْهُ كَمَا يَكْرَهُ أَنْ يُقْذَفَ فِي النَّارِ

"There are three signs that indicate that a person has tasted the sweetness of faith: 1) That he loves Allah and His Prophet more than anything else. 2) He loves a person solely for the sake of Allah. 3) After accepting Islam he hates going back to unbelief as much as he hates going into the Fire." [*Bukhari*, Hadith 15]

It has to be so, because our relationship to the Prophet ﷺ is at the core of our entire religion. He is human, not divine, but he is our connection to the Deity. He relays to us the Word of Allah and he explains what the Word means. He sets a personal example that we look at not just for admiration but emulation. Our relationship to him is legal as well as personal; moral as well as spiritual; intellectual as well as emotional. Allah ﷻ chose him to guide us, educate us, inspire us, and purify us—and we remain indebted forever!

This not only establishes a relationship between a believer and the Prophet ﷺ it also establishes the relationship among the believers, making them one unit because of—in addition to their common faith—their common love for the Prophet ﷺ.

Together these facts explain a Muslim's sensitivity to the honor of the Prophet ﷺ. To begin with, we must remember that the honor of everyone is important. As the hadith reminds us:

> مَا مِنْ امْرِئٍ يَخْذُلُ امْرَأً مُسْلِمًا فِي مَوْضِعٍ تُنْتَهَكُ فِيهِ حُرْمَتُهُ وَيُنْتَقَصُ فِيهِ مِنْ عِرْضِهِ إِلاَّ خَذَلَهُ اللَّهُ فِي مَوْطِنٍ يُحِبُّ فِيهِ نُصْرَتَهُ وَمَا مِنْ امْرِئٍ يَنْصُرُ مُسْلِمًا فِي مَوْضِعٍ يُنْتَقَصُ فِيهِ مِنْ عِرْضِهِ وَيُنْتَهَكُ فِيهِ مِنْ حُرْمَتِهِ إِلاَّ نَصَرَهُ اللَّهُ فِي مَوْطِنٍ يُحِبُّ نُصْرَتَهُ

> "No one forsakes a Muslim whose honor and dignity are under attack except that Allah will also forsake him when he is most in need of Allah's help. And no one helps a Muslim whose honor and dignity are under attack except that Allah will also help him when he is most in need of Allah's help." [*Abu Dawood*, Hadith 4240]

If a Muslim is not supposed to be indifferent when the honor of another ordinary Muslim is under attack, how in the world can anyone expect him or her to be indifferent when the honor and dignity of the Prophet ﷺ himself may be under attack?

As has been noted by someone else, a civilization in which nothing is sacred may have difficulty in understanding the values of a civilization in which sacred is all that counts. But if it cannot understand the logic, because of its own blinders, it will have to come to terms with the facts on the ground: Muslims treat their Prophet, and all the prophets, with utmost respect and they simply cannot tolerate any willful insult and disrespect. To compromise on this issue would tantamount to compromising one's faith. And no one has a right to demand that. The blasphemy laws in Muslim countries like the one in Pakistan, are not only based on solid and agreed upon juristic grounds, they express a fundamental value of the Islamic civilization. We need not offer any apologies for that just because the forces of profanity seem to be powerful.

Some say that since the Prophet ﷺ forgave his worst enemies and never took revenge for himself, any law that prescribed punishment for assaulting the honor of the Prophet ﷺ is clearly against his Sunnah. The premise is true but the conclusion is false. What the prophetic example teaches is that we should also be willing to forgive those who have committed offenses against us, personally—an important message that is generally ignored. On the other hand, we know of Ka'ab bin Ashraf who used to abuse the Prophet ﷺ and instigated others to do so. He was executed by Muhammad ibn Salma ؓ on the orders of the Prophet ﷺ.[24] There are not many such incidents but history records that whenever anyone tried to abuse the person of the Prophet ﷺ the same punishment was meted out to him. As the Persian poet said, "May take liberty with God, Be careful with Muhammad ﷺ."

---

[24] *Bukhari*, Hadith 3731

Acts of Worship

In this section:

- The Purpose of Prayer (Du'a)
- The Key to Paradise
- The Meaning of Ramadan
- Zakat
- The Road from Makkah
- The Power of Du'a

The Purpose of Prayer (Du'a)

فَمِنَ ٱلنَّاسِ مَن يَقُولُ رَبَّنَآ ءَاتِنَا فِى ٱلدُّنْيَا وَمَا لَهُۥ فِى ٱلْءَاخِرَةِ مِنْ خَلَـٰقٍ ۝ وَمِنْهُم مَّن يَقُولُ رَبَّنَآ ءَاتِنَا فِى ٱلدُّنْيَا حَسَنَةً وَفِى ٱلْءَاخِرَةِ حَسَنَةً وَقِنَا عَذَابَ ٱلنَّارِ ۝ أُوْلَـٰٓئِكَ لَهُمْ نَصِيبٌ مِّمَّا كَسَبُواْ ۚ وَٱللَّهُ سَرِيعُ ٱلْحِسَابِ ۝

"From among the people there is (the man) who says: 'Our Lord, give us (your bounties) in this world!' and he will have no share in the Hereafter. And there is (another kind) who says: 'Our Lord, give us good in this world as well as good in the Hereafter, and shield us from the torment of Fire!' To these will be allotted what they have earned. And Allah is Swift in reckoning." [Al-Baqarah, 2:200-202]

الدُّعَاءُ مُخُّ الْعِبَادَةِ

"Prayer (du'a) is the essence of worship." [Tirmidhi, Hadith 3293]

PRAYER IS COMMUNICATION with God. Everyone who believes in God also prays. But "how" and "for what" of prayer depend upon one's concept of God and outlook on life. The pagans of Arabia used to pray as the above verses mention. According to a *Newsweek* survey report, a great majority of Americans also pray, many of them daily. They pray for health, safety, love, and for relief of a "Job-like list of human miseries."[25] Guidance to the Straight Path, protection from Hell, and success in the Hereafter are not mentioned.

What is even more intriguing is the language of the western discourse about prayer. In western literature God is depicted as a wise old man in the sky and prayers appear to be petitions for solution of problems that it is His "duty" to solve. According to the *Newsweek* poll "85 percent of Americans say they accept God's failure to grant their prayers." God's failure? They debate: "Is God unjust or He only appears that way?" Others, like Carl Sagan, who died holding firm to his unbelief, ask: "Does God need to be reminded that someone is sick?"

This is several notches below the level of the pagans of Arabia. At work here is the arrogance of achievements in science and technology. In fact in one case Christian healers joined with scientists to conduct an "experiment" to determine the usefulness of prayer. At the Arthritis Treatment Center in Florida, one group of patients additionally received "healing prayers" from trained professionals of the Christian Healing Ministry (CHM), while the other group only received medical treatment. A year later, a report by CHM declared success while admitting that the study was controversial. Yet it gave opportunity to CHM to market videos and training of professionals who could heal through prayers! One wonders whether to cry at the arrogance of the scientist who is trying to study "God's behavior," or laugh at the marketer trying to sell "healing prayer" to that mindset.

---

[25] "Is God Listening?", *Newsweek*, 31 March 1997

For a believer this is blasphemy of the highest order. Prayer is not a polite demand for rights. God gave us life and everything that we possess, without our having any right to it. It is His design and it is with a purpose. Our conditions of health and sickness, our affluence and poverty, our joys and sorrows, our apparent successes and failures, our gains and losses—all of them are just a test.

$$ٱلَّذِى خَلَقَ ٱلْمَوْتَ وَٱلْحَيَوٰةَ لِيَبْلُوَكُمْ أَيُّكُمْ أَحْسَنُ عَمَلًا وَهُوَ ٱلْعَزِيزُ ٱلْغَفُورُ$$

"He created death and life that He may test you which of you is best in deed. And He is the Powerful, the Forgiving." [Al-Mulk, 67:2]

Our ultimate success or failure—in the Hereafter—will depend solely on how we acted in the different circumstances that He chose for us. Did we seek His help when we needed help or were we too arrogant to ask? Did we accept His Will when things did not turn out our way? Did we show gratitude for His favors or were we proud of our own achievements? And under all circumstances did we follow His commands or were we preoccupied with our demands?

We pray to Him because only He can give. He is not answerable to any authority and everyone is answerable to Him. He has power over everything and none can overpower Him. His knowledge is infinite while ours is infinitesimal compared to His. He is the Lord; we are His slaves. He may grant our prayers here; or He may reward us for them in the Hereafter; or He may give us something better than what we asked for. In any case a praying person can never lose, for prayer is the highest form of submission to Him. "Prophet Muhammad ﷺ was the best of mankind because he was the best in submission to Allah," says Maulana Manzoor Naumani. "Anyone who studies his supplications cannot but

ACTS OF WORSHIP

be awestruck by the perfect understanding of our relationship to the Creator reflected by them."

One of the saddest days in his life came in June 619 CE in his visit to Taif. The pagans of Taif not only mocked his invitation to believe in the one true God, they also sent their urchins to throw stones at him until his shoes filled with blood. In great distress the Prophet ﷺ turned to Allah ﷻ: "O Allah, unto You do I complain of my weakness, of my helplessness, and of my lowliness before men. O Most Merciful of the merciful, You are Lord of the weak. And You are my Lord. Into whose hands will You entrust me? Unto some stranger who will ill-treat me? Or unto an enemy who dominates me? If You are not angry with me then I don't care, but Your favoring help will be easier for me. I take refuge in the light of Your Countenance whereby all darknesses are illuminated and the things of this world and the next are rightly ordered, lest I become the object of Your wrath and anger. To You alone belongs the right to blame and to chastise until Your pleasure is met. There is no power and no might except through You."[26] Moving words!

Thirteen years later the situation had changed completely. All of Arabia had come under the domination of Islam. Paganism had been totally defeated. At the Farewell Pilgrimage about 124,000[27] Companions gathered to perform Hajj with the Prophet ﷺ. And there in the plains of Arafat this was his prayer: "O Allah! You hear me and see me and know everything that I reveal or conceal. None of my affairs is hidden from You. I am a person in distress, a needy

---

[26] *Sirat ibn Hisham*. Vol. 2, p. 33

[27] Reports differ on the number of Companions who attended the Farewell Pilgrimage; numbers ranging from 40,000 to 140,000 have been reported. Such variations in individual estimates of a very large gathering can be understood since no one was taking an exact count. However there is not the least doubt that it was a huge gathering. Sayyidna Jabir ibn Abdullah ﷺ, who gave a detailed eyewitness account, reports: "I saw as far as I could in front of the Prophet ﷺ (and saw nothing but) riders and pedestrians. And the same on his right. And on his left. And behind him." [*Muslim*, Hadith 2137]

person, a beggar, a fearful person. I confess my shortcomings. I entreat You like a humble needy person. I beseech You like a sinful lowly person. I ask You like a person in tribulation whose neck bows before You; who cries in front of You; whose whole body trembles before You. O Allah! Do not leave me frustrated in my prayer, and be the Most Merciful and the Most Gracious to me. O the best of those who are beseeched! O the best of those who give!"[28] Sublime words!

In the best of times, in the worst of times, Prophet Muhammad ﷺ was the same servant of Allah. His supplications remain a living miracle inviting all open-minded people to reflect upon the source of that level of consciousness of Allah ﷻ.

For this ummah, his prayers are one of his greatest spiritual gifts. How unfortunate that any of his followers should remain unlearned about them.

---

[28] *Kanzul Ummal,* Hadith 3614

The Key to Paradise

IN ONE OF HIS circulars Sayyidna Umar ibn Khattab ﷺ sent instructions to all his administrators saying,

إِنَّ أَهَمَّ أَمْرِكُمْ عِنْدِي الصَّلَاةُ فَمَنْ حَفِظَهَا وَحَافَظَ عَلَيْهَا حَفِظَ دِينَهُ وَمَنْ ضَيَّعَهَا فَهُوَ لِمَا سِوَاهَا أَضْيَعُ

"In my opinion, salat is the most important of your obligations. Whoever takes good care of it and safeguards it safeguards his religion and whoever neglects it will neglect other things even more." [*Muwatta Imam Malik*, Hadith 5]

He then added instructions about the times for the five salats and admonition against dozing off before Isha.

This letter from the ruler of a vast empire to the officials of his government—shall we call it Executive Order?—gives us a lot to reflect upon. For salat is among the most emphasized commands in Shariah. Unfortunately it is also a grossly neglected obligation in our life today.

Even a Muslim schoolchild knows that salat is a pillar of Islam. What Sayyidna Umar ﷺ expressed was that it is true at all levels and in all settings, from the private to the public. One cannot build an Islamic life, an Islamic community, an

Islamic institution, or an Islamic government while neglecting or weakening this pillar. It is a measure of its extraordinary status that unlike all other obligations the command for salat was given by Allah ﷻ to Prophet Muhammad ﷺ during his *Mi'raj* (Ascension to the Heavens). Very fittingly so, for salat is the *Mi'raj* of the believer. One begins the salat by standing while facing the Ka'ba or the House of Allah, isolating himself from the worldly affairs, and then addressing Allah ﷻ directly: "O Allah, You are sanctified and (I begin) with Your praise. Your name is Blessed and Your Greatness is Supreme. And no one else is worthy of worship except You." During salat a believer repeatedly stands, bows, and prostrates to Allah ﷻ. Each of these acts brings him closer and closer to his Master and Creator filling him with the feelings of love, devotion, and obedience. The sitting position even includes the re-creation of the conversation that took place between the Prophet ﷺ and Allah ﷻ during the Heavenly Ascent.

Prophet ﷺ: "All greetings, blessings, and good acts are for Allah."

Allah ﷻ: "Peace is upon you O Prophet, and the Mercy, and the Blessings of Allah."

"Peace be with us and unto the righteous servants of Allah. I bear witness that there is no deity except Allah."

"And I bear witness that Muhammad is His servant and messenger."

This closeness is the most valuable gift for the believer. It is the source of all strength and all goodness in his life. It is the light that shows him the right from wrong in all walks of life. It is the river that bathes and cleans him of all sin and contamination. In the hardships of life, it is the source of solace and strength. It is the regulator of the Muslim life, the daily schedule of a believer being built around the five daily salats. It is a source of joy and happiness, of spiritual nourishment and purification. It is the key to all success. It is the key to paradise.

On the other hand, the Qur'an says, "Woe to the worshippers who are negligent in their salat."[29] A hadith says: "Salat stands between man and unbelief." Another hadith says: "Salat is the pillar of religion. Whoever destroys it has destroyed the religion." Another hadith informs us that salat is the first item about which one will be questioned after death. The person who succeeds in this test, will likely pass the subsequent tests. The one who flunks this one has little chance of getting through the rest. Yet another hadith warns us that the person who neglects his salat has walked out of the protection of Allah ﷻ. We can understand the enormity of missing just one salat on purpose from the hadith that says that such a person is like one who lost all his family and all his wealth!

In the presence of all the persuasion and all the admonition about salat in the Qur'an and Hadith, one wonders how could any sane believer be negligent in this matter. To a person who claims to be a believer yet does not offer his salat regularly five times a day, we must ask: What is your justification? The more one thinks about it the more he or she will realize that there is none.

One cannot plead that he did not know about the obligation or its extraordinary importance. Even if an unfortunate Muslim were never to open the Qur'an or a Hadith book in his life, he cannot not notice the call to salat that comes from every masjid throughout the world five times a day. It repeatedly reminds him: "Come to salat. Come to Success." The distribution of masajid in the world today is such that the call to salat can be heard round the clock in a never-ending stream as one moves around the globe. One can begin with the Fajr *adhan* in Indonesia and follow it at small intervals in Malaysia, Bangladesh, India, Pakistan, Afghanistan, Iran, Iraq, Saudi Arabia, Egypt, etc. By that time Zuhr *adhan* has already started in Indonesia. Twenty-four hours later when the Muezzins of Indonesia are

---

[29] Al-Ma'un, 107:4-5

again calling out Fajr *adhan*, the Muezzins in Africa are calling out the *adhan* for Isha. How can one plead ignorance in the presence of this massive and continuous universal call?

One cannot plead that the obligation is too difficult or time consuming. While the obligation remains whether one is healthy or sick, and whether it is rain or shine, Shariah goes to great lengths to accommodate our circumstances. If you cannot stand, you can offer it sitting. Cannot sit? You can offer it lying down. Cannot move? Use whatever gestures are possible. Traveling? Just offer two units instead of four. Cannot figure out the direction of *qibla*? Use your best judgment. Can't use water to purify yourself in preparation for salat? Perform dry ablution.

As people run out of excuses they sometimes try rationalizations. What good is salat if one's mind wanders all over the place? Well our job is to *try* to concentrate not to *achieve* concentration. We are doing our job if we are simply making the effort. Concentration comes through practice but if a person keeps on trying all his life without ever achieving what he considers a satisfactory level of concentration, he has still done his job.

What good is salat if one is still involved in other sins, like the proverbial person who steals and prays? The simple answer is that our lives are combinations of good and evil. Our goal is to increase the good and reduce or eliminate the evil. And that won't happen by putting the good on hold until we can get rid of the evil. Those who put off becoming regular in their daily salat until they straighten out the rest of their life have an excuse for life! It may also be helpful to remember that the greatest theft is that of salat itself.

Salat is indeed the key to paradise. If we valued paradise that would definitely show in the way we guard the key to it!

The Meaning of Ramadan

FASTING DURING RAMADAN was ordained during the second year of Hijrah. Why not earlier? In Makkah the economic conditions of the Muslims were bad. They were being persecuted. Often days would go by before they had anything to eat. It is easy to skip meals if you don't have any. Obviously fasting would have been easier under the circumstances. So why not then?

The answer may be that Ramadan is not only about skipping meals. While fasting is an integral and paramount part of it, Ramadan offers a comprehensive program for our spiritual overhaul. The entire program required the peace and security that was offered by Madinah.

Yes, Ramadan is the most important month of the year. It is the month that the believers await with eagerness. At the beginning of Rajab—two full months before Ramadan—the Prophet Muhammad ﷺ used to supplicate thus: "O Allah! Bless us during Rajab and Sha'ban, and let us reach Ramadan (in good health)."[30]

---

[30] *Kanzul Ummal*, Hadith 18049

The Meaning of Ramadan

During Ramadan the believers get busy seeking Allah's mercy, forgiveness, and protection from Hell-fire. This is the month for renewing our commitment and re-establishing our relationship with our Creator. It is the spring season for goodness and virtues when righteousness blossoms throughout the Muslim communities. "If we combine all the blessings of the other eleven months, they would not add up to the blessings of Ramadan," said the great scholar and reformer Shaikh Ahmed Farooqi (Mujaddid Alf Thani). It offers every Muslim an opportunity to strengthen his *iman*, purify his heart and soul, and to remove the evil effects of the sins committed by him. Ahadith on the merits of this month are well known. For example,

مَنْ صَامَ رَمَضَانَ إِيمَانًا وَاحْتِسَابًا غُفِرَ لَهُ مَا تَقَدَّمَ مِنْ ذَنْبِهِ

"Whoever fasts during Ramadan with purity of belief and with expectation of a reward (from Allah ﷻ) will have his previous sins forgiven." [*Bukhari*, Hadith 37]

مَنْ قَامَ رَمَضَانَ إِيمَانًا وَاحْتِسَابًا غُفِرَ لَهُ مَا تَقَدَّمَ مِنْ ذَنْبِهِ

"Whoever stands in prayers during the nights of Ramadan with purity of belief and expectation of a reward (from Allah ﷻ) will have his previous sins forgiven." [*Bukhari*, Hadith 36]

As other ahadith tell us, the rewards for good deeds are multiplied manifold during Ramadan.

Along with the possibility of a great reward, there is the risk of a terrible loss. If we let any other month pass by carelessly, we just lost a month. If we do the same during Ramadan, we have lost everything. The person who misses just one day's fast without a legitimate reason cannot really make up for it even if he were to fast everyday for the rest of his life. And of the three persons that Prophet ﷺ cursed, one is the unfortunate Muslim who finds Ramadan in good health but does not use the opportunity to seek Allah's mercy.

One who does not fast is obviously in this category, but so also is the person who fasts and prays but makes no effort to stay away from sins or attain purity of heart through the numerous opportunities offered by Ramadan. The Prophet ﷺ warned us: "There are those who get nothing from their fast but hunger and thirst. There are those who get nothing from their nightly prayers but loss of sleep."[31]

Those who understood this, for them Ramadan was indeed a very special month. In addition to fasting, mandatory salat, and extra *Taraweeh* salat, they spent the whole month in acts of worship like voluntary salat, *tilawa* (recitation of Qur'an), *dhikr*, etc. After mentioning that this has been the tradition of the pious people of this ummah throughout the centuries, Maulana Abul Hasan Ali Nadwi notes: "I have seen with my own eyes such *ulama* and *mashaikh* who used to finish recitation of the entire Qur'an everyday during Ramadan. They spent almost the entire night in prayers. They used to eat so little that one wondered how they could endure all this. These greats valued every moment of Ramadan and would not waste any of it in any other pursuit…Watching them made one believe the astounding stories of *ibada* and devotion of our elders recorded by history."

This emphasis on these acts of worship may sound strange—even misplaced—to some. It requires some explanation. We know that the term *ibada* (worship and obedience) in Islam applies not only to the formal acts of worship and devotion like salat, *tilawa*, and *dhikr*, but it also applies to worldly acts when performed in obedience to the Shariah and with the intention of pleasing Allah ﷻ. Thus a believer going to work is performing *ibada* when he seeks *halal* income to discharge his responsibility as a breadwinner for the family. However a distinction must be made between the two. The first category consists of direct *ibada*, acts that are required for their own sake. The second category consists

---

[31] *Musnad Ahmed*, Hadith 9308

of indirect *ibada*—worldly acts that become *ibada* through proper intention and observation of Shariah. While the second category is important for it extends the idea of *ibada* to our entire life, there is also a danger because by their very nature these acts can camouflage other motives. (Is my going to work really *ibada* or am I actually in the rat race?) Here the direct *ibada* comes to the rescue. Through them we can purify our motives, and re-establish our relationship with Allah ﷻ.

Islam does not approve of monasticism. It does not ask us to permanently isolate ourselves from this world, since our test is in living here according to the Commands of our Creator. But it does ask us to take periodic breaks from it. The mandatory salat (five daily prayers) is one example. For a few minutes every so many hours throughout the day, we leave the affairs of this world and appear before Allah ﷻ to remind ourselves that none but He is worthy of worship and of our unfaltering obedience to Him. Ramadan takes this to the next higher plane, providing intense training for a whole month.

This spirit is captured in *I'tikaf*, a unique *ibada* associated with Ramadan, in which a person gives up all his normal activities and enters a masjid for a specific period. There is great merit in it and every Muslim community is encouraged to provide at least one person who will perform *I'tikaf* for the last ten days of Ramadan. But even those who cannot spare ten days are encouraged to spend as much time in the masjid as possible.

Through direct *ibada* we "charge our batteries"; the indirect ones allow us to use the power so accumulated in driving the vehicle of our life. Ramadan is the month for rebuilding our spiritual strength. How much we benefit from it is up to us.

Zakat

MONEY. WHAT DOES Islam say about it? Islam recognizes the value of wealth. It refers to it as:

$$\text{أَمْوَٰلَكُمُ ٱلَّتِى جَعَلَ ٱللَّهُ لَكُمْ قِيَٰمًا}$$

"Your property which Allah has made for you a means of support." [An-Nisa, 4:5]

But it also warns about its dual nature: it could be a blessing or a curse. It is a blessing if used to do some good. Prophet Muhammad ﷺ declared that person to be in an enviable position who has a lot of wealth and he spends it day and night in the cause of righteousness. Otherwise it is a curse. No one who reads the following verse can think of it in any other way:

$$\text{وَٱلَّذِينَ يَكْنِزُونَ ٱلذَّهَبَ وَٱلْفِضَّةَ وَلَا يُنفِقُونَهَا فِى سَبِيلِ ٱللَّهِ فَبَشِّرْهُم بِعَذَابٍ أَلِيمٍ ۝ يَوْمَ يُحْمَىٰ عَلَيْهَا فِى}$$

$$\text{نَارِ جَهَنَّمَ فَتُكْوَىٰ بِهَا جِبَاهُهُمْ وَجُنُوبُهُمْ وَظُهُورُهُمْ ۖ هَـٰذَا مَا كَنَزْتُمْ لِأَنفُسِكُمْ فَذُوقُوا مَا كُنتُمْ تَكْنِزُونَ}$$

"And there are those who hoard gold and silver, and spend it not in the way of Allah. Announce unto them a most grievous chastisement. On the day when it will be heated in the fire of Hell, and with it will be branded their foreheads, their flanks, and their backs. 'This is the treasure that you hoarded for yourselves. Taste then the treasure you hoarded.'" [At-Tauba 9:34-35]

The two characters are brought together in a beautiful juxtaposition in a hadith.

$$\text{مَثَلُ الْبَخِيلِ وَالْمُنفِقِ كَمَثَلِ رَجُلَيْنِ عَلَيْهِمَا جُبَّتَانِ مِنْ حَدِيدٍ مِنْ ثُدِيِّهِمَا إِلَى تَرَاقِيهِمَا فَأَمَّا الْمُنفِقُ فَلَا يُنفِقُ إِلَّا سَبَغَتْ أَوْ وَفَرَتْ عَلَى جِلْدِهِ حَتَّى تُخْفِيَ بَنَانَهُ وَتَعْفُوَ أَثَرَهُ وَأَمَّا الْبَخِيلُ فَلَا يُرِيدُ أَنْ يُنفِقَ شَيْئًا إِلَّا لَزِقَتْ كُلُّ حَلْقَةٍ مَكَانَهَا فَهُوَ يُوَسِّعُهَا وَلَا تَتَّسِعُ}$$

"The case of a miser and a giver of charity is similar to that of two persons clad in armor from their breasts to their collar-bones. Every time the generous person gives charity, his armor expands, until it covers his finger tips and toes. Every time the miser intends to spend something, his armor contracts, every ring of it sinking into his flesh. He tries to loosen it but cannot." [*Bukhari*, Hadith 1352]

It should be remembered that here a generous person is one who spends generously in the path of Allah ﷻ. A miser is one whose love of money keeps him from such spending even though he may be spending lavishly in other areas.

Such love of money is a disease of the heart and the first purpose of charity in Islam is to work as an antidote against that. That is why the Qur'an asked the Prophet ﷺ,

خُذْ مِنْ أَمْوَالِهِمْ صَدَقَةً تُطَهِّرُهُمْ وَتُزَكِّيهِم بِهَا

"Accept charity out of their wealth; you will cleans and purify them by means of it." [At-Tauba, 9:103]

Hence the name zakat (purification) for the main form of that obligation. And it is for this reason that zakat remains obligatory even if there are no needy persons in a community.

Of course, the system of zakat is designed to help the poor and the needy, and it is a highly desirable characteristic of the believers that in addition to prayers and other acts of worship they are always conscious of this duty.

وَفِي أَمْوَالِهِمْ حَقٌّ لِّلسَّآئِلِ وَٱلْمَحْرُومِ

"And in their wealth there is due share for the beggar and the deprived." [Az-Zariyat, 51:19]

They do it for no other motive but to please their Lord.

وَيُطْعِمُونَ ٱلطَّعَامَ عَلَىٰ حُبِّهِۦ مِسْكِينًا وَيَتِيمًا وَأَسِيرًا

إِنَّمَا نُطْعِمُكُمْ لِوَجْهِ ٱللَّهِ لَا نُرِيدُ مِنكُمْ جَزَآءً وَلَا شُكُورًا

"And they feed, for the love of Allah, the needy, the orphan, and the captive, saying: 'We feed you for the sake of Allah alone. No reward do we desire from you, nor any thanks.'" [Al-Insan, 76:8-9]

Charity itself has been a cherished institution in all human societies. It remains so even in the capitalistic society. But without a strong belief in Allah ﷻ and the Hereafter, a charitable act can only be motivated by a desire for fame or some other worldly reward. Human beings are driven by rewards. The only truly selfless act is one in which the reward is sought from Allah ﷻ instead of other human beings. And that is the change in orientation that Islam provides and that remains its most distinguishing feature. Once a goat was slaughtered in the Prophet's household and its meat was distributed. Later on the Prophet ﷺ asked Aisha ؓ what was saved from the goat? "Nothing but a shank," she said. "Everything but the shank," said the Prophet ﷺ. For what was given away in charity was truly saved for the Hereafter.

There are other distinct features of Islam's system of zakat. The Qur'an mentions where it can be used.

$$\text{إِنَّمَا ٱلصَّدَقَٰتُ لِلْفُقَرَآءِ وَٱلْمَسَٰكِينِ وَٱلْعَٰمِلِينَ عَلَيْهَا وَٱلْمُؤَلَّفَةِ قُلُوبُهُمْ وَفِى ٱلرِّقَابِ وَٱلْغَٰرِمِينَ وَفِى سَبِيلِ ٱللَّهِ وَٱبْنِ ٱلسَّبِيلِ}$$

"Charity (zakat) is meant only for the poor, the needy, those working at (collecting and distributing) it, those (possible converts) whose hearts are being reconciled (to yours), for freeing of slaves, for those in debt, in striving along Allah's way, and for the wayfarer." [At-Tauba, 9:60]

These are very precise and specific categories, the seemingly general category of "striving along Allah's way" referring to jihad by consensus of scholars.

We can better appreciate the immense wisdom in this arrangement if we compare it with the tithe. Under that system, adopted by the Christian Church, lay people were forced to pay a tenth of their income to the church to "support the clergy, maintain churches and assist the poor"— mostly in that order. The system led to widespread abuses. It was for this reason that the tithe was abolished in France in 1789 during the Revolution and in other countries after that.

England finally ended it in 1936. It was never accepted in the United States.

Zakat, on the other hand, cannot be used to maintain masajid or support the scholars. Neither can it be used to support the normal functioning of the government. No one can change its rate, sources, or application, which are all predetermined by the Qur'an and Sunnah. All these distinguish zakat as an act of worship rather than a tax and have been responsible for keeping the system mostly free of corruption, even at a time when some Muslim countries have generally fallen victim to the corruption epidemic. Yet the problem is that a very large number of those who should be paying zakat are careless about their responsibility.

To be sure, a Muslim has financial obligations other than zakat, for example to support masajid, schools, and other community projects on an as needed basis, but zakat itself remains the most potent system for addressing the economic problems of the Ummah. With 2.5% of the savings of the rich people throughout the Ummah going to its poor people every year, the basic needs of everyone could be satisfied. In fact if used properly, it could put IMF, the World Bank, and other Shylocks who have been enriching themselves at the expense of the poor out of business in the Muslim countries.

Even for our economic problems, Islam is the solution. If only we would give it a chance.

The Road from Makkah

HAJJ IS OBLIGATORY once in a lifetime on those who can afford it, but it benefits the entire Ummah. Islam's acts of worship have multiple dimensions and they are organized at multiple layers. Daily salat, for example, provides occasion for gathering in the neighborhood masjid five times a day. The Friday salat provides a larger weekly gathering and also includes a *khutbah* to give this gathering a direction and purpose. The twice-a-year Eid salats provide a gathering for the entire city. Hajj is the last in this sequence; an annual worldwide gathering of the entire Ummah at the most sacred of all places.

Its role is that of the heart and liver in the human body. The heart sucks in the tired blood, which is then filtered and rejuvenated by the liver, and sent again to all parts of the body by the heart. Similarly, Hajj brings in members of this ummah, rejuvenates their faith, spiritual energy, and commitment, and sends them back to their communities to spread the blessings far and wide.

Its most powerful message is about *Tauheed* (monotheism) and *Akhirat* (the Hereafter), two of the pillars of faith. If Hajj is a form of jihad, as some ahadith mention, its battle cry is "Labbaik Allahumma Labaik" "I am here O Allah, I am here. There is no partner unto You. All praise and blessings and sovereignty belong to you. There is no partner unto You." From the moment the pilgrim dons his Ihram, he profusely makes this pronouncement during all waking hours until he has stoned the Shaytan on the 10th of Zul-Hijjah.

As for the Hereafter, Hajj is itself a replay of our death and resurrection. The Ihram, the two unstitched pieces of white cloth that replace dress for men, reminds us of the burial shroud. The gathering on the plain of Arafat reminds us of the time when everyone will be resurrected in the Hereafter to stand before Allah ﷻ and give account of their deeds.

Built on these twin foundations of faith is the example of Sayyidna Ibrahim ﷺ that is reflected in many of the rites of Hajj. That example can be summarized in two words: love and obedience. Unwavering love for Allah ﷻ; unfailing obedience to Him. This also is the message of Hajj.

Hajj is at once an intensely personal and a superbly collective act of worship. Today its role in our collective life has been severely watered down by the rulers over the land of Hajj and by an ummah that has lost touch with its mission. Upon arrival the pilgrims are sorted out on the basis of their passports and are reminded at every turn that they are members of a nation-state and not the one Ummah. Every expression that aims at mobilizing this ummah to stand up collectively to the challenges it faces is brutally suppressed during Hajj. The landscape of Makkah and Madinah has also been changed beyond recognition, through obscene attempts at emulating Europe, thereby producing a historic disconnect for the holy land. Today pilgrims have been separated from each other as well as from their glorious history.

So it may be helpful to remind ourselves that Hajj is associated with major turning points and milestones in Islamic history. In fact the history of the Islamic state begins with Hajj. It was here in the 11th year of Prophethood (July 620 C.E) that the first Pledge of Aqaba took place, followed two years later by the second pledge that was the basis for *Hijrah* and the establishment of the Islamic state in Madinah.

Just a decade later, it was here that the mission of the Prophet ﷺ reached its peak when 124,000 Companions performed Farewell Hajj with the Prophet ﷺ in 10 AH.

The *khutbah* of the Prophet ﷺ delivered during the Farewell Hajj is the most important historical document for the entire humanity. It proclaimed: "There is no superiority for an Arab over a non-Arab, nor for a white over a black nor for a black over a white except through *taqwa* (Allah Consciousness)."

It declared the sanctity of life, honor, and property: "O people! Verily your blood, your property and your honor are sacred and inviolable until you appear before your Lord, just as the sacred inviolability of this day of yours, this month of yours and this town of yours."

It set down a fundamental principle of justice: "Beware! No one is responsible for a crime but the person who committed it. Neither the child is responsible for the crime of the father, nor is the father responsible for the crime of his child."

Compared to this proclamation the other celebrated declarations like the Magna-Carta and the Universal Declaration of Human Rights are insincere and juvenile attempts at plagiarizing. The US Declaration of Independence (1776), for example, declared "All men are created equal" but it actually meant "All white men are created equal." Blacks were not included, nor were the natives or any other non-whites.

For a world submerged in total darkness, this new proclamation would have to be spread through the Ummah that was produced out of the *Jahiliya* society through twenty-three years of hard work, sacrifice, and perseverance by the Prophet ﷺ. To them it reminded: "Every Muslim is the brother of another Muslim and all the Muslims form one brotherhood...Take heed not to go astray after me and strike one another's necks." And for the generations to come it also pointed out the way to safeguard this greatest of all revolutions: "I am leaving two things with you such that if you hold on fast to them you will not go astray: the Book of Allah and my Sunnah."

Those standing that day at the plain of Arafat were the best of humanity. They took the torch and spread the light in four corners of the world, ushering in a new era of peace and justice. They liberated mankind from servitude to false gods turning it instead to the service to the Creator.

With the passage of time, their followers gradually became weak in their faith and corrupt in their practices. Darkness returned to the world. Today the world is such a dark place where paganism, Zionism, and racism flourish and the strong devour the weak because "Might is right."

The road from Makkah is full of returning pilgrims who bring back Zamzam, dates, and many souvenirs. These are all great. But what we need the most is the message that was proclaimed there by the Prophet Muhammad ﷺ more than 1400 years ago.

The Power of Du'a

ONCE PROPHET MUHAMMAD ﷺ passed by a people who were suffering from some affliction. "Why don't they make *du'a* (supplication) to Allah for protection," he said. With all the suffering and disasters Muslims are facing in various parts of the world, the question can be directed to all of us today.

It is not that we have forgotten du'a completely; we refer to it regularly. But, our ideas and practice regarding du'a have become distorted. Often it is reduced to the level of a ritual. Generally it is considered when all our efforts have failed—an act of last resort. It is belittled through actions and sometimes even with words. Is it any wonder that today mostly a mention of du'a is meant to indicate the hopelessness of a situation.

What a tragedy, for du'a is the most potent weapon of a believer. It can change fate, while no action of ours ever can. It is the essence of *ibada* or worship. With it we can never fail; without it we can never succeed. In the proper scheme of things, du'a should be the first and the last resort of the believer, with all his plans and actions coming in between.

Du'a is conversation with Allah, out Creator, our Lord and Master, the All Knowing, the All Powerful. This act in itself is of extraordinary significance. It is the most uplifting, liberating, empowering, and transforming conversation a person can ever have. We turn to Him because we know that He alone can lift our sufferings and solve our problems. We feel relieved after describing our difficulties to our Creator. We feel empowered after having communicated with the All Mighty. We sense His mercy all around us after talking to the Most Merciful. We get a new commitment to follow His path for that is the only path for success. We feel blessed with each such commitment.

In every difficulty our first action is du'a, as is our last. We ask Allah ﷻ to show us the way to handle that difficulty; we seek His help in following the path He shows to us; we seek His aid in making our efforts successful. When we fall sick, we know that we cannot find the right doctor without His Will; that the best doctor may not be able to diagnose our condition without His Command; that the best treatment plan will not succeed without His Permission. We make du'a for all of these. We make du'a before we seek medical help, while we are receiving it and after it has been delivered. The same is true of all other difficulties we may encounter.

Du'a is the essence of *ibada*. A person engaged in du'a affirms his belief in *Tauheed* (monotheism) and shuns belief in all false gods. With each du'a his belief in Allah ﷻ grows. He beseeches Him, affirming his own powerlessness. A person seriously and sincerely engaged in du'a understands exactly the relationship between himself and the Creator and affirms it through his actions. That is the essence of worship! Additionally, such a person can never become arrogant or proud, a logical result of true worship.

Du'a is our most potent weapon in all struggles of life as well as in jihad in the battlefield. During the battle of Badr, the Prophet Muhammad ﷺ stood up all night in prayer seeking Allah's help in the battle between unequal armies that would follow the next day. In the decisive battles against the crusaders, Sultan Salahuddin Ayyubi was busy day and night. His days were devoted to jihad. His nights were spent making du'a, crying, and seeking Allah's help.

We should make it a point to make du'a for all things big and small. It is the beginning of wisdom to realize that big and small are arbitrary labels that are totally irrelevant in this context. Nothing is too big for the One we are asking from; nothing is too small for the one who is asking. That is why we have been taught to ask Allah ﷻ when we need something as small as shoelaces. We should ask as a beggar, as a destitute person, for that is what we in reality are in relationship to Allah ﷻ. At the same time we should ask with great hope and conviction that we shall be granted our prayers. We should remember the hadith: "There is nothing more dear to Allah than a servant making du'a to Him." On the other hand, a du'a lacking concentration and conviction is no du'a at all.

We should make du'a at all times, not only during times of distress. The Prophet Muhammad ﷺ said: "Whosoever desires that Allah answers his du'as in unfavorable and difficult conditions, he should make plentiful du'a in days of ease and comfort." Also he said: "The person who does not ask from Allah, Allah becomes angry with him."

We should ask for all of our needs: those related to this world as well as those related to the Hereafter. Those who only concentrate on the former are, in effect, announcing that they don't care for their life in the permanent abode. They should blame nobody but themselves for the total ruin in that world that Qur'an assures us awaits them. Those who only concentrate on the latter are also showing lack of balance, for we need Allah's help to lead a good life here as well.

We should make du'a not only for ourselves but also for our parents, brothers and sisters, spouses and children, relatives and friends, teachers and other benefactors, and destitute and struggling Muslims everywhere. We should pray for them for the good in this world as well as in the Hereafter. The Prophet ﷺ said:

دَعْوَةُ الْمَرْءِ الْمُسْلِمِ لِأَخِيهِ بِظَهْرِ الْغَيْبِ مُسْتَجَابَةٌ عِنْدَ رَأْسِهِ مَلَكٌ مُوَكَّلٌ كُلَّمَا دَعَا لِأَخِيهِ بِخَيْرٍ قَالَ الْمَلَكُ الْمُوَكَّلُ بِهِ آمِينَ وَلَكَ بِمِثْلٍ

"The du'a of a Muslim for his brother (in Islam) in his absence is readily accepted. An angel is appointed to his side. Whenever he makes a beneficial du'a for his brother the appointed angel says, 'Aameen. And may you also be blessed with the same.'" [*Muslim*, Hadith 4914]

In the dark ages that we are living in today, everyday brings fresh news about atrocities committed against our brothers in Palestine, Kashmir, India, Afghanistan, Iraq, Chechnya, etc. And what do we do? We can continue to just feel frustrated and depressed. We can petition the determined perpetrators or a fictional "International Community." We can just forget all this and move on to some other subject. Or we can stand up before Allah ﷻ and pray for His help, Who alone can help. The du'a can change our life, our outlook, and our fate. It is the most potent weapon. But it works only for those who try sincerely and seriously to use it.

Islam is the Solution

In this section:

- ❁ Better, Try to See the Light
- ❁ Islam is the Solution
- ❁ What Does Islam Teach About Justice?
- ❁ The Message of Mercy
- ❁ On Religious Tolerance
- ❁ On Extremism
- ❁ Whose Islam?

Better, Try to See the Light

MODERN DAY CHRISTIANITY and Judaism have been through a series of "reformation" processes. Over the centuries tens of thousands of "reformed churches" and "reformed synagogues" have been established throughout Europe and America. Many see this revision and update as a continuous process.

So, why not Islam?

This question is a perplexing one for those looking at Islam from the outside. Unfortunately for many, it brings rage rather than reflection. Some are driven to do whatever it takes to make it happen. It is a measure of the intensity of such desire that, today, any ignoramus with a Muslim sounding name can become instant celebrity by declaring that Qur'an needs to be updated or Shariah needs to be rethought. In fact during the Satanic Verses affairs, when the entire Muslim world had been outraged by the support for pure filth shown by all sorts of pundits, many of these "experts" were secretly thrilled that the moment had arrived. A professor of Religion at the University of Southern California informed the *Los Angeles Times* readers at that time that the big question the Muslim world was debating was: "Who had really authored the Qur'an."[32]

Such psychotic scholarship has also been enlisted in all kinds of research projects as well as in secret plans by the UN and big powers to find ways of bringing "reform" to Islam. Some come disguised as friends. They appear to applaud Islam's teachings on tolerance and compassion. Islam does preach tolerance for those outside its boundaries. At the same time it is also very sensitive about those boundaries and does not allow them to be blurred in a haze of tolerance. Some point to the principles of ijtihad in Islam. But they fail to realize that ijtihad does not mean second-guessing the Qur'an, Sunnah, or consensus of the Companions. Then there are those who resort to ridiculing Muslims for lagging behind the times. When all else fails, they may simply try to order an abrogation of the Shariah, as the UN is trying to do now under the banner of the Universal Declaration of Human Rights. Wasted efforts, all!

Their fight is with the Qur'an and they only need to turn to the Qur'an to get a response. Here it is, loud and clear:

وَإِذَا تُتْلَىٰ عَلَيْهِمْ ءَايَاتُنَا بَيِّنَـٰتٍ قَالَ ٱلَّذِينَ لَا يَرْجُونَ لِقَآءَنَا ٱئْتِ بِقُرْءَانٍ غَيْرِ هَـٰذَآ أَوْ بَدِّلْهُ ۚ قُلْ مَا يَكُونُ لِىٓ أَنْ أُبَدِّلَهُۥ مِن تِلْقَآئِ نَفْسِىٓ ۖ إِنْ أَتَّبِعُ إِلَّا مَا يُوحَىٰٓ إِلَىَّ ۖ إِنِّىٓ أَخَافُ إِنْ عَصَيْتُ رَبِّى عَذَابَ يَوْمٍ عَظِيمٍ ۝

---

[32] John P. Crossley Jr., "Rushdie Is Only an Early Voice in Islam's Evolutionary Rediscovery of Its Origins," *Los Angeles Times,* March 7, 1989, 7. Such "scholarship" did not hurt his career at all; he has been the director of the School of Religion at USC since 1994, where he has been teaching since 1982 It is also interesting to note that at the time he made that preposterous statement he was chair of the search committee for King Faisal Chair in Islamic and Arabic Studies!

"But when Our clear revelations are recited unto them, those who do not expect to meet Us, say: 'Bring us a Qur'an other than this, or change it.' Say (O Muhammad): It is not for me to change it of my own accord. I can only follow that which is revealed unto me. Lo! If I disobey my Lord I fear the retribution of an awful Day." [Yunus, 10:15]

If the Qur'an could have been changed by worldly powers, it would have been changed long time ago. If it could be made controversial by secretly publishing and distributing corrupt versions, that would have been already done. But not an iota has changed in the Book that was revealed 1400 years ago. It is the only revealed book in the world that exists in the original language of its revelation. And if all the printed copies of it were to be destroyed today, the Book would remain for it is the only Book in the world that is memorized from cover to cover by millions upon millions of people.

And it is the only revealed book that begins with this claim:

"This is the Book whereof there is no doubt; in it is guidance for those who fear Allah." [Al-Baqarah, 2:2]

There is no doubt that it is the Word of Allah. No doubt that it contains the ultimate truth. No doubt that it was sent through the last Messenger of Allah who also explained what it means. No doubt that all success and happiness and bliss lies in faithfully following its commands and all failure and sorrow and misery lies in rejecting it.

You either believe in this statement or you do not. There is no third option.

A Muslim, by definition, is the person who attests to the truth of this statement. He has received Allah's Word through Allah's Messenger ﷺ and he, by force of conviction, submits to this revealed truth. In fact, he stands as a witness to mankind to the truth of this message.

This witnessing is not meant to convert others, but only to deliver the Message, as a trust from Allah ﷻ. The Message has been preserved precisely because no one is allowed to change it to make it attractive to the would-be believers. Muslims do not do in Rome as the Romans do, because then they will have Islam no more. They rise above their surroundings by submitting to the Word of Allah and invite the whole world to the same. Those who accept it do it for their own good; those who reject it do so at their own peril.

So, why is there no "reform" movement in Islam a la Christianity or Judaism? Because the latter lost their scriptures, Islam did not. Words of men replaced the Words of God in their scriptures making the whole thing fallible. One can find hundreds of statements in the Bible that can be tested and found untrue. Or statements that contradict each other. There is not a single such instance in the Qur'an, and there will never be. Islam was never deformed that it should need reform. It is not dated that it should need to be updated. Its message is as true today as it was yesterday. All of its commands are as life-giving today as they were yesterday and they will be tomorrow. It remains as the eternal beacon of light as humanity jumps from one extreme to the other in its ignorance.

Right and wrong are eternal. Definitions of good and evil have to be constant. Otherwise, they will lose all meaning. In a world of shifting standards of good, there is no good. It is a great blessing for humanity that Islam provides that constant.

If the entire world agrees that homosexuality is okay, Islam will still call it a great abomination. If the entire world agrees to destroy the institution of family, Islam will still be there to uphold it. If the entire world agrees that sickness is health and health is sickness, Islam will still be there to remove the confusion and safeguard health. You cannot ban light and legislate darkness. Better, try to see the light yourself.

Islam is the Solution

THE TERM "THIRD WORLD" was coined in 1952, in the wake of the Second World War, to refer to the ex-colonies that were not part of the two newly emerged geopolitical blocs of associated interests. The "Third" then meant the third way.

But, the world order setup by the "First World" in the post-colonial period was even more exploitative than the one that immediately preceded it. It engineered a net transfer of wealth, at an increasing rate, from the poor countries to the rich, making the former poorer and the latter richer. While in 1820 the estimates of disparity of wealth between the richest and the poorest countries in the world were about 3:1, by 1950 the ratio had changed to 35:1, and by 1992 it had reached 72:1. Today it is even higher. Ironically the exploits have earned the exploiters a "respectability" and the exploited a disdain. The term "Third World" has come to signify a rank, as in third class.

Then there are armies of "experts" who have been convincing everyone that the real problem of the exploited countries is that they are too "traditional" and their salvation lies in aping the progressive ways of the West. This is the essence of the modernization theory that seeks to move societies from the "traditional" to the "modern."

This discussion is of special value to the Muslims because all the Muslim countries fall in the "Third World." Today there are generations of educated Muslims who have been convinced that progress equals modernization equals westernization. For every problem they turn to the "First World" for answers, guidance, and assistance. They see their societies as decadent and attribute this decadence to their adherence to traditions and religion. Most of the rulers in the Muslim world today, unfortunately, come from this group. At the same time they claim to be Muslims and servants of Islam.

Maybe we can invite them to shed this hypocrisy and take an objective look at their societies. They may find out that contrary to their thinking, whatever good there is in any society, it comes from Islam. Whatever evils there are come from hypocrisy and defiance of Islam.

It is generally observed that in Muslim societies today people are neither punctual nor value time much. Their leisurely ways are in direct contrast to the world where the creed is that time is money. Islam does not promote this materialistic notion of the value of time, which results in nobody having time for others. But it does teach the value of every moment of our life as providing the opportunity for earning the rewards in the Hereafter. It does require us to be punctual and not to waste time. And it delivers.

In the vast Muslim world there is one enterprise that is extraordinary in its punctuality and discipline. In the big cities or the remotest rural areas, the adhan is called five times a day and the people gather for the congregational prayers at the proper times without fail. Neither excessive cold in the winter nights nor excruciating heat during sizzling summer days keeps them from their sacred duty. This enterprise has not been financed by governments or big businesses. When most people are in their warm beds in their unheated homes, there is a muezzin in every neighborhood who never fails to wake up and remind everyone, "Prayer is better than sleep."

Here is a glimpse of the power of Islam. Can we imagine the situation when not just the muezzin and a small congregation, but the entire population becomes responsive to its duty? Can we imagine when their sense of responsibility goes beyond the salat and covers all aspects of their life?

Equally fascinating is the unparalleled power of Islam in shunning social evils that are consuming the world. Despite their myriad problems, the Muslim lands even today shine as islands of virtue in a deep dark ocean of vice.

Consider alcoholism. In the USA alone, the economic costs of alcoholism and drug abuse are reported to be at a quarter trillion dollar per year. The social and moral costs are additional. But the solution evades the world's most technologically advanced and organized society.

Actually it did try. In 1917, Congress passed the 18th Amendment, prohibiting alcohol. This was after a century of grass roots efforts, which included thousands of societies for prohibition and abstinence pledges in churches. They also allocated $5 million for enforcement to turn the USA into a liquor-free society. A few years later the estimate was $300 million and growing. Organized crime started. Thirteen years later Prohibition was repealed. The "Noble Experiment" had failed miserably.

In contrast, Islam banned alcohol 14 centuries ago among people whose love for alcohol was second to none. In three simple steps, spanning only a few years, alcohol was banished from the Muslim world. Today, despite small areas of infraction, a map of the dry world coincides with the map of the Muslim world. Islam has declared alcohol to be *Ummul-Khabaith* (the root of all evil) and no power on earth can change that designation.

We recently saw a small example of the same miracle with respect to drugs. One command by the Taliban Ameer achieved what hundreds of experts and millions of dollars could not. In the areas under Taliban rule the cultivation of opium stopped. (It continued in areas under the control of the western sponsored Northern Alliance, but that is another story.)³³

Where else but in a Muslim country (Saudi Arabia) can one find jewelry stores without armed guards, closed doors, and elaborate security systems? One of the major crimes against humanity and morality committed by the "First World" has been the exploitation of women in the form of prostitution. Whether it is legal or illegal, whether there are marked red light areas or not, it flourishes everywhere the "First World" has its way. In addition, every area visited by their armies has left behind these centers of filth. Again, the notable exception is the Muslim world.

This world was a dark place, having forgotten or distorted previous prophets' teachings, before Prophet Muhammad ﷺ brought the light. He brought back the message of *Tauheed*, universal brotherhood, compassion, mercy, equality, justice, God consciousness, and morality. As Muslims turned away from Islam, the darkness started to increase again, dividing it into first, second, and third worlds. There is lot of arrogance and ignorance in these ranks. But, Islam again illuminates the way. The solution is there, if only we look in the right direction. Islam is the solution.

---

[33] That was written in 1997. Four years later the USA used its enormous military power to remove the Taliban. And poppy cultivation came back with full force under the patronage of the new rulers.

What Does Islam Teach About Justice?

THERE IS ONE WORD that captures the essence of all Islamic laws and all Islamic teachings; one word that describes the overriding value that permeates all Islamic values. Justice. The Qur'an says:

لَقَدْ أَرْسَلْنَا رُسُلَنَا بِٱلْبَيِّنَـٰتِ وَأَنزَلْنَا مَعَهُمُ ٱلْكِتَـٰبَ وَٱلْمِيزَانَ لِيَقُومَ ٱلنَّاسُ بِٱلْقِسْطِ

"We sent aforetime our messengers with clear Signs and sent down with them the Book and the Balance, so that mankind may stand forth in justice." [Al-Hadeed, 57:25]

The sole purpose of sending the Prophets was to establish justice in the world and end injustice. Broadly speaking, doing justice means giving everyone his due. But this simple statement camouflages all the complexities of life in their myriad and ever-changing relations; all the temptations; all the apprehensions and concerns; all the conflicts and dilemmas. To guide the people, Allah ﷻ sent down the Prophets with clear signs, the Book, and the Balance. The

Book contains the revelations that spell out what's fair and unfair or right and wrong. The Balance refers to our ability to measure and calculate so we can follow the path shown by the Book and explained by the Prophets.

Together these sources taught us what are the rights of Allah ﷻ, of other people, and of our own selves on us and how to balance them. A life lived in obedience to Allah ﷻ, then, is a continuous balancing act, both individually and collectively.

Under normal circumstances many people can be just. But Islam commands its followers to be just even in the face of strong conflicting emotions. In dealing with other human beings, two major impediments to justice are love and hatred. See how the Qur'an teaches us to overcome the first impediment when we are dealing with our closest relatives or even ourselves.

يَٰٓأَيُّهَا ٱلَّذِينَ ءَامَنُوا۟ كُونُوا۟ قَوَّٰمِينَ بِٱلْقِسْطِ شُهَدَآءَ لِلَّهِ وَلَوْ عَلَىٰٓ أَنفُسِكُمْ أَوِ ٱلْوَٰلِدَيْنِ وَٱلْأَقْرَبِينَ ۚ إِن يَكُنْ غَنِيًّا أَوْ فَقِيرًا فَٱللَّهُ أَوْلَىٰ بِهِمَا ۖ فَلَا تَتَّبِعُوا۟ ٱلْهَوَىٰٓ أَن تَعْدِلُوا۟ ۚ وَإِن تَلْوُۥٓا۟ أَوْ تُعْرِضُوا۟ فَإِنَّ ٱللَّهَ كَانَ بِمَا تَعْمَلُونَ خَبِيرًا ﴿١٣٥﴾

"You who believe, stand out firmly for justice, as witnesses to Allah, even though it is against yourself, your parents and near relatives; whether it concerns a rich or a poor man, Allah (stands) closer to them both. Do not follow any passion so that you may deal justly. If you swerve about or turn aside Allah is still informed about whatever you do." [An-Nisa, 4:135]

Here is the resolution from the Qur'an of the perennial conflict between self-interest and justice. Be just, even if it is against your narrowly defined self-interest or of those very close to you. Ignorant people think they are protecting their self-interest by being unjust to others. Their decision to be just or unjust may be based on a cold calculation of self-interest. But real faith in Allah ﷻ elevates one above that narrow-mindedness. These verses remind us that the real protector of interests of all people is Allah ﷻ and He will protect us when we follow His command to be just. The justice demanded by Islam permits no favoritism.

The other equally potent impediment is hatred. Here again Qur'an commands:

يَٰٓأَيُّهَا ٱلَّذِينَ ءَامَنُوا۟ كُونُوا۟ قَوَّٰمِينَ لِلَّهِ شُهَدَآءَ بِٱلْقِسْطِ وَلَا يَجْرِمَنَّكُمْ شَنَـَٔانُ قَوْمٍ عَلَىٰٓ أَلَّا تَعْدِلُوا۟ ٱعْدِلُوا۟ هُوَ أَقْرَبُ لِلتَّقْوَىٰ وَٱتَّقُوا۟ ٱللَّهَ إِنَّ ٱللَّهَ خَبِيرٌۢ بِمَا تَعْمَلُونَ

"You who believe, stand out firmly for Allah, as witnesses to fair dealing, and let not the hatred of others to you make you swerve to wrong and depart from justice. Be just: that is next to Piety: and fear Allah. For Allah is well-acquainted with all that you do." [Al-Ma'idah, 5:8]

In other words you cannot do injustice even when you are dealing with the enemy. The natural, uneducated, and uncivilized tendency is to treat the enemy as less than a human being; one who has no rights and deserves no justice or fairness. It was as true in the pre-Islamic tribal *Jahiliya* (based on ignorance) society as it is today. See how Islam directly curbs it. It is a command to the believers, with a reminder that Allah ﷻ is watching you, that enmity of others cannot be used as an excuse for committing injustices against them.

Justice does require retribution and Islam does call for "an eye for an eye." But it does not mean an innocent eye for an innocent eye; it means the eye of the perpetrator for the eye of the victim. It is amazing how those who call the latter as barbaric, actually rally for the former when a real crisis develops.

Fourteen hundred years ago these commands created a society where rich and poor, friend and foe, Muslim and non-Muslim, the ruler and the ruled were all treated equally and all of them could count on receiving justice. The *qadis* (judges) were independent and no one, including the khalifah was above the law. If a dispute arose between the khalifah and an ordinary person, both had to appear in court and provide their evidence. Islamic history is full of stories of this justice that filled the earth wherever Muslims ruled in their golden era.

Further, this justice was not restricted to the citizens of the Islamic state. Islam declares justice as a fundamental moral value that must extend to everyone, friend and foe alike. Consider just two quick examples from history.

Prominent Companion Hudhayfa ibn Yaman ﷺ and his father were on the way to Madinah when they were stopped by Abu Jahl. He allowed them to continue only on the condition that they would not participate in a battle against his people. When they reached Madinah, the Muslims were facing the battle of Badr in which poorly armed Muslims faced a well-equipped army three times their size. It was a battle in which the very survival of the nascent Muslim community was at stake, and each single person counted tremendously. Yet the Prophet ﷺ did not permit them to join the Muslim army simply because they had given word that they would not!

During the rule of Umar ﷺ at one time the Muslim army in Palestine had to leave because they were needed for a campaign in Syria. As usual the army had collected the *dhimmi* tax from its subjects for providing them with protection. Now when the circumstances forced them to leave, obviously they would not be able to provide the protection. They could have simply left or for better public relations they could have explained the situation and said sorry. But this was the Muslim army. Before leaving they returned all the tax although their subjects were in no position to demand or extract it. The subjects were left crying at this display of justice that they did not expect from even their own co-religionists when they ruled them.

Even during their period of decline, we find sporadic incidents that are just unparalleled. One example from recent history may suffice here. During the British rule in India, once a dispute arose between Hindus and Muslims over a piece of land. Hindus claimed it belonged to a temple while Muslims claimed it to be a masjid. Emotions were high on both sides and the possibility of a riot was real. The English judge could not find any means of ascertaining the truth. It was one group's words against the other's. Finally the judge asked both groups if they could trust the testimony of any person. They could. It was a particular Muslim imam (religious leader) who was known for his piety. The person was requested to come to the court as a witness in a very charged atmosphere, with the entire community urging him to help them win the case through his testimony. His testimony was brief. "The Hindus are right," he said. "The Muslim case is baseless." He had not betrayed the community. He had once more affirmed its unflinching commitment to truth and justice above all else.

That is the justice the world needs today.

إِنَّ ٱللَّهَ يَأْمُرُكُمْ أَن تُؤَدُّوا۟ ٱلْأَمَٰنَٰتِ إِلَىٰٓ أَهْلِهَا وَإِذَا حَكَمْتُم بَيْنَ ٱلنَّاسِ أَن تَحْكُمُوا۟ بِٱلْعَدْلِ إِنَّ ٱللَّهَ نِعِمَّا يَعِظُكُم بِهِۦٓ إِنَّ ٱللَّهَ كَانَ سَمِيعًۢا بَصِيرًا ۝

"Allah does command you to render back your Trusts to those to whom they are due; and when you judge between people, that you judge with justice: verily how excellent is the teaching which He gives you! For Allah is He Who Hears and Sees all things." [An-Nisa, 4:58]

The Message of Mercy

IN THE HADITH LITERATURE there is a category called *musalsal* (continuous). A *musalsal* hadith is such that all its narrations over the centuries shared a common attribute. Some of these ahadith include gestures. For example Anas ﷺ reported a hadith about the handshake of the Prophet ﷺ. "The Prophet's ﷺ hand was softer than silk," he reported. But the report was accompanied by an actual handshake, just like the original. There are people living today who have received this hadith, along with the handshake, through an unbroken chain that goes back to the Prophet ﷺ. This is hadith *musalsal bil masafaha* (continuous with handshake).

It is a fascinating subject. There is no other human being whose words and even gestures have been transmitted through the centuries with such love, devotion, and care. There are so many *musalsalat* that Shah Waliullah has compiled them in a book. Leading the group of *musalsalat* is the hadith known as *musalsal bil awwalia*, (continuously first). It is because for centuries, whenever a teacher of hadith started a new class anywhere in the Muslim world, he always began with this hadith. The practice continues to date in many Islamic religious schools. It is always the first hadith in a new hadith class.

We know that unlike the Qur'an, the order in which ahadith are presented or read is dependent only on the choice of the compiler, teacher, or reader. There is no command that they must be studied in a particular order. So the first hadith became first not because of an explicit injunction, but purely by the choice of those involved in the study. Here is that hadith:

الرَّاحِمُونَ يَرْحَمُهُمْ الرَّحْمَنُ ارْحَمُوا مَنْ فِي الأَرضِ يَرْحَمْكُمْ مَنْ فِي السَّمَاءِ

"Those who have mercy will receive the mercy of the Most Merciful. Have mercy on those who are on earth, the One in Heaven will have mercy on you." [*Tirmidhi*, Hadith 1847]

This is the message from the Prophet ﷺ who was declared by Allah ﷻ to be "Mercy for the worlds." It is just appropriate that his Ummah chose that hadith to be the first for its study. There is no other call for mercy that is more universal or more inspiring. Have mercy on all the people. And do it because you yourself need the mercy of Allah. Be merciful to the other creations so the Creator will have mercy on you. Your mercy should see no bounds. It should reach all human beings. Another hadith in *Bukhari* and *Muslim* states:

مَنْ لاَ يَرْحَمْ النَّاسَ لاَ يَرْحَمْهُ اللَّهُ عَزَّ وَجَلَّ

"The one who has no mercy on other human beings will not receive the mercy of Allah, the Great and Almighty." [*Muslim*, Hadith 4283]

It is important to note that in this second hadith the word used is *nas*, that is people, not just believers.

And not just human beings. But also animals. For "those on earth" include all living things. Once the Prophet ﷺ told the story of a person who had fed water to a thirsty dog by climbing down a well and bringing water in his shoe, and attained salvation for that act. When asked if there is any reward for nice treatment to the animals, he answered that there is reward in being kind to all living creatures.[34] Another hadith tells that a woman was punished for starving a cat to death.[35]

Sometimes people say that Islam taught kindness to animals 1400 years ago while the modern civilization has learned the lesson only now. Only the first part of this statement is true, since the modern civilization has not yet learned the lesson. Its penchant for show biz has resulted in many displays of kindness to animals but they only camouflage the unprecedented cruelty to them. Consider the practice of vivisection, in which live animals are put through torture in the name of medical research. Live and conscious animals are burnt or cut up or tortured in all ways imaginable to see what will happen. The practice was invented by this civilization. It continues today.

When it comes to human beings, the modern civilization decidedly values them less than the animals. That is why there are more people concerned about saving the whales and exotic animals than have been concerned about the Muslims in Bosnia, Kashmir, Palestine or elsewhere. That is why seemingly educated people can painlessly present arguments that the dropping of nuclear bombs on civilians was a good thing. That is why the starving to death of nearly half a million people in Iraq, through economic sanctions, did not raise any serious objections in the "civilized" world. Of course the modern civilization's ruthlessness to other human beings, of different color or religion, exceeds its cruelty to animals. It kills, maims, tortures, and starves to death other human beings because they are "others."

Can this civilization even imagine the outlook and mental make up of a nation that for centuries has begun the study of the traditions of its Prophet ﷺ by recalling this message of universal mercy? Kindness, love, mercy. These are

---

[34] *Bukhari*, Hadith 2363.
[35] *Bukhari*, Hadith 2365.

among the most important defining words for the collective personality of this ummah. Our ummah. We begin every act in the name of Allah ﷻ who is Most Beneficent and Merciful. We invite the entire world to the mercy of its Creator. We show mercy to all the creation. And by doing all that we seek mercy of Allah.

We also show our love for the Creator by being kind to His creations. That is the foundation of real mercy. Our mercy is not a public relations ploy or a propaganda tool. It is not driven by a love of headlines. Such motivations can only create a show of mercy. But the real mercy requires sincerely and a more solid foundation.

In a way mercy is an attribute of power. A helpless, powerless person cannot have mercy on others; he can only ask for mercy. When Muslims had power, the world benefited from their mercy. When they lost it, the world became full of ruthlessness and injustice. That is the world we live in today. It is calling for the return of those who can bring kindness and mercy back. Are we those people? Are we the people who have been informed and inspired by the hadith *musalsal bil awwaliya*?

On Religious Tolerance

WHILE ON HIS DEATHBED, Sayyidna Umar ibn Khattab ﷺ dictated a long will consisting of instructions for the next khalifah. Here is the last sentence of that historic document: "I instruct you on behalf of the people who have been given protection in the name of Allah and His Prophet ﷺ. [That is the *dhimmis* or the non-Muslim minorities within the Islamic state]. Our covenant to them must be fulfilled, we must fight to protect them, and they must not be burdened beyond their capabilities."

At that time Sayyidna Umar ﷺ was lying in pain because of the wounds inflicted on him by a non-Muslim who had stabbed him with a dagger soaked in poison while he was leading the Fajr prayer. It should also be remembered that he was the head of a vast empire ranging from Egypt to Persia. From normal rulers of his time or ours, we could have expected vengeance and swift reaction. (The "enlightened" rulers of today have sent bombers even on suspicion of a murder conspiracy.) From a very forgiving head of state we could have expected an attempt to forget and forgive—and that would be considered noble. But a command to protect the minorities and take care of them?

What is even more remarkable is that for Muslim historians the entire affair was just natural. After all it was the

Khalifah himself who had established the standards by writing the guarantees for the protection of life, property, and religion in decree after decree as Muslims opened land after land during his rule. The pattern established here was followed for centuries throughout the Muslim world.

Of course, Sayyidna Umar ؓ was simply following what he learned from the Prophet Muhammad ﷺ himself. That the protection of life, property, and religious freedom of minorities is the religious duty of the Islamic state. That he personally would be demanding justice in the Hereafter on behalf of a *dhimmi* who had been wronged by a Muslim. That there is no compulsion in religion and that Muslims must be just to friends and foe alike.

The result of these teachings was a Muslim rule that set the gold standard for religious tolerance in a world that was not used to the idea. Not only is the Muslim history so remarkably free of the inquisitions, persecutions, witch hunts, and holocausts that tarnish history of other civilizations, it protected its minorities from persecution by others as well. It protected Jews from Christians and Eastern Christians from Roman Catholics. In Spain under the Umayyads and in Baghdad under the Abbasid khalifahs, Christians and Jews enjoyed a freedom of religion that they did not allow each other or anyone else.

This exemplary tolerance is built into Islamic teachings. The entire message of Islam is that this life is a test and we have the option of choosing the path to hell or to heaven. Messengers were sent to inform about the choices and to warn about the consequences. They were not sent to forcibly put the people on the right path. The job of the Muslims is the same. They must deliver the message of Islam to the humanity as they have received it. They are neither to change it to make it attractive, nor to coerce others to accept it. In addition, the results in the Hereafter will depend upon faith. For all good acts are meaningless in the absence of the proper faith. And faith is an affair of the heart. It simply cannot be imposed.

It is not an idea that followers of other religions have shared with Islam. The result is, Muslim experience in the area of tolerance has been exactly opposite of the rest of the world. As Marmaduke Pickthall noted: "It was not until the western nations broke away from their religious law that they became more tolerant, and it was only when the Muslims fell away from their religious law that they declined in tolerance."

The path that the western world took to provide harmony in society was to banish religion from the public square. For this achievement, it thinks that it has earned lecturing rights over the issue. So it may be good to remember that while it has indeed made huge progress in the area of tolerance during the last century (which should be appreciated), it has a long way to go before it can reach the standards established by Islam. First, while Muslim Personal Law is not recognized in the West, the personal law of non-Muslim minorities has always been recognized in the Muslim world. Second, while throughout Europe and America, Muslims are not permitted to make the call to prayer (*adhan*) on loud speakers, church bells ring freely in the Muslim world. Third, the wide spread anti-Islamic prejudice in the western media is both a cause and a consequence of the underlying intolerance. Fourth, hate crimes are a fact of life in the West although they remain highly under-reported. Fifth, the will to admit this state of affairs is also not sufficiently strong. Again here is just one indication: in 1999 two resolutions were floated in the US Senate and House, titled "A resolution supporting religious tolerance toward Muslims." While the Senate resolution passed, the House resolution was gutted under pressure from several Jewish and Christian groups. That was two years before the fateful September 2001 that "changed everything." Actually it only provided a justification to continue and increase the intolerance that had been going on long before it.

The situation of the rest of the "International Community" is not much different. Today in Germany and France government power is being used to snatch the *hijab* from the Muslim woman's head. Yet the bigots remain convinced that they are champions of both women's rights and tolerance. So they are demanding that the curriculum across the Muslim world be changed to purge intolerance!

For Muslims religious tolerance is not about political posturing. It is a serious religious obligation. They must be a force against all intolerance, even that which is promoted in the guise of tolerance.

On Extremism

وَكَذَٰلِكَ جَعَلْنَٰكُمْ أُمَّةً وَسَطًا

"Thus have We Made of you *ummatan wasatan* (an Ummah justly balanced)." [Al-Baqarah, 2:143]

UMMATAN WASATAN CAN be translated as the middle nation, the best nation, and an Ummah justly balanced. The phrase captures the essence of Islam, which is to shun all excesses. At other places (e.g. Al-Maidah, 5:12) the Qur'an refers to the path it shows as *sawaa-as-sabil*. Abdullah Yusuf Ali explains: "The Arabic word *sawaa* signifies smoothness as opposed to roughness; symmetry as opposed to want of plan; equality or proportion as opposed to want of design; rectitude as opposed to crookedness; a mean as opposed to extremes; and fitness for the object held in view as opposed to faultiness."

Extremism is a product of ignorance. Given two extreme points on a straight line, anyone can point out where the middle point lies. But a person that cannot see the entire line will also miss the middle point. He may be sitting on an extreme edge, yet congratulate himself for being in the middle.

Unlike the line, real life is not one-dimensional. As individuals, we find ourselves being pulled in so many directions by myriad internal and external forces. In a society the complexity increases manifold as these forces intersect in complex ways. When you add their dynamic interrelationship over time, the complexity becomes mind-boggling.

Our own instruments of observation and intellect, wonderful as they are, are simply not up to the task of finding the proper course in this complex, ever-changing, multidimensional maze. There are no satellite observatories, no imaging systems, no supercomputers that can help us find a solution. Yet we know that we do need to find it. Our physical well-being requires that we eat a well balanced diet and follow the course of moderation. Our economic, social, and spiritual well-being similarly demands finding the balanced approach and the moderate course in all these spheres. Our total well-being requires finding the path of moderation for our entire life.

For this we need Divine Guidance. No one is more conscious of this than the believer who turns to Allah ﷻ five times a day with this supplication: "Show us the Straight Path." The path that avoids the extremes of *ifraat* (excess) and *tafreet* (deficiency). Is there another group that seeks the path of rectitude and moderation with the same fervor?

That this is the Ummah justly balanced can be seen by looking at its beliefs and practices.

A large number of followers of other religions who accepted Islam have been impressed by the simplicity, profoundness, clarity, and logical soundness of its belief system. It is in religious belief systems that extremist tendencies take their greatest toll. On the one hand there have been people who worshiped animals, celestial bodies, and forces of nature; on the other there are those who deny even the existence of God. Avoiding these extremes are the shining teachings of Islam. The sun, stars, fire, water, and wind are mere creations of One Almighty God. He alone created the entire universe and He alone is its Lord and

Master. Islamic monotheism is the truth. Atheism and polytheism are extremist distortions of this central truth.

Similar is the case of belief in prophets. On the one hand are people who attributed divinity to prophets, declaring some of them to be son of God; on the other are those who considered these chosen people as ordinary human beings who committed all sorts of sins. There are still others who knowingly persecuted and killed the prophets. Again the truth stands in the middle—as taught by Islam. Allah ﷻ chose messengers from among human beings to convey to them His guidance. They were all humans as they were meant to be exemplars for humanity. Yet they were the best of all humanity and they spoke with Divine Authority. They deserved the deepest love, devotion, and obedience from other human beings. One only needs to contrast the depiction of the prophets in the Qur'an with that in other scriptures to appreciate this difference. The latter shows the distortions produced by human imagination. It shows the extremism that can creep in when God's Words and Teachings are no longer preserved.

It is the same story with religious practices. We see two extremes in Christianity and Judaism. In the former Love replaced Law; in the latter Law turned into a straitjacket that made life unbearable and from which reformists had to seek escape—thereby going to the other extreme. If one were to borrow the language the media uses, routinely and inappropriately, when referring to Islamic law, he would find himself using words like harsh and strict in referring to clause after clause in authentic Jewish law.

Again we see Islam as providing the middle ground between the two extremes. It does provide law and does distinguish between the permissible and the forbidden. But the law is free of that strangulating formalism that is seen as a burden rather than a blessing. The Qur'an mentions it as an important attribute of Prophet Muhammad ﷺ:

$$\text{وَيَضَعُ عَنْهُمْ إِصْرَهُمْ وَالْأَغْلَلَ الَّتِي كَانَتْ عَلَيْهِمْ}$$

"He releases them from their heavy burdens and from the yokes that are upon them." [Al-A'raf, 7:157].

Extremism is inherently unstable. Its injustices invoke a rebellion and a counter trend. Thus we see that the western world has gone from the pleasure-is-sin asceticism of yesteryears to the sin-is-in liberalism of today. In these wanderings from one extreme to another, the extremist tendencies themselves have not been overcome. Rather, they have produced unprecedented social upheaval at home and unprecedented exploitation and injustices abroad. Islamic history is free of such wanderings, as one would expect of a religion that came to show the middle path.

$$\text{فَمَن كَفَرَ بَعْدَ ذَٰلِكَ مِنكُمْ فَقَدْ ضَلَّ سَوَاءَ السَّبِيلِ}$$

"But if any of you, after this, resists faith, he has truly wandered from the Path of Rectitude." [Al-Maidah, 5:12]

Whose Islam?

WHENEVER THERE IS any talk of following Islam in the collective life of any Muslim country, one inevitably hears a rhetorical question. Whose Islam? Always the question is posed by those who want an easy out. But in addition to antipathy or hostility to Islam, which is generally recognized, it also shows an intellectual dishonesty that is not as widely perceived.

Actually the question is borrowed from elsewhere—without the least effort to judge its applicability in case of Islam. Nevertheless, it is a valid question when posed in the context of, say, Hinduism, Christianity, or Judaism. Hinduism cannot even agree on its own definition or its articles of faith. ("Hinduism is whatever a Hindu believes in.") There is no unified code or source for a code, just some vaguely defined cultural traditions.

In case of Christianity, the Bible could be a central unifying instrument. The trouble is there is not one, but hundreds of them —none of them in the original language of its revelation. Whose Bible? Whose translation? Whose interpretation? The same is true of Judaism, where even the question, who is a Jew? remains a bone of contention. (The common ground in Israeli Jewry is not based on theology but only on a common goal of oppressing the non-Jews.)

Whose Islam?

In fact it was the problems with and within Christianity that lead to the doctrine of separation of Church and State in the United States. A little bit of history may be helpful here. A lot of those who came to the United States from Europe were religious people. For example, in 1630 when John Winthrop reached Massachusetts Bay, the would-be governor of the new colony declared to his followers: "We are entered into Covenant with Him...we shall be as one body, always having before our eyes our Commission from God to walk in His ways and to keep His Commandments and His Ordinance and His Laws...so that the Lord, our God may bless us."

But not everyone agreed on what was presented as "His Laws." After all, these were personal opinions of the religious authorities. What else could one expect in the absence of a well-preserved revealed text and well-preserved prophetic interpretation of that text. An obvious problem with this is that you can have as many contending interpretations as there are experts—and vested interests—willing to define them. Thus the question, whose religion? became relevant and there was no practical answer. As religion became a divisive force that could not hold the country together, it had to be relegated to the private space to protect it as well as the State. So a century and a half after Winthrop, the framers of the US Constitution firmly embedded the doctrine of separation of Church and State in it.

Exactly the opposite is true in the case of Islam. Here Allah's Book has been miraculously preserved in the original language of its revelation, as has been the language of its revelation itself. The sayings of the Prophet ﷺ along with a complete account of his life down to the smallest details have also been preserved. As even a child knows, the question, whose Qur'an? is as absurd as the question, whose Bible? is relevant. The Shariah is rooted in the Qur'an and Sunnah. With the twin rock-solid foundations plus historic continuity, Islam remains a sure and uncompromised source of guidance unlike any other.

Aren't there big differences between various schools of Islamic Law? Not only are there various schools, but also there are divisions within the schools themselves, some might point out. For example in the countries of the Indian subcontinent where the great majority of Muslims belongs to the Hanafi school, there seems to be this unbridgeable chasm between the Deobandi and Barelwi groups. What is generally not realized is that there is no difference on issues of law or *fiqh* between these groups. While there is disagreement between them over certain practices, they rely on the same authorities, quote from the same books, and follow the same exact code of law.

The four major schools of *fiqh* certainly have differences between them. Yet the relevance of these differences to implementing Islam in a society is vastly exaggerated, while the common ground between them is ignored. Just consider, are there any differences between them regarding the articles of faith? The pillars of Islam? The meaning of good and evil? The definition of right and wrong? Sources of law? Moral values? The role of government? The relationship of individual and the society? The role of women in the society? The fact is that on all of these issues there is no difference between them. Yet these are central issues when organizing the collective life of any society.

For example, reforming the education system based on Islam means helping the students develop an Islamic outlook. In science they should see the signs of Allah ﷻ. In history they should see the working of Allah's Laws that determine the rise and fall of nations. Reforming the media means aligning their methods and goals with Islamic morality, throwing out a system that appeals to people's baser emotions as a means to attracting their attention and their money. Reforming the economic system means replacing the injustice and irresponsibility of a *riba* (interest) based system with the justice and responsibility taught by Islam. It means developing a society in which affluence and poverty are not viewed as achievements and failures but only as different conditions that carry with them different sets of rights and responsibilities.

Now let us ask, which of the above is hampered by the differences between various Islamic schools? Which of these require us to ask the question, whose Islam? before we can proceed?

In map making, the prevalent European Mercator projection system introduces distortions making some areas much bigger and others much smaller. For example Greenland is in reality much smaller and Africa is much bigger than the maps show. A similar distortion has been introduced in the religious maps of the Muslim world that vastly enlarge our areas of disagreement and tremendously reduce our common ground, thereby portraying the picture of "so many irreconcilable versions of Islam." That, unfortunately, sometimes the distortions may be done by insiders does not change the fact of distortion. It is time we realized that there is something wrong with that picture and with the question, whose Islam?

The Choice is Yours

In this section:

- Lowest of the Low
- The Choice is Yours
- The Road to Paradise

Lowest of the Low

لَقَدْ خَلَقْنَا ٱلْإِنسَٰنَ فِىٓ أَحْسَنِ تَقْوِيمٍ ۝ ثُمَّ رَدَدْنَٰهُ أَسْفَلَ سَٰفِلِينَ ۝ إِلَّا ٱلَّذِينَ ءَامَنُوا۟ وَعَمِلُوا۟ ٱلصَّٰلِحَٰتِ فَلَهُمْ أَجْرٌ غَيْرُ مَمْنُونٍ ۝

"We have indeed created man in the best of molds. Then reduced him (to be) the lowest of the low. Except for those who believe and do righteous deeds: for they shall have a reward unfailing." [At-Tin, 95:4-6]

PHILOSOPHERS AND THINKERS have always been wondering and arguing about the nature of man. Is man evil by nature? Is he a born sinner? Is he intrinsically good? Or, as the postmodernists are now saying, is there even such a thing as good and evil? To them, just like beauty, good and evil are in the eye of the beholder.

Inevitably for the secular minds, the point of reference is the animals. Biologically man is also an animal, albeit a civilized animal. A social animal. A tool-using animal. The most intelligent animal. One with a sense of morality. Similarly, when we see a person doing some horrible violence the immediate word that comes to mind about the perpetrator is animal. Those committing such heinous crimes cannot be human beings. They are animals.

Both characterizations miss the reality. When good, man is not just an animal with a sense of morality. When bad, man is not just a beast.

Consider the butchery that went on not too long ago under the media spotlight in Bosnia and Kosova, or away from the attention of the media in Kashmir, Palestine, Iraq, or a dozen other places in the world. What animal is capable of committing such horrors? Animals kill for food or territory but they do not commit massacres, plot massive starvation of their enemies, invent tools and techniques of torture, or establish rape camps. There is no animal that has ever committed the atrocities that the human-looking perpetrators in all these places have committed.

Similarly, consider the wickedness of another group of actors in the same drama. Their purpose was to help destroy the Muslims and bury once for all their desire for—as well as their legal and moral right to—liberation from Serb tyranny, while appearing to be helping them. Both in Bosnia and Kosova, Muslims would have been in much better position had there been no "International Community" at all. Again, such chicanery is only possible in the human world. While stories invented by human beings tell of wickedness of animals, in reality animals do not hatch conspiracies, or appear to be your friends when they are actually trying to hurt you. There are no spin doctors or "media experts" in the animal kingdom. It is humans, not crocodiles, that shed the proverbial "crocodile tears."

On the other hand, consider the cases of extreme sacrifice, perseverance, courage, restraint, kindness, and altruism shown by human beings during the darkest moments of history. Even more, consider the near universal appreciation of these attributes. How can a being capable of doing so much evil also show love for so much good? Simply because Allah ﷻ has endowed us with the potential for reaching the greatest heights or the lowest depths. In the first case man becomes higher than the angels. In the second case, he becomes the lowest of the low. Which of the two paths we follow is up to us as God has given us the freedom to choose between them.

As the Qur'an tells us, Allah ﷻ has created man in the best mold. This refers to the potential for goodness built into human nature. All the goodness we see in the world today or find in the pages of history is a result of this innate goodness. It was because of that potential that angels were asked to bow down to Adam ﷺ. By nature angels never commit any sin. Human beings, who have been given the freedom of choice by their Creator, have the potential of surpassing the angels in goodness when they follow the path of obedience to Allah ﷻ out of their free will. The best expression of that goodness was in the Prophets of Allah, peace on all of them. The best of the Prophets was Prophet Muhammad ﷺ. Thus we see that during his *Mi'raj* he went to the point where angel Jibreel ﷺ was not even allowed.

The goodness of the rest of us can only be derived from the Prophetic goodness. For the humanity now the path to goodness is through following the teachings and example of the Last Messenger ﷺ. To the extent that one follows him in beliefs and actions, one will attain his or her potential.

Of course, human beings have freedom to choose another path, rejecting belief in One True God and refusing to obey Him. Instead of worshiping God, they can worship and obey their own lusts and desires. They can do whatever pleases them or feels good. In their pursuit of power, wealth, or sensory pleasures, they can choose to ignore all moral values or ethical principles. This road is wide open too. Those who follow it will become the lowest of the low.

The same freedom of choice that has been given to the human beings also requires that those who choose the second path not be punished right away. Thus, we see that people get away with murder here. Crime and wrongs seem to pay. Little do the perpetrators realize that their victories and gains are fleeting; they will be gone before they know it. Then they will suffer the eternal doom that they had earned. And the never-ending reward will only be for those who chose the first path.

This is the central teaching of Islam.

$$\text{إِنَّا هَدَيْنَٰهُ ٱلسَّبِيلَ إِمَّا شَاكِرًا وَإِمَّا كَفُورًا}$$

"We have guided him along the (right) path, whether he is thankful or thankless." [Al-Insan, 76:3]

Man has been shown the Way through Revelation brought to him by the Prophets. If he is grateful, he will accept the Guidance, follow the path of righteousness and be successful both here and in the Hereafter. If not, he will face eternal doom and a never-ending Blazing Fire.

Today the affairs of this world are being controlled by the lowest of the low and the daily news is a reminder of that tragic fact. This should not make us lose hope, but only make us redouble our efforts to follow and promote the path of Belief and good deeds.

The Choice is Yours

AN ARTICLE IN THE *Detroit News* once contrasted the lives of two ordinary persons from Palestinian refuge camps in Jordan. Two persons joined by faith and circumstances, yet separated by choices of their lifestyles. One awakened at 4 a.m. every day and walked a mile to the masjid for the Fajr prayers. At that time, the other was often just getting to sleep, capping off another night of drinking and socializing at a bar that catered to tourists and wealthy Palestinians. One kept abreast of the latest political developments in the Middle East to "ensure our future liberation from Israel." The other, "like many in his Heineken-drinking clique, is oblivious to the latest showdown between the United States and Iraq and the subsequent peace brokered by the United Nations. But ... knows all the words to the latest music videos." One wore a beard. The other religiously shaved it before happy hour, "because the real hot girls like soft skin." One was concerned about moral decadence and the mortal danger it presents to "their country and their afterlife." The other asked, "Why shouldn't we enjoy ourselves? Come on, you only live once, right?"

The article titled "Partying versus Praying" was pleasantly free of the propaganda overtones characteristic of the mainstream media reports about the Muslim world. In a

THE CHOICE IS YOURS

typical piece, the first person would have been depicted as a "fundamentalist," a fanatic, a "bad guy" who is danger to himself and to the world. The second person would, of course, be the "good guy"—the friendly, "civilized" person who needs encouragement and support. In contrast, here was an objective observation about the clash of two currents. Its objectivity compels those it reports about, to reflect on their situation.

In a way, the story captures the current state of the entire Ummah. For today, the Ummah is a big refuge camp: robbed, wounded, tortured, expelled, dispossessed, and disenfranchised. And just like the refuge camp it has two powerful but exactly opposite currents: One represents awakening, turning to Allah ﷻ, overcoming the base desires, and preparing for liberation from slavery, both physical and intellectual. The other represents falling asleep, turning away from Allah ﷻ, and "enjoying" the slavery. This is a clash between piety and profanity, between light and darkness, between the path to Paradise and the way to Hell.

It is born of the freedom of choice that has been given to every human being. Allah ﷻ has created two possible destinations for all human beings, and there are two opposite paths leading to them.

وَهَدَيْنَٰهُ ٱلنَّجْدَيْنِ ۝

"We have shown him the two paths." [Al-Balad, 90:10]

إِنَّا هَدَيْنَٰهُ ٱلسَّبِيلَ إِمَّا شَاكِرًا وَإِمَّا كَفُورًا ۝

"We have guided him along the (right) path, whether he is thankful or thankless." [Al-Insan, 76:3]

The first path leads to success, the other to failure.

The Choice is Yours

$$\text{وَنَفْسٍ وَمَا سَوَّاهَا ۝ فَأَلْهَمَهَا فُجُورَهَا وَتَقْوَاهَا ۝ قَدْ أَفْلَحَ مَن زَكَّاهَا ۝ وَقَدْ خَابَ مَن دَسَّاهَا ۝}$$

"By the Soul and the proportion and order given to it, and its inspiration as to its wrong and its right. Truly he succeeds that purifies it and he fails that corrupts it." [Ash-Shams, 91:7-10]

The Qur'an is very emphatic that those who choose the disparate paths cannot be alike, either here or in the Hereafter:

$$\text{أَمْ نَجْعَلُ الَّذِينَ ءَامَنُوا۟ وَعَمِلُوا۟ الصَّالِحَاتِ كَالْمُفْسِدِينَ فِى الْأَرْضِ أَمْ نَجْعَلُ الْمُتَّقِينَ كَالْفُجَّارِ ۝}$$

"Shall We treat those who believe and do good deeds like mischief-makers on earth? Shall We treat the pious as the wicked?" [Sad, 38:28]

$$\text{أَفَمَن كَانَ مُؤْمِنًا كَمَن كَانَ فَاسِقًا ۚ لَّا يَسْتَوُۥنَ ۝}$$

"Is someone who is a believer like someone who has been acting immorally? They are not alike." [As-Sajda, 32:18]

$$\text{أَفَمَن يَعْلَمُ أَنَّمَا أُنزِلَ إِلَيْكَ مِن رَّبِّكَ الْحَقُّ كَمَنْ هُوَ أَعْمَىٰ ۚ إِنَّمَا يَتَذَكَّرُ أُو۟لُوا۟ الْأَلْبَابِ ۝}$$

"Is someone who knows that what has been revealed unto you (O Muhammad), from your Lord is the Truth, like someone who is blind? Only the people of understanding respond to the advice." [Ar-Ra'd, 13:19]

يَوْمَ يَتَذَكَّرُ ٱلْإِنسَٰنُ مَا سَعَىٰ ۝ وَبُرِّزَتِ ٱلْجَحِيمُ لِمَن يَرَىٰ ۝ فَأَمَّا مَن طَغَىٰ ۝ وَءَاثَرَ ٱلْحَيَوٰةَ ٱلدُّنْيَا ۝ فَإِنَّ ٱلْجَحِيمَ هِىَ ٱلْمَأْوَىٰ ۝ وَأَمَّا مَنْ خَافَ مَقَامَ رَبِّهِۦ وَنَهَى ٱلنَّفْسَ عَنِ ٱلْهَوَىٰ ۝ فَإِنَّ ٱلْجَنَّةَ هِىَ ٱلْمَأْوَىٰ ۝

"The Day when Man shall remember all that he strove for, and Hell-fire shall be placed in full view for him who sees. Then, for such as had transgressed all bounds, and had preferred the life of this world, the abode will be Hell-fire; and for such as had entertained the fear of standing before their Lord and had restrained their soul from lower desires, their abode will be the Garden." [An-Nazi'at, 79:35-41]

It is, then, for each one of us to make up our mind regarding our destination and to check whether we are moving in its direction. Of course, the choice would not be difficult if we were only looking at the destination. No one in his right mind would choose Hell over Heaven or eternal failure over success. But the eternal success requires us to go uphill. It takes effort and patience. The journey to hell, on the other hand, is downhill. One can just slide to it. And so, weak and prone to temptations that we are, we slip. That slip alone would not be that much of a problem, because one can also recover from it through repentance. The real problem occurs when we lose all sense of direction and purpose and start thinking that our fall is our rise.

To complicate matters further, today big outside forces are also busy at work to smooth our slide and cheer us at our fall. It is a juggernaut of unbelievable proportions and unprecedented wickedness. The television and music videos, present everywhere and all the time, are part of it. The UN Social Action Program and its plans for "development" and "empowerment" are part of it. The various NGOs working for "human rights," "women's rights," or whatever rights, are part of it. All those propaganda pieces that praise "moderates" and demonize "fundamentalists" are part of it.

Of course none of that can do any harm to us if we are willing to cut through the haze and see things for what they are. It is Allah's promise that both paths will remain open to us. It is our choice. The young Palestinian man who walks a mile to the masjid three to five times a day has made his choice. So have thousands upon thousands of others like him in the Ummah who have decided to shun evil and follow the path of piety and righteousness. So can the millions of others who are just wandering around.

Let us remember: We cannot get to the high ground by taking the low road. We cannot win our Creator's pleasure by disobeying Him. We cannot enter Paradise by being ambivalent about it. The clash between the two lifestyles here is actually the clash between two afterlives. And the choice is ours.

The Road to Paradise

AN ADVERTISING SLOGAN from an international beverage company makes its case in just three words: "Obey Your Thirst." Although these words are meant to produce an impulsive reaction rather than reflection, it would be good, and immensely more refreshing and rewarding if, for a change, we did the exact opposite. For, this is the battle cry of the pop culture. Of course the ad never explains why we must obey our thirst.

In fact, this has been the central obsession of *Jahiliya* societies throughout history: eat, drink, and be merry because tomorrow we die. Do whatever pleases you. You live only once so make the most of it. Obey your desires.

Today's society has taken this old obsession to unbelievably new heights (or depths). Ad men make a living out of provoking thirsts of all kinds. It has been developed into both a scientific discipline and an art form. The best available technologies, talents, and resources of all kinds are used to promote one message: indulge your desires.

If this unprecedented pursuit could produce happiness, these would have been the happiest times in the entire history of mankind. It is no secret that it is not so. If there were a Misery Index to gauge the despair and gloom of individuals and communities, we would find that it is also at an all time high. This road has never led to true happiness. And it never will.

Actually, this road leads straight into eternal Hell. The warnings are posted all along this road and have also been communicated to us by Messengers of Allah. That is why the Prophets are called *nadheer* (warners). The entire mission of the Last Messenger of Allah ﷺ was to warn us about the road that leads to Hell and show us the path that leads to Paradise. His teachings remain with us so we can avoid the peril. He informed us: "The Fire has been surrounded by lusts and desires and the Paradise by hardships."[36] Another hadith explains this further.

لَمَّا خَلَقَ اللَّهُ الْجَنَّةَ وَالنَّارَ أَرْسَلَ جِبْرِيلَ إِلَى الْجَنَّةِ فَقَالَ انْظُرْ إِلَيْهَا وَإِلَى مَا أَعْدَدْتُ لِأَهْلِهَا فِيهَا قَالَ فَجَاءَهَا وَنَظَرَ إِلَيْهَا وَإِلَى مَا أَعَدَّ اللَّهُ لِأَهْلِهَا فِيهَا قَالَ فَرَجَعَ إِلَيْهِ قَالَ فَوَعِزَّتِكَ لَا يَسْمَعُ بِهَا أَحَدٌ إِلَّا دَخَلَهَا فَأَمَرَ بِهَا فَحُفَّتْ بِالْمَكَارِهِ فَقَالَ ارْجِعْ إِلَيْهَا فَانْظُرْ إِلَى مَا أَعْدَدْتُ لِأَهْلِهَا فِيهَا قَالَ فَرَجَعَ إِلَيْهَا فَإِذَا هِيَ قَدْ حُفَّتْ بِالْمَكَارِهِ فَرَجَعَ إِلَيْهِ فَقَالَ وَعِزَّتِكَ لَقَدْ خِفْتُ أَنْ لَا يَدْخُلَهَا أَحَدٌ قَالَ اذْهَبْ إِلَى النَّارِ فَانْظُرْ إِلَيْهَا وَإِلَى مَا أَعْدَدْتُ لِأَهْلِهَا فِيهَا فَإِذَا هِيَ يَرْكَبُ بَعْضُهَا بَعْضًا فَرَجَعَ إِلَيْهِ فَقَالَ وَعِزَّتِكَ لَا يَسْمَعُ بِهَا أَحَدٌ فَيَدْخُلَهَا فَأَمَرَ بِهَا فَحُفَّتْ بِالشَّهَوَاتِ فَقَالَ ارْجِعْ إِلَيْهَا فَرَجَعَ إِلَيْهَا فَقَالَ وَعِزَّتِكَ لَقَدْ خَشِيتُ أَنْ لَا يَنْجُوَ مِنْهَا أَحَدٌ إِلَّا دَخَلَهَا

"When Allah created the Garden and Fire, He sent Angel Jibreel (Gabriel) to the Garden and said, 'Look at it and at what I have prepared in it for its inhabitants.' So he went and looked at it and at all that Allah had prepared in it for

---

[36] *Bukhari*, Hadith 6006

its inhabitants. Then he returned and said, 'By Your Honor, whoever hears about this place will enter it.' Then Allah surrounded the Garden with hardships and said, 'Go back and look at what I have prepared in it for its inhabitants.' So he went back and it had been surrounded with hardships, so he returned to Allah and said, 'By Your Honor, I am afraid now that no one will be able to enter it.'

Then Allah said, 'Go to the Fire and look at it and at what I have prepared in it for its inhabitants.' And parts of it were piled up over other parts. So he returned and said, 'By Your Honor, no one who hears about it will ever enter it.' Then Allah surrounded the Fire with all kinds of lusts and desires and said, 'Go back to it.' So he went back. This time after looking at it Jibreel said, 'By Your Honor, I am afraid that no one will be able to avoid it.'" [*Tirmidhi*, Hadith 2483]

These ahadith so beautifully and powerfully capture the test of life. The path to Hell is a slippery downhill slope. It looks attractive and promises instant satisfaction. It makes us feel good just like the drug addicts feel good when they go on a high, oblivious of the ruin that awaits them. This is the path of hedonism, consumerism, and materialism. It promises "liberation" from all norms, moral values, obligations, and higher authority, so we can become slaves of our own desires. This is the path to eternal doom and gloom. On the other hand, the path to Paradise is most definitely uphill. It requires sacrifice and self control, patience and perseverance, obedience and submission to our Creator, and hard work and firm commitment. It requires giving up instant satisfaction so we can get eternal satisfaction. It is paved with stumbling blocks and hardships. But should we choose our destination simply on the basis of how easy it is to get there?

Although Hell is a greater horror than the worst horror all human minds put together can ever imagine, it is easier to avoid, as we have been told about paths leading to it and given the freedom of choice to avoid those paths. Although Paradise is a greater treasure than all human minds put together could ever imagine, the journey to Paradise is easier than the journey to treasure islands found in fables where the seekers have to find the path on their own. Here we have been shown the path and taught through Prophetic example how to travel on that path. Yes, the lure of worldly pleasures is always great. That is by design or there would be no test. But then this is a fair test. We have been given the capability to shun the temporary pleasures and embrace the temporary pains by remembering the eternal ones. All it takes is belief, commitment, and seeking help from Allah ﷻ and we can overcome the roadblocks.

Our success lies not in obeying our thirsts but in controlling them in obedience to Allah ﷻ. Our goal is not to maximize our pleasures here, but to reach the house of eternal pleasures. Once we embrace this perspective, it brings joy to this life as well, but it is a materially different kind of joy than one finds in obeying one's basal desires. The Prophet ﷺ said, "The coolness of my eyes lies in offering salat."[37] On the other hand, the Qur'an tells us that salat is a burden except on those who have fear of Allah ﷻ in their hearts. Clearly, what brings joy to a healthy person may not bring joy to a sick person. The joy righteousness brings to this life is the joy of the person who is awake and alert. In contrast the pleasure brought by satisfying our lusts is like the "pleasure" of a drunkard who has fallen in a sewer. He may be sound asleep but can anyone who knows the reality of his situation envy him?

Obeying our thirsts means falling asleep in that unseemly place. Let us heed the wake-up call from the Prophet ﷺ:

مَا رَأَيْتُ مِثْلَ النَّارِ نَامَ هَارِبُهَا وَلَا مِثْلَ الْجَنَّةِ نَامَ طَالِبُهَا

"I have not seen anything as dreadful as the Fire whose evader is asleep and anything as desirable as Paradise whose seeker is asleep." [*Tirmidhi*, Hadith 2526]

---

[37] *Nasa'ee*, Hadith 3878

Self Reform

In this section:

- Reward Only from Allah ﷻ
- On Intentions and Actions
- Virtues, Real and Apparent
- Istighfar: Seeking Forgiveness from Allah ﷻ
- Humility in Knowledge and Arrogance in Ignorance
- Do We Mind Our Language?
- The Value of Words
- Good Muslim, Good Human Being
- No Haya, No Life
- Taqwa is for Everyone
- Dhikr: Remembering Allah ﷻ
- On Arrogance, Ignorance, and Inferiority Complex
- Time is Life
- Preparing for Death
- Natural Disasters: Test, Punishment, or Blessing?
- Seeking Halal Earning
- Sunnah and Bid'ah
- On the Dress Code
- All Virtues, Big or Small
- Amr-bil-Maroof
- What is Tasawwuf?

Reward Only from Allah ﷺ

ONE OF THE MOST important teachings of Islam has been captured in a well-known hadith in a few words. Sayyidna Umar ibn Khattab ؓ narrates: I heard Allah's Messenger ﷺ saying,

إِنَّمَا الأَعْمَالُ بِالنِّيَّاتِ وَإِنَّمَا لِكُلِّ امْرِئٍ مَا نَوَى

"The reward of deeds depends upon the intentions. And every person will get the reward according to what he intended." [*Bukhari*, Hadith 1]

Because of the great significance of this hadith, many hadith compilers including Imam Bukhari have chosen to begin their compilations with it. It reminds us to keep our intentions pure, to avoid contaminating our motives, and to seek Allah's pleasure and nothing else when performing an act of virtue. The message is central to all Islamic teachings and is repeated at many places in the Qur'an. For example:

$$\text{فَمَن كَانَ يَرْجُواْ لِقَآءَ رَبِّهِ فَلْيَعْمَلْ عَمَلاً صَالِحًا وَلاَ يُشْرِكْ بِعِبَادَةِ رَبِّهِ أَحَدًا}$$

"So whoever looks forward to the meeting with his Lord, let him work righteousness and associate none as a partner in the worship of his Lord." [Al-Kahf, 18:110]

A few verses earlier we are told that the worst losers in the Hereafter will be the people whose efforts were lost in this world while they were thinking that they were doing good. Their actions might have been good, but their intentions were not and so those actions will carry no weight in the Hereafter.

It is a terrible possibility that all of our good deeds might be wiped out because of a corruption of our motives. To avoid that fate, one must know the danger and be on the lookout for it at all times. Every believer knows that we should be performing the acts of worship solely to seek Allah's pleasure. We may begin a good deed for the sake of Allah ﷻ alone. But there may be other worldly rewards associated with the same act and we may start enjoying them and even seeking them without any realization that a switch has taken place internally. Many such rewards are intangible: fame, glory, appreciation, recognition, honor. They satisfy our deepest hidden desires. They are hard to detect and harder to repel. Besides, the chance of getting caught by others is so small. The net result is that we may be under the illusion that we are performing a certain act of virtue for the sake of Allah ﷻ, but we might actually be in it for the praise from people.

The Qur'an and Hadith warn us that that is *shirk*, or associating partners with Allah ﷻ. And *shirk* is the most severe and unforgivable sin anyone can commit. A hadith informs us that such people would be asked to go get their rewards in the Hereafter from the people for whose sake they were performing those virtues. Another hadith tells us that the first three people to be thrown in the Hell would be believers, known for their virtue. One would be a scholar of the Qur'an who had learned and taught it. Another would be a philanthropist who had spent tremendous wealth in charity. The third would be a mujahid who fought and gave his life in the path of Allah ﷻ. But in reality all were looking for fame and recognition instead of truly seeking Allah's pleasure.

The impact of these teachings on our elders has been profound. They always prayed for *ikhlas* (sincerity) in all their good deeds. They always monitored their own motives carefully and ruthlessly. They were always concerned that carelessness here could lead to disaster. Through such concern their lives became totally devoted to Allah ﷻ.

Just two accounts from the recent past may illustrate this devotion. Once Shah Ismail Shaheed Dehalvi (d. 1831 CE) delivered a *khutbah* at the Jamia Masjid in Delhi, India. Afterwards as the people dispersed and he was about to leave, a villager met him at the door. "Has the *khutbah* ended?" he asked. Upon being told that it had, the villager expressed his disappointment for missing it, for which he had come from a long distance. Shah Ismail introduced himself to the villager and told him not to worry for he would repeat the *khutbah* for him. Then he sat down with the stranger right there, on the stairs, and repeated his entire *khutbah* for the next couple of hours. Someone later expressed great puzzlement that he repeated the entire *khutbah* for just one person. "I had spoken earlier also for the sake of the One," he replied softly.

The other incident is equally telling, although from an opposite direction. As a young teacher, Maulana Ashraf Ali Thanvi (d. 1943) once invited his mentor and *ustaz* Sheikh-ul-Hind Maulana Mahmood-ul-Hasan (1851-1920) to speak to a distinguished gathering in Kanpur, India. As he states, his purpose was to impress the people with the academic caliber of Deoband as it was not getting much respect from them yet. Without mentioning his motive, he did ask his *ustaz* to tailor the discourse to the needs of an educated audience. Maulana Mahmood-ul Hasan did proceed with the lecture but then abruptly stopped when he had just begun to discuss some fine academic points. "I am sorry I am unable to continue," he said and sat down. It was not just disappointing; it was disastrous. After the program he was asked what happened. "I stopped because I had started to get a feeling that I was now speaking only to show my academic prowess," he told Maulana Ashraf Ali Thanvi. "I was not sure I was still speaking for the sake of Allah."

In addition to so powerfully warning us of the danger of the corruption of our motives, Islam also dispels a commonly held illusion, that there is such a thing as true selflessness or altruism. Normally what passes for such attributes is a trait that thrives on advertisement. Many of life's evils are based on a distorted and unsustainable idea of virtue. Instead of allowing us to hide our desire for reward behind high-sounding phrases, Islam teaches us to be true to ourselves. We should seek our rewards, because that is built into our nature, but we should seek them from our Creator and Lord, not from other destitute people like ourselves.

That is why all the prophets told the people:

$$فَإِن تَوَلَّيْتُمْ فَمَا سَأَلْتُكُم مِّنْ أَجْرٍ ۖ إِنْ أَجْرِىَ إِلَّا عَلَى ٱللَّهِ$$

"But if you turn away no reward have I asked of you: my reward is only due from Allah." [Yunus, 10:72]

$$وَيَٰقَوْمِ لَآ أَسْـَٔلُكُمْ عَلَيْهِ مَالًا ۖ إِنْ أَجْرِىَ إِلَّا عَلَى ٱللَّهِ$$

"And O my people! I ask you for no wealth in return: my reward is from none but Allah." [Hud, 11:29]

$$قُلْ مَا سَأَلْتُكُم مِّنْ أَجْرٍ فَهُوَ لَكُمْ ۖ إِنْ أَجْرِىَ إِلَّا عَلَى ٱللَّهِ$$

"Say: No reward do I ask of you: it is (all) in your interest: my reward is only due from Allah." [Saba, 34:47]

Reward Only from Allah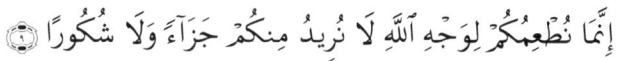

That is why the Qur'an quotes the truly generous persons feeding the hungry as saying:

$$\text{إِنَّمَا نُطْعِمُكُمْ لِوَجْهِ ٱللَّهِ لَا نُرِيدُ مِنكُمْ جَزَآءً وَلَا شُكُورًا}$$

"We feed you for the sake of Allah alone: no reward do we desire from you, nor any thanks." [Al-Insan, 76:9]

On Intentions and Actions

THE HADITH ABOUT intentions is so important, some scholars have expressed the opinion that it encompasses fully one third of Islamic teachings. It is one of the most remembered and quoted ahadith and one that is frequently quoted in its original Arabic even by non-Arabic speaking Muslims. There is hardly a Muslim who has never heard it. While all this attention to its words is superb, unfortunately we have not done as much to understand its implications and let that understanding inform our actions.

From the Islamic perspective our actions can fall in one of three categories and our intentions have different implications for each of them. In the first category are the religiously mandatory acts or the voluntary acts of worship (like voluntary salat). In the second category are the permissible acts that include most of the mundane activities in life, like eating, drinking, sleeping, earning a living, and raising a family. The third category consists of prohibited acts.

The most direct application of this hadith is to the first category. It tells us that such deeds must be performed for the sole purpose of pleasing Allah ﷻ for even the slightest

On Intentions and Actions

corruption of our motives could destroy them. The five pillars are the prime example of such deeds. For example if a person offers salat (ritual prayers) to be recognized as a pious person, he has not only destroyed his salat, he has committed the unforgivable sin of associating partners with Allah ﷻ. For he was praying for the sake of others. The same is true of Hajj, and *hijra*, and jihad, and charity, etc.

The Qur'an explains it further through a beautiful simile. It compares the case of two persons engaged in what would appear to be identical acts of charity. Both spend money to help the needy. One does it purely for the sake of Allah ﷻ; the other has the goal of getting a good name from it.

يَٰٓأَيُّهَا ٱلَّذِينَ ءَامَنُوا۟ لَا تُبْطِلُوا۟ صَدَقَٰتِكُم بِٱلْمَنِّ وَٱلْأَذَىٰ كَٱلَّذِى يُنفِقُ مَالَهُۥ رِئَآءَ ٱلنَّاسِ وَلَا يُؤْمِنُ بِٱللَّهِ وَٱلْيَوْمِ ٱلْءَاخِرِ ۖ فَمَثَلُهُۥ كَمَثَلِ صَفْوَانٍ عَلَيْهِ تُرَابٌ فَأَصَابَهُۥ وَابِلٌ فَتَرَكَهُۥ صَلْدًا ۖ لَّا يَقْدِرُونَ عَلَىٰ شَىْءٍ مِّمَّا كَسَبُوا۟ ۗ وَٱللَّهُ لَا يَهْدِى ٱلْقَوْمَ ٱلْكَٰفِرِينَ ۞ وَمَثَلُ ٱلَّذِينَ يُنفِقُونَ أَمْوَٰلَهُمُ ٱبْتِغَآءَ مَرْضَاتِ ٱللَّهِ وَتَثْبِيتًا مِّنْ أَنفُسِهِمْ كَمَثَلِ جَنَّةٍۭ بِرَبْوَةٍ أَصَابَهَا وَابِلٌ فَـَٔاتَتْ أُكُلَهَا ضِعْفَيْنِ فَإِن لَّمْ يُصِبْهَا وَابِلٌ فَطَلٌّ ۗ وَٱللَّهُ بِمَا تَعْمَلُونَ بَصِيرٌ ۞

"You who believe, do not cancel your acts of charity by reminders of your generosity or scolding like someone who spends his money simply for people to see it while he does not believe in Allah and the Last Day. He may be compared to a boulder covered with some soil, which a rainstorm strikes and leaves bare. They cannot do anything with whatever they have earned. Allah does not guide such disbelieving folk. Those who spend their wealth seeking Allah's approval and to strengthen their souls may be compared to a garden on a hilltop; should a rainstorm strike it, its produce is doubled, while if a rainstorm does not strike it, then drizzle does. Allah is Observant of anything you do." [Al-Baqarah, 2:264-265]

Charity is an important example because here the chances of corruption of our motives are especially high due to the very nature of the act. We deal with other people who may thank and recognize us and we may begin to love and seek that appreciation. What is more, we may brush aside any qualms by assuring ourselves that the publicity is only meant to inspire others.

If we keep this background in mind, we can begin to see the now nearly routine practice of holding a fundraising dinner—by the Muslims living in the West—very differently. It is obvious that this is not a Muslim institution; they borrowed it from their host countries. And they did so without much thought. For here are its underlying ideas. First, a nice dinner in a nice restaurant is a way of putting people in the mood. Second, advertising each donation is a means of inspiring others as well as rewarding the donors. Third, high-pressure techniques, like putting people on the spot, are quite productive.

Each of these elements is poles apart from Islamic teachings. A Muslim gives out of concern for his Hereafter, not by being lulled into giving by posh surroundings. He knows that the reward for his donation depends upon the sincerity with which it is given and not its monetary amount. He is fully aware that this sincerity and purity of intention are his most important assets, for without them his most generous donation may bring nothing but disaster. A person with such concerns would be very leery of going to a fundraising dinner in its present form.[38]

Often times this hadith is invoked in a twisted manner; with reference to the third category of deeds (the prohibited acts), for example. When we commit a mistake, we try to assuage our guilt feelings by assuring ourselves that we meant no harm. For our failures or shortcomings, we have the satisfaction that our intentions were good. In the worst case we may interpret the hadith to suggest that the ends justify the means. We need to remember that sheer good intentions do not repair a bad act. If we do not perform our salat or sacrifice or Hajj correctly, mere good intentions will not make them right. The extreme case is that of justifying a known prohibited act based on good intentions. "It is like playing games with the religion," says Maulana Manzoor Naumani. He goes on to add that such an act could tremendously add to one's burden of sin.

With regard to the second category (permissible mundane acts) our intentions have a potential for turning them into acts of worship. This is also an aspect we ignore to our own loss. For here is the possibility of turning every moment of our life into an act of worship through a change in our intentions. For example, when a believer goes to his place of work with the intention of fulfilling his religious responsibility to provide for his family and earn *halal* living, he may be engaged in the same physical activity as the next person but his outlook is very different. And so is his reward! Through this small effort we could really be living for a higher purpose. And at a higher level.

---

[38] For more on the subject see "The Fundraising Dinner", which begins on page 402.

Virtues, Real and Apparent

HE WAS A CONTEMPORARY but not a Companion of the Prophet ﷺ. Seeing the Prophet ﷺ, undoubtedly, would have been the greatest achievement of his life. For any believer no event could have been of greater emotional or spiritual value than a chance to see the last of the Messengers of Allah in person, to shake hands with him, to listen to him, and to learn directly from him. But Owais Qarni's mother was old, blind, and disabled. He had to constantly take care of her and that responsibility did not permit him to take the trip from Yemen to Madinah. He missed the chance to become a Companion—the highest category of any group of believers. But his piety earned him the title of *Khairut Tabi'een* or "The Best of the Successors" from the Prophet ﷺ himself. Later when he did visit Madinah, Sayyidna Umar ؓ sought him and asked him to pray for him, explaining that he made the request for prayers because the Prophet ﷺ had advised him to do so.

The story obviously tells us about the status of mothers in Islam and the virtue of serving one's parents. But there is even a bigger lesson here. Sometimes there is a fine line between apparent virtue and real virtue; between what we

Virtues, Real and Apparent

like to do and what we must do; between religion as hobby and religion as the serious business of obedience to Allah ﷻ. This is a delicate issue because the conflict between duty and desire may be camouflaged by the apparent virtuosity of the deeds. To detect the difference and make the right choice we need balance, sensitivity, and wisdom—qualities that are central to Prophetic teachings.

Jihad in the battlefield is a very important Islamic institution and the Qur'an and Hadith are full of merits of those who are willing to lay their lives to uphold Truth and fight falsehood. Yet there were occasions when the Prophet ﷺ sent back aspiring *mujahids* to their homes to take care of their old parents when the parents really needed them. To a mere general, the soldier who had demonstrated his devotion to the battle by overcoming his personal ties would have been even more valuable.

Voluntary fasts and salats, especially night salats, are highly emphasized in Islam's system of worship as the means of attaining closeness to Allah ﷻ. They have special blessings precisely because of their voluntary nature. Yet when some Companions decided to fast everyday and pray all night, they were admonished. To a mere religious leader who was promoting these particular forms of worship, the more his followers indulged in them, the better.

In declaring Prophet Muhammad ﷺ as the most influential person in history, Michael Hart, in his famous book admits that he is the only person who has been equally successful in both religious as well as secular spheres. Actually not only did Prophet Muhammad ﷺ excel as the best human being and the best leader in all areas of life, he demonstrated and taught an unprecedented balance between conflicting real-life requirements. There is simply no other example of that achievement in the entire history. What is more, he inculcated that wisdom in the Companions and their followers. Anyone who looks at this aspect of the Prophet's life with an open mind will find himself declaring, "I bear witness that Muhammad ﷺ is Allah's servant and Messenger."

SELF REFORM

There have been great warriors and there have been people with remarkable self-restraint, but where do we find an example like that of Sayyidna Ali ﷺ who, in the heat of a fight left his subdued opponent when the latter spat at him in desperation. To the perplexed enemy he explained that he was fighting for the sake of Allah ﷻ not for his ego. His commitment was not to the fight, it was to serving Allah ﷻ.

Consider a small incident from the life of the great scholar, mujahid, sufi, and jurist Abdullah ibn Mubarak. Among his many virtues is that he was fond of performing Hajj regularly and even paid the expenses of all the members of his Hajj group. During one such trip he saw that at a stopover the people of another caravan threw a dead chicken in the trash. Moments later a little girl emerged from a nearby house and rushed home with the dead bird. Curious, Abdullah ibn Mubarak followed her. He found that the girl lived with her widowed mother and they had no source of income. They had been starving for days. Seeing this he gave all the money he had for the Hajj trip to the poor family and returned home. The Hajj, being voluntary, was a personal passion. It meant a lot and he had already undertaken a big part of the difficult journey. But when faced with the need of a destitute family, he immediately knew what he had to do. His commitment was not to the Hajj trip, it was to serving Allah ﷻ.

Today as individuals and groups we seem to be lacking that perspective. We have heard that something is good but we do not know its limits nor do we realize how it fits in the big picture. Examples abound. Some of us have heard that leaving home to invite people to the religion is a great act. It indeed is. *But not if one's own family needs him and leaving it alone will expose it to dangers.* In those cases it would be "performing a hobby and not doing a duty," says Mufti Taqi Usmani. A group learns that we need to establish an Islamic state. Another realizes that we need to restore *Khilafah*. Both are right. But then they put these goals to the exclusion of everything else and develop elaborate philosophies to justify that distortion.

In the best case we are wasting resources by having the wrong priorities. In the worst case we are putting a religious cover on our own desires, without even realizing it. In each case the solution begins with a critical self-examination. It would help to occasionally ask ourselves what would we do if we were in the place of Owais Qarni? Or Abdullah ibn Mubarak?

Istighfar: Seeking Forgiveness from Allah

إِنَّ ٱللَّهَ يُحِبُّ ٱلتَّوَّٰبِينَ وَيُحِبُّ ٱلْمُتَطَهِّرِينَ

"Truly, Allah loves those who repent, and He loves those who purify themselves." [Al-Baqarah, 2:222]

عَنْ عَائِشَةَ أَنَّ رَسُولَ اللَّهِ صَلَّى اللَّهُ عَلَيْهِ وَسَلَّمَ كَانَ يَقُولُ اللَّهُمَّ اجْعَلْنِي مِنَ الَّذِينَ إِذَا أَحْسَنُوا اسْتَبْشَرُوا وَإِذَا أَسَاءُوا اسْتَغْفَرُوا

Aisha ؓ reports that the Messenger ﷺ used to say: "O Allah! Make me among those who, when they commit an act of virtue, feel good, and when they commit a mistake, seek forgiveness." [*Ibn Majah*, Hadith 3810]

TAUBA (REPENTANCE) AND *istighfar* (seeking forgiveness from Allah ﷻ) are among the most meritorious acts of virtue for the believers. *Tauba* means feeling remorse for our actions or omissions. *Istighfar* means expressing that remorse in words and begging Allah for forgiveness.

The act for which we perform *tauba* and *istighfar* is not necessarily a sin, or an act of disobedience to Allah; it also includes our shortcomings. As we realize Allah's immense favors to us, all of our thankfulness and devotion clearly appears to be inadequate. As we realize the Grandeur of Allah, Most High, our acts of worship and obedience clearly are seen to be insufficient. The higher a person is on the scale of *taqwa*, piety and God consciousness, the greater is this sense of inadequacy. Consequently the greater is his practice of *istighfar*.

That is why all the prophets preached and practiced *tauba* and *istighfar*. We do not have to invent any sins — inherited or personal—to explain their repentance. In fact all the prophets were free of sin, as Allah appointed them as role models for humanity and Allah did not send defective role models.

The leader of all the prophets was Prophet Muhammad a fact that was also symbolized in his leading of all the prophets in salat in Jerusalem during *Isra*. And what did the prayer leader of the prophets use to do after every prayer? He used to say "*astaghfirullah*" (I seek Allah's forgiveness) three times! This is the *istighfar* that comes out of the highest level of God consciousness! He taught us to perform *istighfar* profusely, as he himself practiced. The Companions have reported that he used to do *istighfar* hundreds of times during the course of a day.

Tauba and *istighfar* are the essence of our servitude and submission to Allah.

Istighfar is also a means of enhancing that consciousness of Allah and strengthening our relationship with Him. We turn to no one except Allah in repentance. We confess our deepest errors, shortcomings, failures, and sins to Him and Him alone. (In contrast, Christianity made a fatal mistake when it instituted confession to priests. As Martin Luther (1537) observed, "What torture, rascality, and idolatry such confession has produced is more than can be related.") We seek His forgiveness, knowing that He alone has knowledge about all our deeds and thoughts and He alone can forgive us and save us from the consequences of our actions. *Istighfar*, thus, is a most intimate conversation with Allah ﷻ. And during that conversation we are at our humblest. We can see why *tauba* and *istighfar* are the essence of our servitude and submission to Allah ﷻ!

We need *istighfar* to constantly purify and cleanse our heart. We are not born in sin, but we are born in weakness. We are prone to fall prey to the many temptations that are part of our test in this life. And when we do fall and commit a sin, it produces a dark spot in our heart. A famous hadith, reported by Abu Hurairah ؓ describes this process. When a person shows remorse and repents, that dark spot is removed. Otherwise it will stay there and grow with each additional sin. A time may come when his heart is full of darkness because of un-repented sins.[39] We can see this gradual darkness of the heart as people advance in their sinful behavior. In the beginning they have a lot of inhibitions. They commit the wrong hesitatingly and feel bad about it. If they do not turn back, they get used to it, so it just feels normal. Then a stage comes when vice becomes virtue and virtue vice. They defend and advocate evil and shun good.

Today, unfortunately, we see so many examples of this all around us. In the "everything goes" postmodern world, good and evil do not mean anything anymore. Then there is a whole crop of misguided psychologists who are ready to assure you that the only guilt you should feel is for feeling guilty in the first place! Is it any wonder that in the English language the word sin is now normally used to describe things that are delicious, attractive, fun, and highly desirable? That this darkness of the heart should be considered enlightenment only completes the inversion.

---

[39] *Tirmidhi*, Hadith 3257

But there is hope for those who seek hope. No matter how corrupt we might have become, we can always make a U-turn. We can repent and seek forgiveness from our Beneficent and Merciful Creator Who is always ready to forgive those who turn to Him in sincerity.

$$\text{قُلْ يَـٰعِبَادِىَ ٱلَّذِينَ أَسْرَفُواْ عَلَىٰٓ أَنفُسِهِمْ لَا تَقْنَطُواْ مِن رَّحْمَةِ ٱللَّهِ ۚ إِنَّ ٱللَّهَ يَغْفِرُ ٱلذُّنُوبَ جَمِيعًا ۚ إِنَّهُۥ هُوَ ٱلْغَفُورُ ٱلرَّحِيمُ}$$

"O my servants who have transgressed against their souls! Despair not of the Mercy of Allah. For Allah forgives all sins: for He is Oft-Forgiving, Most Merciful." [Az-Zumar, 39:53]

Further a hadith declares:

$$\text{التَّائِبُ مِنْ الذَّنْبِ كَمَنْ لاَ ذَنْبَ لَهُ}$$

"A person who has repented from a sin is as if he had never committed that sin." [*Ibn Majah*, Hadith 4240]

And this:

$$\text{لَوْ أَخْطَأْتُمْ حَتَّى تَبْلُغَ خَطَايَاكُمُ السَّمَاءَ ثُمَّ تُبْتُمْ لَتَابَ عَلَيْكُمْ}$$

"If you were to sin until your sins reached the sky and then you repented, Allah would (still) accept your repentance." [*Ibn Majah*, Hadith 4238]

The Prophet Muhammad ﷺ has taught us many words of repentance and it is good if we learn, understand, and use them. Of these one has been mentioned as *syedul-istighfar*:

SELF REFORM

اللَّهُمَّ أَنْتَ رَبِّي لا إِلَهَ إِلاَّ أَنْتَ خَلَقْتَنِي وَأَنَا عَبْدُكَ وَأَنَا عَلَى عَهْدِكَ وَوَعْدِكَ مَا اسْتَطَعْتُ أَعُوذُ بِكَ مِنْ شَرِّ مَا صَنَعْتُ أَبُوءُ لَكَ بِنِعْمَتِكَ عَلَيَّ وَأَبُوءُ لَكَ بِذَنْبِي فَاغْفِرْ لِي فَإِنَّهُ لا يَغْفِرُ الذُّنُوبَ إِلاَّ أَنْتَ

"O Allah! You are my Lord. There is no God except You. You created me and I am Your slave. To the best of my ability, I will abide by my covenant and pledge to You. I seek Your protection from the evil that I create. I acknowledge Your favors to me and I admit my sins. So please forgive me for indeed no one can forgive sins except You."

A hadith explains its extraordinary significance:

مَنْ قَالَهَا مِنْ النَّهَارِ مُوقِنًا بِهَا فَمَاتَ مِنْ يَوْمِهِ قَبْلَ أَنْ يُمْسِيَ فَهُوَ مِنْ أَهْلِ الْجَنَّةِ وَمَنْ قَالَهَا مِنْ اللَّيْلِ وَهُوَ مُوقِنٌ بِهَا فَمَاتَ قَبْلَ أَنْ يُصْبِحَ فَهُوَ مِنْ أَهْلِ الْجَنَّةِ

"Whoever says this with complete faith and sincerity in the morning and dies before the evening will enter Paradise. Whoever says it during the night and dies before the morning will enter Paradise." [*Bukhari*, Hadith 5831]

This powerful du'a is our daily pledge of allegiance. We will do well to memorize it in Arabic and never let a day or night go by without saying it with full consciousness.

Humility in Knowledge and Arrogance in Ignorance

IMAM MALIK BIN ANAS (93-179 AH) was one of the greatest Islamic scholars of all times. Among his 1300 disciples were people from all walks of life: rulers, judges, historians, sufis, poets, and scholars of Qur'an, Hadith, and *fiqh*. The Khalifah attended his class as an ordinary student along with others.

In the best traditions of this ummah Imam Malik considered his knowledge as a trust. When he knew something to be right or wrong, no intimidation could stop him from declaring so. It was his fatwa that divorce given under compulsion is invalid that earned him the wrath of the ruler (as it implied that pledge of allegiance given under compulsion was also invalid). He was punished with lashes and at every strike he said, "I am Malik bin Anas and I declare that divorce given under compulsion is invalid."

Yet it was the same Imam Malik who was more likely to say "*la adree*" (I don't know) or "*la ahsin*" (I don't know it very well) in response to the constant flow of queries directed toward him. Once a person approached him and told him that he had come from Marrakesh—after a six month journey—only to ask a question. "My people back home are waiting for your answer," he said. After hearing the question Imam Malik replied, "Please tell your people that I do not know the answer to your question." In one case he was asked forty-eight questions and in response to thirty-two of them he said, "I don't know." It was commonly said that if somebody wrote down Imam Malik's answers to questions, he could easily fill pages with "I don't know" before writing a real answer.

The reason for this extraordinary care was nothing but a deep sense of accountability before Allah ﷻ. It was the caution of a person who was standing between Hell and Heaven, fearful that one wrong step could lead him to the former. "Before you answer a question about Religious Law, visualize that you are standing at the gates of Hell and Heaven," he used to advise others.

Of course, he was not alone. Ibn Jareej used to attend the majlis (sitting) of Abdullah ibn Umar ﷺ. "In answer to more than half the questions he used to say I don't know." Ibn Abi Layla saw 120 Companions. "Whenever one of them was asked a question he wished that someone else would answer it."

Nor was this caution restricted to *fiqh* (Islamic Sacred Law). In interpreting the Qur'an or the Hadith, they exercised the same care. Imam Muslim whose *Sahih Muslim* is unanimously considered the second of the two most authentic collections of Hadith, had set for himself only the task of hadith collection, leaving the job of interpreting them to others. He was so concerned about this that he did not even divide the book into chapters for such classification would amount to interpretation.

They were the authoritative source on Islamic teachings, having devoted their lives to learning and practicing them. They knew very well the tremendous burden inherent in a statement that begins with "Allah says," or "The Prophet ﷺ

says." For here stating something that is not so means that a person is incorrectly attributing something to Allah ﷻ or the Prophet ﷺ. What can be a greater sin than that! They always remembered that it is *haram* to give fatwa without knowledge. They always remembered the hadith,

$$\text{مَنْ قَالَ فِي الْقُرآنِ بِغَيْرِ عِلْمٍ فَلْيَتَبَوَّأْ مَقْعَدَهُ مِنْ النَّارِ}$$

"Whoever says something in interpreting the Qur'an without knowledge should find his place in the Fire." [*Tirmidhi*, Hadith 2874]

Fast forward to today and you are in a totally different world, where there are innumerable "experts" who are willing to interpret the Qur'an and Hadith, give *fatwas*, even do *ijtihad*—all without the benefit of even the minimum religious education and training. If such a person is a good writer or speaker, that is qualification enough. For the audiences today readily confuse eloquence with scholarship. If the "expert" also carries the magic title "Dr." that certainly fills any gaps in his authority. It does not matter whether his educational achievement may be in gynecology or business administration, journalism or nuclear science, physics or animal husbandry.

The results have been disastrous. The vast confusion and ignorance of even elementary subjects in religious teachings among the seemingly "educated" classes today is unprecedented. Today one can find all sorts of un-Islamic ideas and practices, conjectures, whims, and desires finding approval in the "ijtihaddom" that has been concocted. What is more we also make a virtue out of this catastrophe by bragging that we have broken the "shackles of blind following" and opened direct access to the original sources of Islamic teachings. But no amount of bragging can hide the fact that this is the equivalent of allowing unlicensed and untrained people to practice medicine. Although in this case the resulting death and injury is not physical and is therefore less visible.

The reasons for this malaise are complex but two stand out. First, the schooling of our "educated" people included very little or none of Islamic education. Plainly, we do not know and we do not know that we do not know. Second, many of us harbor great mistrust of those who have received formal Islamic education. In turn this is also based on ignorance of what constitutes such education. It is a distant world, a black box, and all we know is that there is something wrong with it.

For a change let us visit a *darul-uloom* where they are screening candidates for admission to the next *ifta* class. The top scorers from the regular *alim* course were given a test and just the top ten scorers from the test will be brought for interview. They are tested not only for their knowledge of Arabic and religious texts but also their ability to understand complex real-life situations and to communicate well. Once they graduate, they will do an internship for years under qualified and experienced muftis. But even the best of their teachers will consult others when they face a difficult issue. After exercising the best of caution they will learn to say "Allah knows best" at the end of their answers.

It is not to say that the decline of Muslim political power and the general decline of Muslim civilization has had no effect on this area of activity or our *darul-iftas* are running problem free. But can anyone in all honesty declare that an untrained and uneducated alternative is better? There is a famous saying in Urdu. "A pseudo doctor is danger to life. A pseudo religious scholar is danger to faith." Do we know the danger?

Do We Mind Our Language?

إنَّ لِكُلِّ دِينٍ خُلُقًا وَخُلُقُ الْإِسْلَامِ الْحَيَاءُ

"Every religion has a distinct moral call and the moral call of Islam is *haya*." [*Ibn Majah*, Hadith 4171]

HAYA IS AN ALL-ENCOMPASSING Islamic concept that includes modesty, decency, and inhibition against sin. It is an inner feeling; a state of mind that reflects itself in myriad ways. Among other things, it shows itself in the language one uses.

How should one communicate about morally sensitive and delicate subjects? Anyone can be crude, explicit, and vulgar. But Islam civilizes this aspect of our life also and teaches us to be refined, subtle, and indirect. As a result, the language of Islamic societies has been the language of *haya*. They do not talk about some subjects, (not publicly at least), not because of ignorance, but because they know. When there is need to talk about sensitive subjects, they are mentioned in a language that is as fully clothed as decent men and women should be.

Such *haya* in the language is both a consequence of and a contributor to the *haya* in the society. It is difficult to nurture *haya* in actions if it is not cultivated in words also. The life of *haya* requires an environment of *haya* and our ways of communication are a very important determinant of that environment. Thus, it stands to reason that the discourse of a people whose distinct moral call is *haya* would also reflect that cherished distinction.

Today, three factors have begun to change this. First, there is a blow-back effect from emerging Muslim presence in western countries. The languages and the discourse here have had as much regard for *haya* as one can find on a hot summer day on a beach in Europe or the USA. The prevailing forms of expression about delicate issues are as subtle as a sledgehammer. This is probably an inherent inability of the language in its current state of development. Moreover, being explicit and crude is considered a virtue by the "open society." To its convoluted logic inhibitions are a sickness and having taboos is taboo. The atmosphere is clearly hostile to *haya*. Unfortunately, as emerging communities within this landscape Muslims have had little time for scrutiny; they have borrowed the vocabulary and idiom without questioning.

Another reason for this attitude is the "accent complex" of immigrant communities. Immigrants know that their acceptance in the society depends upon their ability to speak the language like the natives. This builds pressures for assimilation as far as language is concerned. When it remains within healthy limits it provides a positive force for gaining command over the language. But when it exceeds those limits it becomes a complex: we just don't want to sound different. Period. That is why many of us avoid words of blessings when writing in English, even though that has been a cherished and extremely valuable Islamic tradition. That is why we avoid titles of respect in places where we would be routinely using them if we were conversing in Arabic, or Urdu, or Farsi, etc. And that is why it does not occur to us to deviate from the prevalent modes of expression even on intimate subjects.

One can see the results of this attitude in the most unlikely places: *Jumu'ah Khutbahs,* religious talks and writings, and religious discussion groups. Normally we do not recognize these changes because we have become accustomed to them. So one example might help. In 1947, when British India was partitioned into Pakistan and India, rogues and fanatics targeted women in addition to men and children. The tragedy was remembered, but it was always referred to as the "violation of women" or "sacrifice of honor." In contrast, during the Bosnia tragedy, everyone was using the R-word. Matter of fact. Mechanical. Indifferent to *haya*.

This is just a symptom of a widespread problem. One can routinely find today in the religious Q & A columns published in Muslim newspapers and magazines, explicit language about the most intimate matters. In the past, such issues were discussed only privately, or in specialized text. They were never considered appropriate for mass media.

Second, the emerging communication technologies, because of the lopsided international power structure, have effectively put Muslims at the receiving end of the global media. This global media is alien to the ideas and ideals of *haya*. It is spreading its *haya*-hostile language with impunity. To make matters worse, most Muslim media outlets today act simply as clipping services for the global media. All they can do is translate and in doing that they are unwittingly (carelessly?) creating a new *haya*-neutral or anti-*haya* vocabulary even in the languages that hitherto were influenced by Islamic moral teachings. Thanks to the careless Muslim journalists, the R-word has become a common word in Pakistan also.

The issue of media is, of course, a much bigger issue. Our subservience here has crippled our ability not only to know about ourselves but also to think for ourselves. We let the labels carefully crafted by the global media machine to color our understanding of the world around us. We let its language, its images, its tone, and its modes of expression dictate to us what we will focus on and what we will talk about and how, when we do.

Third, there is a deliberate effort by powerful forces to destroy the moral fiber of all societies, especially the Muslim societies, for strategic reasons. The machinery of this social engineering project is gigantic and one of its main goals is to corrupt the discourse by using all means possible. The notorious "sex education" and "family welfare education" schemes are just one example of this effort[40]. The NGO's the international "aid agencies," and the UN have been working feverishly to introduce all the wrongs in the name of rights. Together they act as one big Commission For the Elimination of All Forms of *Haya* And Morality From the World. Sadly they have discovered that most obscene of ideas and expressions magically become legitimate, even respectable, when broadcast from their "respectable" platforms.

Overall, the result has been alarming. It is robbing our children and youth of their innocence. It is robbing our societies of their sense of *haya* and Islamic morality. When a people forget their distinct moral call, they are a people lost. We should watch our language before we talk our way into that disaster.

---

[40] It is also interesting to note that the phrase "education" is added to precisely those subjects that don't fall under it! We don't say chemistry education or math education., because chemistry and math are valid subjects for education.

The Value of Words

مَنْ كَانَ يُؤْمِنُ بِاللَّه وَالْيَوْمِ الآخِرِ فَلْيَقُلْ خَيْرًا أَوْ لِيَصْمُتْ

"Whoever believes in Allah and the Last Day should say something good or keep quiet." [*Bukhari*, Hadith 5994]

FAMOUS COMPANION Sayyidna Muadh ibn Jabal ﷺ once asked the Prophet ﷺ, "Tell me about an act that will cause me to enter Paradise and be protected from the Fire." "You have indeed asked something profound," responded the Prophet ﷺ. "But it will be easy on whom Allah makes it easy. Worship Allah and do not associate any partners with Him. Establish regular salat, pay zakat, fast during Ramadan, and perform Hajj." Then he asked, "Shall I not tell you about the doors of good? Fast is a shield (against sins and against Hell-fire); charity extinguishes sins like water extinguishes fire; and the midnight salat (the voluntary *Tahajjud* salat)." Then he recited this verse:

تَتَجَافَىٰ جُنُوبُهُمْ عَنِ ٱلْمَضَاجِعِ يَدْعُونَ رَبَّهُمْ خَوْفًا وَطَمَعًا وَمِمَّا رَزَقْنَٰهُمْ يُنفِقُونَ ﴿١٦﴾

"They slip quietly away from their beds to appeal to their Lord in fear and anticipation and spend (charitably) whatever We have provided them with." [As-Sajda, 32:16]

SELF REFORM

Then he continued: "Shall I tell you about the beginning, the mainstay and the high point of this? The beginning is (acceptance of) Islam; its mainstay is salat; its highest point is jihad."

Then the Prophet ﷺ asked: "Shall I tell you about the thing on which all this depends?" He, then held his tongue and said "Guard this." Sayyidna Muadh ibn Jabal ؓ asked: "Shall we be questioned about our utterances?" On this the Prophet ﷺ said, "Most people will be thrown into Hell—face down—because of the transgressions of their tongues."[41]

The ability to speak and express themselves separates human beings from animals. The proper use of this great gift—or its absence—separates the good and successful people from the bad and unsuccessful ones.

Sayyidna Muadh's ؓ question was about eternal success. In response, the hadith mentions both mandatory and voluntary good deeds that cover a person's entire life. But then we are reminded that the outcome of all these depends upon guarding our tongue. In other words carelessness with the tongue can poke holes in all of our good deeds.

Another hadith highlights the same issue in a different way:

إِذَا أَصْبَحَ ابْنُ آدَمَ فَإِنَّ الْأَعْضَاءَ كُلَّهَا تُكَفِّرُ اللِّسَانَ فَتَقُولُ اتَّقِ اللَّهَ فِينَا فَإِنَّمَا نَحْنُ بِكَ فَإِنِ اسْتَقَمْتَ اسْتَقَمْنَا وَإِنِ اعْوَجَجْتَ اعْوَجَجْنَا

"Every morning, when the son of Adam wakes up, all the limbs plead with his tongue: 'Fear Allah for our sake, for our fate is tied to yours. If you remain upright so shall we. And if you go astray so shall we.'" [*Tirmidhi*, Hadith 2331]

Yet another hadith reminds us about the far reaching consequences of the words we utter.

---

[41] *Tirmidhi*, Hadith 2541

The Value of Words

إنَّ الرَّجُلَ لَيَتَكَلَّمُ بِالْكَلِمَةِ مِنْ رِضْوَانِ اللَّهِ عَزَّ وَجَلَّ مَا يَظُنُّ أَنْ تَبْلُغَ مَا بَلَغَتْ يَكْتُبُ اللَّهُ عَزَّ وَجَلَّ لَهُ بِهَا رِضْوَانَهُ إِلَى يَوْمِ الْقِيَامَةِ وَإِنَّ الرَّجُلَ لَيَتَكَلَّمُ بِالْكَلِمَةِ مِنْ سَخَطِ اللَّهِ عَزَّ وَجَلَّ مَا يَظُنُّ أَنْ تَبْلُغَ مَا بَلَغَتْ يَكْتُبُ اللَّهُ عَزَّ وَجَلَّ بِهَا عَلَيْهِ سَخَطَهُ إِلَى يَوْمِ الْقِيَامَةِ

"Sometimes a person says something pleasing to Allah, the Great and Almighty, but he does not realize how far his words will go. Yet it earns him the Pleasure of Allah until the Day of Judgement. On the other hand sometimes a person says something displeasing to Allah, the Great and Almighty, although he does not realize how far his words will go. Yet it earns him the Wrath of Allah until the Day of Judgement." [*Musnad Ahmed*, Hadith 15291]

The pre-Islamic Arab society was a very vocal society. While reading and writing were not that common, people did pride themselves in their facility with words—both prose and poetry. A person commanded respect based on his command over words. Using power of words only, they could sink reputations, start wars, and impact life in a similar fashion as the modern media has come to demonstrate on a much larger scale. Then, as now, it was raw power like the power of the beasts of the jungle.

Islam tamed this beast. It reminded us that each and every word we utter is being recorded by the angels and one day we will have to stand accountable for all this record. It reminded that a person's greatness lies not in how powerful he is with words but in how careful is he with them. It reminded that it is better to keep silent than to say something bad. And it is better to say something good than to keep quiet.

The social revolution it engendered was unprecedented. It produced a people who truly understood the value of words and who were as pious with them as they had been powerful. Their silence was the silence of quiet reflection. And they spoke only when they could improve the silence. Is it any wonder that even their extempore statements were pearls of wisdom.

Today, everywhere there are schools that can teach one how to read, write, and speak a language. But their students will never learn how to civilize this raw power; to use it only in promoting truth and spreading virtue; to never use it for promoting falsehood or spreading evil. There is a lot of unlearning we have to do if we want to get out of this. It is a costly mistake for a believer to think that talk is cheap; that you can say whatever is expedient without any concern for any consequences beyond the immediate ones.

Such attitudes, prevalent today, lead to all kinds of sins: vain pursuits, gossip, dishonesty, insincerity, arrogance, belittling others, backbiting, spreading scandals and corruption, telling lies. Each of these has been clearly defined as a deadly sin by the Qur'an and Hadith. The treatment for each of these sins begins with learning the Islamically responsible use of the tongue. Then there are secondary problems caused in turn by these. In fact most of the problems in the family and the society are either created or augmented by the irresponsible use of the tongue.

Modern communication technologies have made it possible for messages to be transmitted instantaneously all over the globe. But as the world marvels at these achievements, it continues to confuse the speed of a message with its quality and value. We pride ourselves on the ability to spread trash around the world at the speed of light. Witness the rubbish that continues to dominate the Internet alone. We are amazed by the sophisticated techniques of telling lies in a convincing manner. Witness the modern mainstream media machine and its hold on our thoughts and actions.

The "information age" is begging for the moral guidance of Islam.

Good Muslim, Good Human Being

IHSAN IS A SPECIAL Islamic term, defined by the famous hadith known as the *Hadith-Jibreel*. Once Angel Jibreel ﷺ visited the Prophet ﷺ in the guise of a man and in the presence of Companions. This happened toward the end of the Prophetic mission and its purpose was to summarize some fundamental teachings of Islam for the education of all of us. Jibreel ﷺ asked questions about Islam, *iman*, *ihsan*, the Day of Judgement, and Fate. Regarding *ihsan*, the Prophet ﷺ responded: "It is that you worship Allah as if you are seeing Him. For though you see Him not, verily He is seeing you."[42] Obviously, our worship will be at its best when performed with that feeling. *Ihsan*, therefore, means striving for excellence in achieving piety, through an overwhelming feeling of closeness to Allah ﷺ.

For anyone seeking spiritual purification, this is the goal. Abdul-Hameed Siddiqi, well known for his English translation of *Sahih Muslim*, notes that what is implied by the term *tassawuf* is nothing but *ihsan*. With that in mind we can understand the joy of the person who once reported to his

---

[42] *Muslim*, Hadith 9

mentor that he had achieved *ihsan* in his salat. He felt being in the presence of Allah ﷻ every time he stood up for salat. "It is great that you should feel that way while praying," his mentor replied. "But, do you have the same feelings when you are dealing with others? Have you attained *ihsan* in relations with your spouse and children? In relations with friends and relatives? In all social relations?" To the perplexed disciple he went on to explain that one must not restrict the concept of *ihsan* to the performance of salat. The term is general and applies to all endeavors in our life.

The sufi mentor in this story was Dr. Abdul Hai Arfi, himself a disciple of Maulana Ashraf Ali Thanvi. One of the many great contributions of Maulana Thanvi was that he reintroduced Islamic teachings regarding social relations and dealings with others as a religious issue. His message: you must become a good human being before you can ever become a good Muslim. This message destroys a disastrous and tragic misconception that reduces Islam to only the performance of the ritual acts of worship—the pillars—thus robbing it of much of the rest of the building. (Some others try to construct the building without the pillars—an even more devastating and futile act—but that is another subject.) A very important and integral section of that building deals with our social relations. It is concerned with how we behave in the family. How we interact with relatives, friends, neighbors, colleagues, and all the rest of humanity.

The cornerstone of Islamic teachings in this area is the requirement that we do not cause anyone any harm through our words or actions. A famous hadith states,

الْمُسْلِمُ مَنْ سَلِمَ الْمُسْلِمُونَ مِنْ لِسَانِهِ وَيَدِهِ

"A Muslim is the one from whose hands and tongue other Muslims are safe." [*Tirmidhi*, Hadith 2551]

This hadith clearly describes this as a defining trait of a Muslim. While it refers to "other Muslims," scholars agree that it is a general requirement that equally applies to all non-

Muslims except those who are at war with them. A person who through his intentional or careless actions or words inflicts unjustified pain on others is not worthy of being called a Muslim.

We can begin to appreciate the value of this teaching by realizing that most problems in our lives are man-made. Life can become living hell if there are problems within the family: the tensions between the spouses, the frictions between parents and children, the fights between brothers and sisters and other relatives. Today these are common stories everywhere. But can these problems occur and reach the intensity they do if everyone is genuinely concerned about not hurting others? The same applies to relations between friends, neighbors, colleagues, and communities.

Islam wants to build a society that is a model of civility, courtesy, and consideration for others. It does so by emphasizing these attributes as a matter of faith. One hadith says that *iman* (faith) has seventy-seven branches. The highest one is the declaration that there is no God except Allah ﷻ and the lowest one is the removal of harmful objects from the path. This is being considerate. And obviously, there is no trace of *iman* below this.

We see this consideration for others throughout the life of the Prophet Muhammad ﷺ. Of course, such an attitude shows itself in "minor" details. For example, whenever the Prophet ﷺ visited a group where some people were asleep and others were not, he would greet them with a low enough voice so those awake could hear him while those asleep would not be disturbed. Every night when he used to get up for *Tahajjud* (midnight prayer)—a voluntary salat for the rest of us—he would walk out of the bed very quietly so as not to disturb his sleeping wife.

Whenever he saw someone commit a wrong that needed to be corrected in public for the education of others, he would mention it in general terms, not naming the person who did it. This last practice also shows the two extremes in this regard that must be avoided. On the one hand is the temptation to compromise on the issue of right and wrong to avoid hurt feelings. On the other is the temptation to correct the wrong with total disregard to the fact that one might be insulting or injuring the other person. While we may see these extreme attitudes in people who seem to be poles apart in terms of their practice of religion, both stem from the same narrow vision of religion that holds our dealings with others as worldly affairs, outside the realm of Islam!

It is good to remember that Islam is a way of life. We must submit our whole life, not a small subset of our choosing, to the commands and teachings of Allah ﷻ and His Prophet ﷺ. Our commitment to Islam must not only be life-long but also life-wide.

No Haya, No Life

Imam Shu'bah ibn Hajjaj was riding his horse when Abdullah intercepted him. Abdullah was a known street urchin. Not only was he given to a life of sin, he was also unabashed about it. Imam Shu'bah knew that trouble was ahead when Abdullah stopped him.

Shu'bah (d. 100 AH) is known as *Amirul Momineen fil Hadith*. He is one of the foremost scholars of the science of Hadith criticism. Abdullah knew his stature as a great Hadith scholar, but he was bent on having some fun. "Shu'bah! Tell me a hadith," he said with mischief in his eyes. "This is not the way to learn Hadith," Imam Shu'bah replied. "You are going to tell me a hadith or else…" Abdullah threatened. When Shu'bah realized that he could not talk his way out of this he said: "OK, I'll tell you a hadith." He then narrated the isnad (a chain of narrators) and then the hadith: "If you have lost *haya* then do whatever you feel like."

Abdullah's demeanor changed suddenly. It was as if the Prophet ﷺ had himself caught him in his mischief and was speaking to him: "Abdullah, if you have lost *haya* then do whatever you feel like." He was totally shaken. "I just wanted to cause trouble for you," he admitted, "but please extend your hand. I want to repent."

This hadith turned a life around. Abdullah, the street urchin, became a student and then a great scholar of Hadith. Today he is known as Shaikh Abdullah ibn Maslamah Qa'nawi. His name can be found repeatedly in *Sihah Sitta* or the six most authentic collections of Hadith, especially in the collection of Imam Abu Dawood who was his disciple.

What is *haya*? It is normally translated as modesty or inhibition but neither word conveys the same idea as *haya*. Modesty suggests shunning indecent behavior but it also implies bashfulness based on timidity. That is why the adjective based on its opposite, immodest, is sometimes also used as a compliment suggesting courage. Inhibition is defined as "conscious or unconscious mechanism whereby unacceptable impulses are suppressed." This is a very neutral definition with no reference to right or wrong. So one finds psychiatrists "helping" their patients overcome inhibitions.

In contrast to the moral ambiguity of these words, *haya* refers to an extremely desirable quality that protects us from all evil. It is a natural feeling that brings us pain at the very idea of committing a wrong.

Along with its unique connotation comes the unique value of *haya* in Islam. Prophet Muhammad ﷺ said:

$$إِنَّ لِكُلِّ دِينٍ خُلُقًا وَخُلُقُ الإِسْلامِ الْحَيَاءُ$$

"Every religion has a distinct moral call and the moral call of Islam is *haya*." [*Ibn Majah*, Hadith 4171]

Another famous hadith says:

$$الإِيمَانُ بِضْعٌ وَسَبْعُونَ أَوْ بِضْعٌ وَسِتُّونَ شُعْبَةً فَأَفْضَلُهَا قَوْلُ لا إِلَهَ إِلاَّ اللَّهُ وَأَدْنَاهَا إِمَاطَةُ الأَذَى عَنْ الطَّرِيقِ وَالْحَيَاءُ شُعْبَةٌ مِنْ الإِيمَانِ$$

"There are more than seventy branches of *iman* (faith). The foremost is the declaration that there is no god except Allah and the least of it is removing harmful things from the path. And *haya* is a branch of *iman*." [*Muslim*, Hadith 51]

As some *muhaditheen* (Hadith scholars) point out, the number seventy is a figure of speech. What the hadith tells us is that the declaration of faith is the most important part of *iman* but that is not all. *Iman* also has to reflect itself in all kinds of actions in real life. Moreover, *haya* is a centerpiece of most of the actions that *iman* calls for. It is the basic building block of Islamic morality. When it is lost everything is lost.

Based on such teachings, Islam brought about a moral revolution of unprecedented dimensions with *haya* as its cornerstone. The pre-Islamic *Jahiliya* society of Arabia knew the word but did not understand its meaning. Nudity, the antithesis of *haya*, was not only common in every day life, it was even part of the most important religious ritual of *tawaf* (circumbulation of *Ka'bah*). So were all the other evils that flow from it. Islam exterminated all of those evils and changed the society in such a way that *haya* became one of its most cherished values. To this day in Friday *Khutbahs* around the world, the third khalifah Sayyidna Uthman ﷺ is mentioned as the person with the best *haya* (*asdaquhum haya*). Is there any other religion that celebrates *haya* like that?

Islam's laws about *hijab*, its ban against free mixing of men and women, its teachings about relations between men and women—all of these reflect a deep concern for *haya*.

For men and women who have not lost their *haya*, these come naturally. There is a moving story from the earlier Islamic period about a woman who learned that her young son had been lost in a battle. She ran in a panic to confirm the news, but before that she took time to make sure that she covered herself fully in accordance with the newly revealed laws of *hijab*. She was asked how did she manage to do that in a time of great personal tragedy. She replied, "I lost my son, but I did not lose my *haya*."

And for centuries afterwards Muslim societies did not lose their *haya*. When Muslim lands came under the western colonial rule about three centuries ago, they were faced with a civilization that was no different than the pre-Islamic *Jahiliya* society on the issue of *haya*. While it did not have a better morality, it did have better guns. At the gunpoint of military and political domination, Muslim societies were made to lose their grip on *haya* on the collective scale. The powerful and attractive media became an important instrument in this war. First it was books, magazines, and newspapers. Then radio. Now it is television. Together they projected ideas and images detrimental to *haya*. They made indecency attractive. The pace was increased tremendously by television, which has shown more firepower than all the previous media combined. Now Internet is competing with it as the new purveyor of porn.

When historians write about the moral decline in Muslim societies in the twentieth century, they will probably underscore television in subverting the moral fabric of society. We can get a sense of the rapidity of our fall by realizing that what was unthinkable just a decade ago has become routinely accepted today. In some cases, we seem to have lost all control. Isn't it shocking that while contraceptive ads cannot be shown on television in the United States or the United Kingdom, they are freely shown in the Islamic Republic of Pakistan?

We can get out of the morass by making *haya* as our number one concern in both individual as well as public lives. There is no Islamic life without Islamic morality. There is no Islamic morality without *haya*.

Taqwa is for Everyone

يَـٰٓأَيُّهَا ٱلَّذِينَ ءَامَنُوا۟ كُتِبَ عَلَيْكُمُ ٱلصِّيَامُ كَمَا كُتِبَ عَلَى ٱلَّذِينَ مِن قَبْلِكُمْ لَعَلَّكُمْ تَتَّقُونَ ۝

"O ye who believe! Fasting is prescribed to you as it was prescribed to those before you, so that you may develop *taqwa*." [Al-Baqarah, 2:183]

THIS VERSE MAKES two statements. First, fasting is for everyone. Second, the purpose of fasting is to develop *taqwa*. It should be obvious then, that taqwa is for everyone!

In other words, taqwa (God consciousness, fear of Allah, righteousness) is not required just of a select group of religious people who would then be called *muttaqeen* (possessors of taqwa). Rather, every believer has to become *muttaqi* for the success in the Hereafter is only for the *muttaqeen*.

A Hindu may say that certain injunctions of his religion (for example not eating meat) do not apply to him because he is not a Brahmin. So can a Buddhist or a Christian. As the *Britannica* notes, Hinduism, Buddhism, and Christianity (especially the Roman Catholic and Eastern Orthodox branches), among others, stress "separation, even polarization, between the life of the person who has a sacred vocation and that of the ordinary man." Not Islam. Islam eliminates that polarization.

The point is emphasized heavily in the Qur'an, where the word taqwa and its variations have been used 151 times. It commands:

$$\text{يَٰأَيُّهَا ٱلَّذِينَ ءَامَنُوا۟ ٱتَّقُوا۟ ٱللَّهَ وَلْتَنظُرْ نَفْسٌ مَّا قَدَّمَتْ لِغَدٍ}$$

"O you who believe! Have taqwa of Allah and let every soul look to what provision he has sent forth for the morrow." [Al-Hashr, 59:18]

It asks us to choose between taqwa and its absence by presenting a very moving example:

$$\text{أَفَمَنْ أَسَّسَ بُنْيَٰنَهُۥ عَلَىٰ تَقْوَىٰ مِنَ ٱللَّهِ وَرِضْوَٰنٍ خَيْرٌ أَم مَّنْ أَسَّسَ بُنْيَٰنَهُۥ عَلَىٰ شَفَا جُرُفٍ هَارٍ فَٱنْهَارَ بِهِۦ فِى نَارِ جَهَنَّمَ}$$

"Which then is best? He that lays his foundation on taqwa of Allah and His Pleasure? Or he that lays his foundation on the edge of a crumbling bluff so it crumbles along with him into Hell-fire." [At-Tauba, 9:109]

It reminds us that the eternal bliss is only for the *muttaqeen*:

$$\text{وَسَارِعُوٓا۟ إِلَىٰ مَغْفِرَةٍ مِّن رَّبِّكُمْ وَجَنَّةٍ عَرْضُهَا ٱلسَّمَٰوَٰتُ وَٱلْأَرْضُ أُعِدَّتْ لِلْمُتَّقِينَ}$$

"Hasten towards forgiveness from your Lord and a Garden broader than Heaven and Earth, prepared for the *muttaqeen*." [Al-i-'Imran, 3:133]

Of course in every race some people get ahead while others lag behind. So with the race for taqwa. Obviously some people will develop more taqwa than others. Though taqwa is also a state of the heart[43], and we cannot judge the taqwa of others, many aspects of taqwa have a reflection in our behavior. So it is natural and normal for us to recognize the differences in achievement of those in the race. But those of us lagging behind cannot pretend that we are not in the race at all. For there is no other race!

We are all in it together. The rich and the poor, the educated and the un-educated, the leader and the follower, the writer and the reader, the preacher and the listener, the ruler and the ruled, the old and the young, the man and the woman, all must develop taqwa. The most honored, in the sight of Allah, is the believer with the most taqwa.[44] The Islamic society is a taqwa-conscious society, conferring its highest respects on those considered to be highest in taqwa. Without it the best achievements in other areas of life mean little.

While all this is obvious in principle, in practice many of us seem to have accepted the idea that *muttaqeen* are a separate class of people, different from the rest of us, the ordinary Muslims. This has been a very devastating import from Christianity and Hinduism. While Islamic Shariah has been one integral entity, this devious mechanism has allowed us to develop our own individual Shariahs by picking and choosing from the Shariah what we might think is appropriate for the "ordinary Muslim." Such reasoning provides a ready-made justification for our sins, shortcomings, and weaknesses. All of them end with: "After all I am not a *muttaqi*."

---

[43] Al-Hajj, 22:32
[44] Al-Hujurat, 49:13

SELF REFORM

The flip side of taqwa is sin. And the mentality that made taqwa the burden of a small group of religious people has also imported another term into contemporary Islamic discourse: self-righteousness. These days this seems to be the most potent weapon of anyone being challenged for introducing a deviation in the Shariah. Those challenging must be self-righteous. A most despised species!

The Qur'an does prohibit us from making claims of self-purity.

$$فَلَا تُزَكُّوٓا۟ أَنفُسَكُمْ ۖ هُوَ أَعْلَمُ بِمَنِ ٱتَّقَىٰٓ$$

"Hold not yourself purified. He knows best who has *taqwa*." [An-Najm, 53:32]

Being a major sin as it is, one has to be extremely careful in blaming others for committing it simply because they are challenging what they consider as *munkar* or evil. The Qur'an does mention the use of that allegation in history. When Prophet Lut ﷺ admonished his nation for indulging in the abomination of homosexuality, they fought back by blaming the Prophet to be self-righteous.[45]

Once Qadi Ibn Abi Lailah refused to accept the testimony of Imam Abu Hanifa in a case because of an incident. The previous day both were walking together when they passed by some women who had been singing. The women stopped as they saw them. As they passed by them, Imam Abu Hanifa said, "Good," meaning it was good that they had stopped. But Qadi Ibn Abi Lailah thought that Abu Hanifa had praised their singing and on that basis declared him a *fasiq* and therefore unfit as a witness. Here was one of the greatest jurists, scholars, and a very pious person being publicly declared a *fasiq*. One can imagine some of today's intellectuals having a field day by bringing the counter charge of self-righteousness against the Qadi. But what did Imam Abu Hanifa do? He simply explained his comments and was

---

[45] An-Naml 27:56

allowed to proceed with the testimony. It is hardly an isolated incident. In Islamic history, despite very open and fierce debates, we do not find anyone resorting to the charge of self-righteousness against his opponents.

Why? The charge comes from a universe where polarization between the religious and the ordinary lives is stressed, for it is possible that some will falsely claim to be adhering to a higher standard and therefore be guilty of self-righteousness. In Islam there is only one Shariah and one scale for righteousness for everyone.

Dhikr: Remembering Allah ﷻ

THE SHEPHERD WAS approached by a lone traveler in the desert. "I am hungry and have run out of food. Could I milk one of your sheep?" The shepherd replied that he was not the owner of the sheep and could not let anyone milk them without the owner's permission. The owner would surely notice it and would not like it. The traveler had an idea. "Why don't you sell one of them to me. When the owner asks, you can tell him that a wolf killed it. Wolves attack the herds all the time. I'll satisfy my hunger. You'll get the money. We'll both profit." The shepherd strongly refused saying, "But what about Allah!" Strangely, the traveler was pleased to hear that. "As long as there are people like you in the Ummah, wolves won't kill the sheep," he said.

The shepherd was, of course, not aware that he was talking to the Ameer-ul-Momineen Umar ؓ who kept his finger on the pulse of his people. It was the spontaneous, natural reaction of a believer who remembered Allah ﷻ. And the comment came from the person who knew the value of that remembrance. Today we find wolves killing the sheep everywhere. Corruption has become commonplace in most parts of the Muslim world. Why? Because most of us have moved away from that remembrance that was the protection against sin and corruption!

The journey of life is beautifully described in the Qur'an as a constant toil, at the end of which we are going to meet our Creator.

يَٰٓأَيُّهَا ٱلْإِنسَٰنُ إِنَّكَ كَادِحٌ إِلَىٰ رَبِّكَ كَدْحًا فَمُلَٰقِيهِ ۝

"O mankind, Verily you are ever toiling on towards your Lord—painfully toiling—and you shall meet Him." [Al-Inshiqaq, 84:6]

The person who remembers Allah ﷻ, then, is the person who keeps his eyes on his destination. The journey is arduous. The distractions are many. Satan and our own desires are constantly trying to steer us away from our goal. But the stakes are extremely high. And a vigilant and wise person will never lose sight of his destination. Such is the person who remembers Allah ﷻ all the time.

إِنَّ فِى خَلْقِ ٱلسَّمَٰوَٰتِ وَٱلْأَرْضِ وَٱخْتِلَٰفِ ٱلَّيْلِ وَٱلنَّهَارِ لَءَايَٰتٍ لِّأُو۟لِى ٱلْأَلْبَٰبِ ۝ ٱلَّذِينَ يَذْكُرُونَ ٱللَّهَ قِيَٰمًا وَقُعُودًا وَعَلَىٰ جُنُوبِهِمْ

"Behold! In the creation of the Heavens and the Earth, and the alternation of night and day, there are indeed Signs for men of understanding—men who remember Allah standing, sitting, and lying down on their sides." [Al-i-'Imran, 3:190-191]

SELF REFORM

This remembrance or *dhikr* is itself the source of strength for the believer. According to one *hadith-e-qudsi*, Allah ﷻ says: "I am with my servant as long as he remembers Me."[46]

It is for this reason that a distinction is made between other ritual acts of worship, and *dhikr*. We are not required to engage in the former excessively. In fact we are cautioned against that possibility. But we are asked to perform *dhikr* profusely—keeping our heart and tongue busy in that remembrance all the time. We simply cannot overdo it. In fact Prophet Muhammad ﷺ said:

لَيْسَ يَتَحَسَّرُ اَهْلُ الْجَنَّةِ اِلاَّ عَلَى سَاعَةٍ مَرَّتْ بِهِمْ لَمْ يَذْكُروا اللّٰهَ تَعَالَى فِيْهَا

"The people of Paradise will not be sorry for anything except for the moments (in this life) that passed by in which they did not remember Allah, Most High."
[*Tabrani* 20/94]

How can we remember Allah ﷻ when we cannot see Him and cannot even visualize His Person? There are two answers. First, we look at His creations, for the creations remind one of the Creator. The verses of Al-i-'Imran quoted above mention this, as do numerous other verses throughout the Qur'an. The more we look at the grand design of the universe, the more we are reminded of the Designer. How many forces must come together with perfect coordination before a seed can sprout? What keeps this immensely complex and constantly expanding universe work so flawlessly? There are pointers to the Creator on every square inch of this universe in all things ranging from the simplest to the most complex. In fact the Arabic word for the universe (*alam*) comes from the root *ilm* or knowledge; it is the name of that by means of which the Creator is known, just like *khatam* is a name of that by means of which one seals.

---

[46] *Bukhari*, Hadith 6856

Unfortunately when the western civilization took the lead in science this connection was severed. As the Qur'an mentions:

$$وَكَأَيِّن مِّنْ ءَايَةٍ فِى ٱلسَّمَٰوَٰتِ وَٱلْأَرْضِ يَمُرُّونَ عَلَيْهَا وَهُمْ عَنْهَا مُعْرِضُونَ ۝$$

"And how many Signs in the Heavens and the Earth do they pass by? Yet they pay no attention to them." [Yusuf, 12:105]

For the Muslim scientists today, a prime task must be to remove this ignorant de-linking. It is a sign of wisdom that a person looks at the universe and says *Subhan-Allah*, Glory be to Allah.

Second, we recall Allah's blessings on us. The fact is that we cannot fully encompass the blessings of a single moment in our life. Right now somebody is reading these lines. We take the act for granted and think nothing of it. But let us pause and reflect on it. The eyes have to be working for us to recognize the printed characters. The brain has to be working for us to translate the images of characters we see on paper into meaningful statements that they stand for. We need peace of mind to reflect on it. We need available time to even begin the process. None of these is of our own making.

Most of us are lucky enough to get food everyday. Again, we just take it for granted. But let us reflect on the process of production of food materials, cooking and preparation of our meals, and its consumption and digestion by our body—and we may begin to realize the blessings that we are receiving in one bite of the simplest food we may eat! It is a sign of wisdom that a person realizes all this and says *Alhamdulillah*, Praise be to Allah.

Subhan-Allah, *Alhamdulillah*, *Allahu Akbar*—these are some of the forms of *dhikr* of Allah. To pronounce them is *dhikr* by the tongue. To understand and reflect on them is *dhikr* by the heart. Both forms are highly desirable and they reinforce each other. Repetition by the tongue engraves the words in the heart. Understanding and reflection brings life to the spoken words. Together, they help us keep our eyes on our destination through the journey of life. They help us develop and strengthen our relationship with Allah ﷻ, thereby bringing peace of mind and protecting us from the evil temptations. And we can hope that a person who always remembered that he has to meet with Allah ﷻ will not be disappointed when that time comes.

The unlettered shepherd was a greater man of understanding than the "greatest great" who does not remember Allah ﷻ. If only we can understand.

On Arrogance, Ignorance, and Inferiority Complex

IT HAS BEEN CALLED *ummul-amradh*, or the root of all sicknesses of the heart. Prophet Muhammad ﷺ warned that a person having even an iota of it in his heart shall never enter paradise. This deadliest of all sins is *kibr*, or arrogance.

No one likes arrogance—in others. We never like a person who is haughty, too proud, or condescending. We detest a person who belittles us and has a huge ego. Similarly we love people who are humble, polite, and easy to talk to. We love people who give us respect and honor. Thus if we follow the principle of treating others the way we like to be treated, most of these problems might be cured easily.

In reality, the treatment of *ummul-amradh* requires a deeper look. For that we need to appreciate the difference between *adaab* or manners, on the one hand and *akhlaq* or morals on the other. While *adaab* deal with one's external disposition, *akhlaq* as defined by Islam deal with our inner thoughts, feeling, and attitudes. In a healthy personality, the manners and morals are in harmony. But it is also possible to

SELF REFORM

have the former without having the latter. The first concerns itself with how a person deals with others. The second is concerned with what a person thinks of himself. Two persons showing humbleness in their dealings with others may have exactly opposite ideas in their minds. One may do it out of his or her "generosity"; the other may do it because he genuinely thinks that he is not better than the other person. The first person only has a shell of humbleness, which will crumble when tested. It is the second person that is really free of arrogance.

Real greatness belongs only to Allah ﷻ, our Lord, Creator, and Master. Human beings are just a creation of Allah—and a very small creation in comparison to the unimaginably vast universe. Anyone who understands this will realize that our proper status is only that of the servants of Allah. In fact for a Muslim the real human model is none other than Prophet Muhammad ﷺ who is the greatest of all human beings. His greatness lies in being the humblest of all servants of Allah! It is impossible for any person who has this consciousness to entertain any notions of his own greatness.

This leads us to the definition of *kibr*, given in a famous hadith:

الْكِبْرُ بَطَرُ الْحَقِّ وَغَمْطُ النَّاسِ

"*Kibr* is knowingly rejecting the Truth and belittling other people." [*Muslim*, Hadith 131]

This hadith exposes two strains of this deadly disease, both dealing with our exaggerated ideas of self-importance. The first suggests that I am more important than the Truth. The second suggests that I am more important than other people.

We know about the Quraish and Jews of Arabia who had come in contact with Prophet Muhammad ﷺ and who knew in the heart of their hearts that he indeed was the Messenger of Allah. Their arrogance, though, kept them from accepting it. History has recorded statements from some of them who said they knew he was the Promised Prophet, but that they would keep on opposing him to maintain their leadership.

While that was the most blatant form of arrogance, we can witness the same attitude on a smaller scale in our discussions and arguments. A person realizes that he was wrong, but then his pride keeps him from admitting it. No matter how polite or "humble" that person may appear to be ordinarily, this test shows the presence of arrogance in his heart. It is arrogance that keeps a person from saying, "I was wrong."

The second strain involves our feeling of superiority with respect to other people. Islam's teaching is that one should never consider oneself greater than other people, because that judgment will come from Allah ﷻ, and Allah ﷻ alone, on the Day of Judgment. None of us knows what our end will be, whether we will end up being a winner or a loser over there. The person who appears to be nobody here may end up with eternal bliss because of his goodness that only Allah ﷻ knew. The person who is a big shot here may end up among the sinners who will be punished there, because of his evil that only Allah ﷻ knew. How foolish, it is then to congratulate ourselves over our fleeting "superiority."

What if a person does have edge over another person in measurable worldly terms? How then can he not consider himself superior than the other person in that respect? The point is sometimes made in jest: it is difficult to be humble when you are so great. Islam does not ask us to reject reality and imagine we don't have what we really do. Rather it asks us to take a deeper look at the reality and not be misled by a superficial perception of it. And the simple reality that escapes many is that our health, wealth, talents, and power are not of our own creation. God gave those to us as a test and He can take them back whenever He wills. Those who are conscious of this reality, their blessings will produce gratitude in them; those who are blind to it will develop pride and arrogance.

While throughout history humanity had agreed on the evil of arrogance and the virtue of humbleness (despite its failures in practice), the modern age has seen new dogmas that aim at changing the definitions of good and evil. Humbleness is no longer desirable. Rather, one has to avoid "Inferiority Complex." Alfred Adler (1870-1937) gave us that term. According to him, life is a continuous struggle to move from a position of inferiority to a position of significance. Those who fail to make the progress, develop inferiority complex, which can be treated by increasing self-esteem. Unfortunately today such pseudo-science is accepted as gospel truth.

The truth is, a humble believer is a happy, content, grateful person who thanks God for his blessings and has no notions of his own superiority. He puts his trust in Allah ﷻ and that trust sustains him through all the ups and downs in life. He becomes neither depressed nor arrogant. He is remarkably free of all complexes. On the other hand, problems arise when we turn away from reality. For it is the false notions of superiority or of one's entitlements in life that lead to frustrations and complexes.

Time is Life

وَٱلْعَصْرِ ۝ إِنَّ ٱلْإِنسَٰنَ لَفِى خُسْرٍ ۝ إِلَّا ٱلَّذِينَ ءَامَنُوا۟ وَعَمِلُوا۟ ٱلصَّٰلِحَٰتِ وَتَوَاصَوْا۟ بِٱلْحَقِّ وَتَوَاصَوْا۟ بِٱلصَّبْرِ ۝

"By the time. Verily Man is in a state of loss. Except such as have Faith and do righteous deeds and exhort one another to Truth and exhort one another to endurance."
[Al-Asr, 103:1-3]

TIME IS MONEY. So goes the most repeated metaphor for time in the English language. There is some truth in it as time can be used to produce wealth and wasting time may also mean losing opportunities for wealth production. Yet this metaphor also implies something about the purpose of life itself that we should examine carefully. If a child says that money is candy, he'll be right in the sense that money can be used to buy candy. But adults will laugh at him because the statement implies that candy is the most important object that money can buy. Similarly "time is money" implies that money is the most important object in life: one must value time as he or she values money.

Historically this has been one of the key metaphors driving the engine of Industrial Revolution and technological development in the past few centuries. A lot of inventions and new technique have aimed at saving time and therefore money. And certainly the list of such inventions and their achievements in speed are mind-boggling. Today men, materials, and ideas can be moved from one place to another at an astonishing speed. The tasks that used to take months and years can be finished in minutes. And yet there is something ironic about all this development. Despite the tremendous explosion in timesaving gadgets, life has become busier than ever before. Overall we can't show much for all the time that has been saved.

We are very busy, but at the end of the day we can't tell what we have been busy doing. Where all the saved time has gone? In what way our lives have become more productive? Just imagine how Internet has made it possible for information to move all over the world in seconds. And then see how the same medium is being used to waste countless hours in frivolous discussions in chat rooms or meaningless net surfing! The juxtaposition of the time saving and time wasting nature of the same tool brings in full focus the basic problem with the prevalent ideas of time itself.

One may think that the metaphor is not to be blamed for this waste. After all "time is money" would seem to suggest that no time should be wasted. Actually belittling time by equating it with money allows whiling it away when one has made the money he needs. So people talk about "killing time" and the need for the gadgets that let them kill time. One has to consider time to be much more important than money not to waste it like this!

To put things in perspective a quick historic comparison is in order. Consider the period of early Muslims when none of these technological marvels were available. There is a common notion that people then leisurely lived in sleepy little towns and had little to do. Actually that was a period of unprecedented activity in all aspects of life. Theirs was a period of intense military and political activity during which nearly half the known world came under the banner of Islam. Coming from a most backward part of the world, they introduced a new civilization to the world that was proud of its civilization and its military might. In personal life they used to spend a lot more time in worship than we do, most of them spending long hours of their nights in individual prayers. This would seem to leave a lot less time for other pursuits in life. We also know that means of communications were so poor then, that sometimes they had to travel on horseback for weeks or months to go to another area, say, to collect a report of a hadith from someone who had heard it directly from the Prophet ﷺ. Yet during this period and despite all the logistics problems, together they collected the hundreds of thousands of ahadith that have been compiled into various collections and are available today! And this is just one aspect of their work! How in the world did they find time for that?

The answer is simple. They were driven by a different metaphor for time. They valued it as the gift whose proper or improper use would determine the outcome for the eternity. They had listened to the Prophet ﷺ when he said,

نِعْمَتَانِ مَغْبُونٌ فِيهِمَا كَثِيرٌ مِنَ النَّاسِ الصِّحَّةُ وَالْفَرَاغُ

"There are two blessings that most people are deluded by: health and available time." [*Bukhari*, Hadith 5933]

They took his advice very seriously when he said,

اغْتَنِمْ خَمْسًا قَبْلَ خَمْسٍ : شَبَابَكَ قَبْلَ هَرَمِكَ ، وَصِحَّتَكَ قَبْلَ سَقَمِكَ ، وَغِنَاكَ قَبْلَ فَقْرِكَ ، وَفَرَاغَكَ قَبْلَ شُغْلِكَ ، وَحَيَاتَكَ قَبْلَ مَوْتِكَ

"Value five things before five other things: youth before old age; health before sickness; affluence before poverty;

leisure before becoming too busy; and life before death."
[*Mustadrak Al-Hakim*, Hadith 7846]

Abdullah bin Hasn ﷺ reports that whenever two Companions met they would not depart until they had recited Surah al-Asr to each other reminding themselves of the eternal loss that everyone faces if we waste away our time in foolish pursuits. They did not waste any moment of their life in gossips, useless talks, or meaningless pursuits.

The difference is clear. We may have a fast car, but if we are riding it for the joy of speed driving, not because we want to get there, we'll never get there. The success of our elders or *salaf* lay in their overriding sense of purpose and accountability and their concern with using their time very carefully.

Coming closer to our own period we find other examples of a similar nature. Consider the case of Maulana Ashraf Ali Thanvi (d. 1943). On the surface he just ran a small monastery and a religious school and was given to spending long periods of time in individual worship. But he also authored about 1200 publications ranging from small booklets to encyclopedic works like *Bahishti Zewar*, which has seen millions of copies in print. He also used to answer all his mail everyday, which consisted of dozens and sometimes hundreds of pieces. And he taught many generations of scholars! His secret? A strict discipline born of a deep concern about accountability for time.

We are becoming older every day. One day our time will be up and we'll leave this world forever. What happens afterwards will depend solely on how we use all the moments available to us before that certain but unknown moment comes. Time is life. What is at stake is the entire eternity.

Preparing for Death

"Suppose you learn today that you have only one more day to live; you'll die tomorrow. How will you spend your last day?" This interview question was posed long before the age of the mass media. The interviewer approached prominent scholars and people known for their virtuous lives with the idea that he would compile their answers in a book. Such a book would provide the readers with inspiration for the most important virtues.

But the most inspiring response came from the person who did not provide a wish list of virtuous deeds. He was the great *muhaddith* Abdur Rahman ibn abi Na'um and he replied: "There is nothing that I could change in my daily schedule learning that it is my last day. I already spend everyday in my life as if it is going to be my last."

Death is the most certain aspect of life. According to the latest statistics, 6178 people die in the world every hour. These are people of all ages, dying of all causes. Some of these deaths will make headlines. The great majority will die quietly. Yet everyone will enter his grave the same way. Alone. At the time appointed by God. Science and technology can neither prevent nor predict death. It is solely in the hands of the Creator.

SELF REFORM

$$\text{يَا أَيُّهَا النَّاسُ إِن كُنتُمْ فِي رَيْبٍ مِّنَ ٱلْبَعْثِ فَإِنَّا خَلَقْنَٰكُم مِّن تُرَابٍ ثُمَّ مِن نُّطْفَةٍ ثُمَّ مِنْ عَلَقَةٍ ثُمَّ مِن مُّضْغَةٍ مُّخَلَّقَةٍ وَغَيْرِ مُخَلَّقَةٍ لِّنُبَيِّنَ لَكُمْ ۚ وَنُقِرُّ فِي ٱلْأَرْحَامِ مَا نَشَآءُ إِلَىٰٓ أَجَلٍ مُّسَمًّى ثُمَّ نُخْرِجُكُمْ طِفْلًا ثُمَّ لِتَبْلُغُوٓا۟ أَشُدَّكُمْ ۖ وَمِنكُم مَّن يُتَوَفَّىٰ ۖ وَمِنكُم مَّن يُرَدُّ إِلَىٰٓ أَرْذَلِ ٱلْعُمُرِ لِكَيْلَا يَعْلَمَ مِنۢ بَعْدِ عِلْمٍ شَيْـًٔا ۚ}$$

"O mankind! If you are in doubt concerning the Resurrection, then lo! We have created you from dust, then from a drop of seed, then from a clot, then from a little lump of flesh shapely and shapeless, that We may make it clear for you. And We cause what We will to remain in the wombs for an appointed time, and afterward We bring you forth as infants, then give you growth that you attain full strength. And among you there is he who dies young, and among you there is he who is brought back to the most abject time of life, so that after knowledge he knows naught!" [Al-Hajj, 22:5]

We see it happening all the time. Yet it is amazing how we feel that it won't happen to us. At least not anytime soon. We bury our own friends and relatives but think that we'll live forever. Our attitudes about death defy all logic. In a way we recognize it and even plan for it. We take out life insurance policies. We may do estate planning. Businesses and governments have contingency plans to carry out their operations in case of sudden loss of their leaders. But this is recognition of death as an end point of this life. Where we fail is in recognizing it as the beginning of another life that will never end and where we'll reap what we sow here.

A central teaching of Islam is that it is our recognition of and preparation for that eternity that must separate those who are smart from those who are not. As the Prophet ﷺ said:

$$\text{الْكَيِّسُ مَنْ دَانَ نَفْسَهُ وَعَمِلَ لِمَا بَعْدَ الْمَوْتِ}$$

"Truly smart is the person who controlled his desires and prepared for life after death." [*Tirmidhi*, Hadith 2383]

There is a moving story about Bahlool, who, in his innocence seems to be on the opposite end of the scale of worldly-smartness. Khalifah Haroon-ur-Rashid had given him access to his court probably because his naiveté was a source of entertainment to him. Once the Khalifah gave him a walking stick saying, "It is meant for the most foolish person in the world. If you find a person more deserving of it than yourself, pass it on." Several years later Haroon-ur-Rashid fell seriously ill and no medical treatment seemed to work. Bahlool visited him and inquired about his condition. The conversation went something like this:

> Haroon: "No treatment is working. I see my final journey ahead of me."
> Bahlool: "Where are you going?"
> Haroon: "I am going to the Other World."
> Bahlool: "How long will you stay there? When will you come back?"
> Haroon: "No one ever comes back from that world."
> Bahlool: "Then you must have made special preparations for this journey. Did you send an advance group to take care of you once you arrive?
> Haroon: "Bahlool, you have to go there alone. And no I did not make any preparations."
> Bahlool: "Ameer-ul-Momineen! You used to send troops to make extensive preparations for you for even short trips of only a few days. Now you are going to a place where you'll live forever but you have made no preparations! I think I have found the person more deserving of the stick that you had given me some years ago."

This story speaks to all of us. We may not be kings but we do plan our trips of even a few days very carefully. How about preparing for the journey into eternity? How about making the concern for the Hereafter the cornerstone of our lives here?

Actually, that concern can change our lives here as well. This world is an abode of deception. Here we are not punished the moment we commit a sin. This fools us into thinking that we can get away with it. Remembering death is the antidote for that deception. A person who remembers that he will have to stand before his Creator and be accountable for his actions simply cannot defy God!

In the story of Pharaoh, we learn that when he saw death approaching he declared belief in the God of Moses. Before that he had been fooled by his apparent power. His repentance came too late but it did show how his arrogance and intransigence evaporated when faced with the certainty of death.

It is amazing how a lot of our own "confusions," frivolous arguments, excuses (for why we cannot do this or avoid that), or plane laziness can melt away when we visualize ourselves in our grave! Death settles lot of arguments. Its remembrance can do that too—before it is too late. He was indeed a very wise person who spent everyday of his life as if it was going to be his last day. But that certainly should be the goal for all of us!

Natural Disasters: Test, Punishment, or Blessing?

WITHIN THE SPACE of a few seconds on 16 August 1999 an entire city was demolished and an entire country was badly shaken. The 7.4 earthquake in Turkey that left an estimated 200,000 people homeless, killed 17,000, wounded about 50,000 people, and caused more than $6.5 billion in damages was called as the "disaster of the century" by authorities. Quite naturally, Muslims the world over felt the pain and sufferings of their brothers and sisters in Turkey.

No one can predict or prevent an earthquake. But even if we were able to predict their occurrence, as we can such natural disasters as hurricanes or floods, they would remain a reminder of how fragile we really are. Our ability to harness the forces of nature can give us the illusion that we are the masters of the universe. But this ability is granted by God and only to the extent that He Wills. The power of the most arrogant and "mighty" kings, presidents, military generals, or armies of all sorts combined together is nothing compared to the Power of Allah as manifested by a small earthquake.

As a result of the earthquake even some of the fanatically anti-Islamic generals of Turkey suddenly, though temporarily, remembered Allah ﷻ. Such flashes of faith are common. The most die-hard atheist or skeptic may suddenly find Allah ﷻ when faced with an extreme suffering or danger. It is a testimony to the belief in Allah ﷻ that has been built into our nature by the Creator. But as soon as the danger subsides, many go back to their old ways. Then they begin to rationalize the reactions they had during the moment of truth. They start suggesting that natural disasters are just random events that show the power and fury of a blind nature that scientists hope to tame completely one day.

To the non-believers it seems like that. They point out that an earthquake—or any natural disaster for that matter—hits the sinners and saints alike. It makes no distinction between a believer and a non-believer. Further, they say it makes no sense, because they cannot make any sense out of it.

We should know the hollowness of these assertions. To say that something has no logic because we cannot understand its logic is to show arrogance, not wisdom. As for the first assertion, it is not true that these events have the same impact on the believers as the non-believers. For the fact is that the two groups of people do not look at events in life, including disasters, the same way; they do not draw the same conclusions from them; and they do not end up in the same place with respect to them. While the shaking of the ground may shake the world of the non-believer, it strengthens the faith of the believer who knows that not a leaf can fall on the ground without the Will of Allah. It is because of our very limited knowledge and understanding that many events appear to us to be random and devoid of purpose. In reality all events in this universe happen only by leave of the All-Knowing, All-Wise, All-Powerful God. There is a purpose behind all of this and understanding that purpose enables us to cope with them.

Natural Disasters: Test, Punishment, or Blessing?

Why do sufferings happen in this life? There are two answers.

For the believers they are a test of patience and submission to the Will of Allah.

$$\text{وَلَنَبْلُوَنَّكُم بِشَيْءٍ مِّنَ ٱلْخَوْفِ وَٱلْجُوعِ وَنَقْصٍ مِّنَ ٱلْأَمْوَالِ وَٱلْأَنفُسِ وَٱلثَّمَرَاتِ ۗ وَبَشِّرِ ٱلصَّابِرِينَ ۝ ٱلَّذِينَ إِذَآ أَصَابَتْهُم مُّصِيبَةٌ قَالُوٓا۟ إِنَّا لِلَّهِ وَإِنَّآ إِلَيْهِ رَاجِعُونَ ۝}$$

"Indeed We shall test you with something of fear and hunger, some loss of goods, lives, and the fruits (of your toil), but give glad tidings to those who patiently persevere. Who say, when afflicted with a calamity: 'To Allah we belong, and to Him is our return.'" [Al-Baqarah, 2:155-156]

All hardships in life—over which we have no control—thus become an opportunity for gaining rewards in the Hereafter by exercising patience. Islam, as we know very well, means submission to Allah. It means submission to the *Command* of Allah in areas within our control. It means submission to the *Will* of Allah in areas beyond our control.

For the sinners they are a punishment:

$$\text{وَلَنُذِيقَنَّهُم مِّنَ ٱلْعَذَابِ ٱلْأَدْنَىٰ دُونَ ٱلْعَذَابِ ٱلْأَكْبَرِ لَعَلَّهُمْ يَرْجِعُونَ ۝}$$

"And indeed We will make them taste of the lighter chastisement before the greater chastisement in order that they may repent and return." [As-Sajda, 32:21]

But even this punishment will turn out to be a mercy for those who heed the wake-up call and mend their ways; it will spare them the much greater punishment in the Hereafter.

According to clear Islamic teachings in both the Qur'an and the Hadith, every hardship in life—sickness, accidents, monetary losses, natural disasters, difficulties of all kinds—can be either a punishment or a blessing in disguise. There is no difference in the appearance of the two. The plague killed thousands of the Companions of the Prophet ﷺ during the time of Sayyidna Umar ؓ as it did thousands of nonbelievers in other parts of the world. But who can say that these were the same incidents, with the same consequences?

How do we, then, know whether a particular suffering is a punishment or a blessing for us? By examining our own feelings. If the suffering brings us close to Allah ﷻ; if we find ourselves turning to Him in prayers and repentance; if we feel the pain yet do not complain about the "injustice" of nature to us; if we submit and patiently persevere, then the suffering is indeed a blessing in disguise that will bring tremendous rewards in the Hereafter. On the other hand if as a result of the hardship we turn away from Allah ﷻ; if we complain and ask "why me?"; if our focus is only on apparent causes and remedies and not on the Creator who Creates and Controls the causes themselves, then these are the signs that, God forbid, the suffering is a punishment and a greater punishment awaits us in the Hereafter!

The earthquake in Turkey has no doubt entailed massive human suffering. But the greater tragedy will be if we fail to learn from the "disaster of the century," and remain stubborn about our crooked ways of disobedience to Allah ﷻ and defiance of His Shariah. The earthquake that will take place on the Day of Judgment will be much, much stronger; on that day the whole earth will be shaken. And there will be no end to the sufferings it will cause to those who refuse to learn from the much smaller earthquake now.

Seeking Halal Earning

ACCORDING TO ABDULLAH ibn Masud ﷺ Prophet Muhammad ﷺ said: "Seeking *halal* earning is a duty after the duty." In other words working to earn a *halal* living is itself a religious obligation second in importance after the primary religious obligations like prayers, fasting, and Hajj.

This brief hadith contains three very important messages. First, it points to the Islamic way out of the apparent dichotomy between the material and the spiritual worlds. We often see them working in opposite directions. Indulgence in the material world does lead one away from the spiritual world. Spiritual uplifting seems to accompany a tendency to distance oneself from the material pleasures. There is a conflict, but is there a contradiction also? Is it possible to resolve the conflict in a way that one can take care of both? Or are they mutually exclusive? This has been a central question for all religions and many in the past suggested the second answer, making hermits as the ideal for the humanity. Unfortunately not much humanity is left when one moves too far in this direction. One can read today the horror stories of Christian and Hindu monks, among others, who tried to seek spiritual purification this way.

As a reaction, others took the other course, making material pleasures the goal of this life. The western civilization today is the prime example of that. Its toll on human spirit and morality is well known and is a constant reminder that something is wrong here as well.

In between the two extremes Islam points out the Straight Path. Man is both a material and a spiritual being. The solution does not lie in denying the material needs and desires but in denying their claim to primacy. They are part of being but not the reason or goal of being. As long as they are kept in place, they are an important part of our life. The problem is not money but the love of it. Wealth itself is not bad. In fact the Qur'an refers to it as "...your wealth which Allah has made for you a means of support."[47]

And another hadith praises the merits of "the *halal* wealth of a pious person." The effort to earn a living is not only not against spirituality, it is a religious obligation!

But this earning must be through *halal* means. This is the second message of this hadith. Our obligation is not just to make money but to make *halal* money. This is a broad statement that is the basis for reforming a society's economic life. Not every business idea or possible business enterprise is good for the society. And the decision regarding right and wrong here cannot be left to the so-called market forces. Right and wrong in the economic life, as in all life, must be determined by a higher source. The Shariah (Islamic Sacred Law) guides us regarding *halal* and *haram* in business enterprises and practices, and at both individual and collective levels we must follow that guidance.

At times that guidance may conflict with the prevailing practices. For example *riba* (interest), gambling, pornography, and liquor are *haram*, and no matter how attractive the financial rewards of engaging in those enterprises may seem to be, a Muslim must refrain from them. This is the economic struggle of a believer, and it is obvious why it should be carried out as a religious obligation. At the individual level the obligation is to engage in *halal*

---

[47] An-Nisa, 4:5

professions and businesses. At the collective level the obligation is to establish a system that facilitates such individual efforts and discourages their opposite.

Sometimes we lose balance between obligations at the two levels. Obviously our ultimate responsibility is at the individual level; in the Hereafter we will be asked about what we did in our personal lives. At the same time, in the era of multi-national companies, CNN, IMF, World Bank, and WTO, it is obvious that individual efforts alone cannot steer the economic life of a society in the direction of *halal*. Why has avoiding interest become so difficult today? Not because of its inherent merits as a healthy financial instrument but because it is entrenched in the system. Can we build an Islamic life style when the CNN is advertising the opposite in the most enticing ways 24 hours a day in our homes? Can we resolve the issues of *halal* and *haram* in taxation[48] in Muslim countries when the national budgets and tax decisions are dictated to these countries by the IMF and the World Bank? Obviously the struggle to avoid *haram* individually must, of necessity, include the struggle to change the system that forces *haram*.

Third, all this effort for *halal* earning should not eclipse our primary religious obligations. Indulgence even in a purely *halal* enterprise should not make us miss our salat, or Hajj, for example.

This point is more important than we may realize at first. In recent times, some Islamic movements made the error of suggesting that the primary acts of worship like salat were not meant for their own sake, but were there to prepare us for the real challenge of establishing an Islamic state. The statement was made to persuade the audiences to join such movements but the speakers had been carried away and in effect it would result in an inversion of the relationship between the two. The result is that those drawn to collective struggles, in

---

[48] Jurists say that taxes may be permissible if they are necessary, reasonable, fair, within the ability of the payers, and if the means of collection are not harsh. Otherwise they are unjust and *haram*.

political or economic arenas, sometimes may ignore their primary religious responsibilities, in favor of the "bigger" struggle. This hadith may help us set our priorities right: the economic endeavor is a duty *after* the primary duties. And let us remember: in economics, as well as in religion, getting the priorities right is part of being right.

Sunnah and Bid'ah

ONCE SOME JEWISH scholars said to Sayyidna Umar ibn Khattab ﷺ, "The Qur'an contains a verse that if it had been revealed to us, we would have designated a day to celebrate its revelation." Upon inquiry they mentioned the verse:

$$ ٱلۡيَوۡمَ أَكۡمَلۡتُ لَكُمۡ دِينَكُمۡ وَأَتۡمَمۡتُ عَلَيۡكُمۡ نِعۡمَتِي وَرَضِيتُ لَكُمُ ٱلۡإِسۡلَٰمَ دِينٗا $$

"This day I have perfected your religion for you, and completed my favor towards you, and have chosen for you Islam as your religion." [Al-Ma'idah, 5:3]

"Yes, I know, the time and place when it was revealed," he replied.

Indeed it was a historic day. It was the day of *Arafah* during the Farewell Hajj of Prophet Muhammad ﷺ. This verse announced the completion of a historic process that had started with the coming to earth of Sayyidna Adam ﷺ. Allah ﷻ sent His guidance with him and informed him that in the generations to come there would be additional messengers. The process continued through the 124,000 prophets who were sent to different lands at different times.

SELF REFORM

It culminated with the coming of the Last Messenger, Muhammad ﷺ. He received revelations over a twenty-three year period. Then during the Farewell Hajj, on the plain of Arafat, in the presence of nearly 124,000[49] Companions, this verse announced that it was all done!

The full significance of this message must never escape us. Islam is unlike all previous revealed religions in one crucial respect. All of them came with expiration dates. Islam has none. The Guidance from Allah ﷻ had been completed. The religion had been perfected. There would be no new message, no new prophet, no new Shariah, and no new command until the Last Day! The Straight Path has been laid out. Our job is only to follow it, not to try to discover new paths. In Jumu'ah *khutbahs* the Ummah has been repeating the ahadith:

وَإِيَّاكُمْ وَمُحْدَثَاتِ الأُمُورِ فَإِنَّ كُلَّ مُحْدَثَةٍ بِدْعَةٌ وَكُلَّ بِدْعَةٍ ضَلَالَةٌ وَكُلَّ ضَلالَةٍ فِي النَّارِ

"I warn you of the newly invented matters (in the religion), for every newly invented matter is *bid'ah*, and every *bid'ah* is misguidance, and every misguidance is in the Fire." [*Abu Dawood*, Hadith 3991 and *Nasa'ee*, Hadith 1560]

In Islamic terminology, Sunnah and *bid'ah* are antonyms. Sunnah literally means path, and it is the path shown to us by the Prophet ﷺ. This includes the Shariah teachings derived from the Qur'an, Hadith, the consensus of the Companions, and the *ijtihad* of the qualified imams. *Bid'ah* means something new but in Islamic terminology it means adding or changing articles of faith or religious practices. It can take many forms. One may change the occasion of a prescribed act, thereby extending it to occasions for which it was not meant. One may add restrictions on a desired act

---

[49] Regarding the number of Companions who attended the Farewell Hajj, see footnote on page 88.

that the Shariah had not imposed. One may change the style or form of such an act. One may start doing something collectively that was to be performed individually. Or one may change the Shariah status of an act from permissible to mandatory. Of course, one may also add a ritual where none existed. These are all forms of *bid'ah*. They are all forbidden.

Bid'ah is like fake currency that tries to drive out the good currency. By design it has the appearance of a virtuous religious act. But it lies outside the Shariah. So do its sources, which, in a great number of cases can be traced to non-Islamic influence from surrounding communities with which Muslim communities historically came into contact. Hence the telltale signs that set it apart from Sunnah. First, *bid'ahs* normally vary from region to region—and over time—revealing their local, non-Islamic source. This is unlike the genuine religious practices that maintain the same form everywhere. No matter where he comes from, a follower of, say, Hanafi *fiqh*, will be offering salat in exactly the same way, right down to the minutest detail—like when to raise the index finger. In contrast, the *bid'ah* practices surrounding, marriage or death in the Indo-Pak subcontinent vary from those in Arabia or Africa.

Second, the *bid'ah* practices are largely transmitted through oral tradition. Many of these have a pseudo-legal, ritualistic framework of their own, but one would be hard pressed to find it in the standard legal texts! Rather it lives in the folklore. Consider the practice of shaking hands after finishing the salat. Open the chapter on salat in your *fiqh* book. It lists all the steps, in great detail, involved in offering salat. Does it mention the handshake as well? No. The handshake comes from folklore, not from an authentic text, a clue that it may be a *bid'ah*, which it is. Similarly consider the rituals normally performed upon the death of a person. Again the *fiqh* books describe in great detail how the funeral and burial should be done. But do they also mention that on the third day (or the tenth or the fortieth), a gathering should be arranged where participants should recite the Qur'an for the benefit of the deceased and after which they should be served with dinner? Again the answer is no. Again the reason is that all of these common practices are not part of the Shariah. They are an addition or *bid'ah*.

One factor that helps the propagation of *bid'ahs* is the attitude that treats religion as hobby rather than as the serious business of submitting to the command of Allah ﷻ. Pure submission may be "boring." It demands sacrifice. *Bid'ahs* are fun. On top of that they "promise" reward in the Hereafter. This makes the *bid'ah* more deadly than ordinary sins. From an act we know to be a sin, we can repent. But how can one repent from a wrong that he considers to be right?

But in reality *bid'ahs* are a tremendous burden. Islamic teachings are simple and easy and life would be much simpler if all *bid'ahs* were removed from it. When a person dies, Islam teaches that others should be providing food to the bereaved family. *Bid'ah* requires the exact opposite, that the bereaved should feed all the visitors—a widespread practice in the Muslim communities in Asia. Other *bid'ahs* are also like that. A burden. And the burden in the Hereafter will be much bigger, for "every *bid'ah* is in the Fire."

On the Dress Code

WHAT WOULD YOU think of a home that provided no shelter and no privacy? What would you think of a meal that provided no nourishment and no energy? It does not take much to realize that if one were in the business of selling any of these he would go bankrupt very quickly. Yet, amazingly the rules seem to be different when it comes to another basic need: clothing, especially women's clothing. Every year fashion centers in Europe and America come up with the latest designs. And what have they designed? Another way of *not* covering the body; the dress equivalent of the home that provides no shelter and no privacy.

One might ask, if a person did not want to cover himself or herself why would he or she buy anything, least of all expensive fashions, to achieve that? If we think about it, we may see the tension between two forces. All human beings (except for the handful of deviants who call themselves naturalists) have an inborn sense of shame. People of all religions agree on the need to cover themselves in public. Yet we also find a force that promotes nudity. Our clothing designs reflect different levels of compromise between these opposing forces.

Why? What is going on?

SELF REFORM

Science cannot answer the question. It cannot trace the origins of forces that take place deep in our mind. In addition, most of the scientific establishment is still dominated by the ideas of Darwinism which is a system of belief not science. Their beliefs keep them from dealing honestly with a simple fact: while all other animals have a skin that provides them protection against the elements, human beings don't. Monkeys can live without clothing, human beings cannot.

The Qur'an answers the question. Our bodies did not develop our skin—so thin and fur free that it requires external covering for protection—because of some unexplained evolutionary accident. Our Creator designed it this way so we will always need clothing. He also put in us the sense of shame that forces us to cover ourselves. On the other hand, the first act of Satan was to cause Adam and Eve to expose themselves:

فَدَلَّىٰهُمَا بِغُرُورٍ ۚ فَلَمَّا ذَاقَا ٱلشَّجَرَةَ بَدَتْ لَهُمَا سَوْءَٰتُهُمَا وَطَفِقَا يَخْصِفَانِ عَلَيْهِمَا مِن وَرَقِ ٱلْجَنَّةِ ۖ

"So by deceit he brought about their fall: when they tasted of the tree, their shameful parts became manifest to them, and they began to sew together the leaves of the Garden over their bodies." [Al-A'raf, 7:22]

This is the source of the tension we see. Two opposing forces: good and evil.

With that background we can understand the importance of clothing.

يَٰبَنِىٓ ءَادَمَ قَدْ أَنزَلْنَا عَلَيْكُمْ لِبَاسًا يُوَٰرِى سَوْءَٰتِكُمْ وَرِيشًا ۖ وَلِبَاسُ ٱلتَّقْوَىٰ ذَٰلِكَ خَيْرٌ ۚ

On the Dress Code

"Children of Adam! We have sent you down clothing with which to conceal your private parts and to dress up in. Yet the clothing of heedfulness is best!" [Al-A'raf, 7:26]

The address here is to all humanity, emphasizing thereby the universal human need to cover ourselves properly. The Qur'an then warns that Satan was not finished after his first attempt:

$$\text{يَٰبَنِىٓ ءَادَمَ لَا يَفْتِنَنَّكُمُ ٱلشَّيْطَٰنُ كَمَآ أَخْرَجَ أَبَوَيْكُم مِّنَ ٱلْجَنَّةِ يَنزِعُ عَنْهُمَا لِبَاسَهُمَا لِيُرِيَهُمَا سَوْءَٰتِهِمَآ}$$

"Children of Adam! Do not let Satan tempt you in the same manner as he got your two ancestors out of the Garden, stripping them of their clothing, in order to show them their private parts." [Al-A'raf, 7:27]

Once we realize the nature of the dress issue, it is natural that we should turn to our Creator to seek guidance for the proper dress code. Qur'an and Sunnah have provided ample guidance on the subject which can be summarized in four essential principles.

Our dress must cover our body adequately. Again we cannot determine what is adequate cover on our own, as any witness to the misery of those who have tried it can readily ascertain. Shariah, as always, takes us out of this misery by defining it for us. For men, it is the middle part of the body from navel to knee. For women, it is the entire body except hands and face. These parts must never be exposed to any other person (except in case of genuine need e.g. medical treatment). In addition, the cloth must be neither see-through nor tight fitting.

Our dress should provide adornment. It should provide for decent appearance. Our appearance should not be an eyesore for decent human beings. For men, this extends the coverage requirements to include most of the body. For

SELF REFORM

women, the essential requirement is that their dress should identify them as respectable ladies who would be honored not harassed. Additionally, *hijab* rules aim at protecting them from the gaze of other men.

Our dress should establish our Islamic identity. At the least it should not identify us as followers of another religion. But, additionally it should positively identify us as Muslims.

The design of our dress must avoid three deadly sins: showoff, arrogance, and self-indulgence. These are very serious diseases of the heart in their own right that we must avoid at all times. Our garments provide an easy opportunity to nurture them. Hence the need to be extra cautious. Sayyidna Abdullah ibn Abbas ؓ said,

$$كُلْ مَا شِئْتَ وَالْبَسْ مَا شِئْتَ مَا أَخْطَأَتْكَ اثْنَتَانِ سَرَفٌ أَوْ مَخِيلَةٌ$$

"Eat what you feel like and wear what you feel like as long as you avoid two things: extravagance and arrogance." [*Bukhari*]

At the risk of stating the obvious one should be reminded that this statement establishes an overriding concern that limits our choices within the realm of what is considered *halal*. It does not do away with the distinction between *halal* and *haram*.

As one implication of this general requirement, men are also required not to wear their lower garments below the ankle. (Many well-meaning Muslims today have been persuaded that this is a petty issue. This misgiving can be put to rest if we just refer to the hadith of Jabir ibn Sulaym ؓ in *Abu Dawood*. He asked the Prophet ﷺ for some advice when parting with him after his very first meeting. Of the six pieces of advice given him one was: "Never let your lower garment go below the ankles because that is arrogance. And Allah does not like arrogance." Another was "Never belittle a good deed.") [50]

Islam has not prescribed a particular dress style, giving us ample room to accommodate our needs, circumstances, and tastes. However, these principles are for everyone and forever. Any garment that accommodates these principles will be Islamic. This is the Islamic formula to dress for success. Eternal success.

---

[50] *Abu Dawood*, Hadith 3562

All Virtues, Big or Small

A BIG HANG UP of our times—sometimes found even in those involved in Islamic work—is the focus on doing something big. We want to be associated with big projects. We want to serve the cause of Islam in a big way. Big deeds, big rewards. Big success, here and in the Hereafter. Who can argue with that?

Well, though the logic appears to be bullet proof, there actually is a problem with it. It assumes that the reward for a good deed is based on its value as perceived by us. In reality, the reward for every good deed is based on the actual goodness in it and only Allah ﷻ can judge that. That is why even after performing the greatest meritorious acts, our *salaf* (predecessors) used to be worried whether or not their deeds would be accepted. At the same time they approached even the smallest virtues with the enthusiasm of a desperate person who knows he needs all the help he can get. They had fully understood the message that many seemingly great deeds may not carry much weight in the Hereafter because of some inherent flaw that the doer may not even be aware of. Yet it is possible for some apparently minor charitable act to save a believer from Hell. For example one hadith in *Bukhari* and

All Virtues, Big or Small

Muslim mentions the case of a woman of ill repute who once helped a thirsty dog by making extra effort to fetch water from a well. She was saved from Hell for that small kindness alone.

What is the point of this hadith? It is beautifully stated in another hadith:

$$\text{لَا تَحْقِرَنَّ مِنْ الْمَعْرُوفِ شَيْئًا}$$

"Never belittle any good deed." [*Muslim*, Hadith 4760]

We should always remember these golden words of wisdom from the Prophet ﷺ. Every good deed, no matter how small, has the potential of becoming our ticket to Paradise. It just depends upon the situation in which it was performed and the level of sincerity in our heart. Feeding water to a thirsty dog is not an extraordinary event per se, but in the particular case mentioned in the hadith it became large enough to wipe out all the sins of a very sinful person.

It certainly does not mean that we should become complacent with sins in the hope that some small kindness will wipe them out. No one who remembers this warning by the Prophet ﷺ can do that:

$$\text{الْعَاجِزُ مَنْ أَتْبَعَ نَفْسَهُ هَوَاهَا وَتَمَنَّى عَلَى اللَّه}$$

"Really frustrated will be the person who follows his own desires (in violation of Allah's commands) yet entertains the wishful thinking that Allah will forgive him." [*Tirmidhi*, Hadith 2383]

Rather the point is that we should never miss an opportunity to do some good by considering the act too small. We should never consider any good act beneath us.

For who knows the true value of a small kindness or small virtue? One may simply say Alhamdulillah (Praise be to Allah) with such an intense feeling that it alone tilts the scale in his or her favor in the Hereafter. Helping a destitute person with a small amount of money or just some kind words, greeting a stranger, visiting the sick, joining in the funeral, consoling someone going through difficulty, removing something harmful from the path, making a quiet prayer for someone in need of help, forgiving a person who has hurt us—none of these will make big headlines but all of them can bring about major change in our lives.

What is true about good is also true about evil. What seems to be a minor evil may not be small in terms of its consequences both here and in the Hereafter. As the Qur'an mentions:

$$وَتَحْسَبُونَهُ هَيِّنًا وَهُوَ عِندَ ٱللَّهِ عَظِيمٌ$$

"You reckoned it was trifling although it was most serious in the sight of Allah." [An-Nur, 24:15]

Small sins, if we become comfortable with them, may lead us to bigger and bigger sins. "The difference between a major and a minor sin is like the difference between a big and a small burning piece of charcoal," says Maulana Ashraf Ali Thanvi. "Who would willfully pick the burning charcoal with his bare hand because it is small?"

The Qur'an does make a distinction between minor and major sins, but that distinction is meaningful only when the sin just happened, not when it was committed on purpose. A sin, any sin, is by definition an act of disobedience. It may be forgiven when it resulted from human weakness. But when performed with a "so what" attitude, it becomes defiance—and thus a major sin.

We can begin to grasp the wisdom behind this teaching by considering what happens in real life. Our minds are fascinating machines that are always receiving and generating all kinds of ideas. It would be a rare person who never received any idea for either virtue or vice. An action idea can come from any source: something we read or heard; a conversation with a friend or a stranger; some quiet

All Virtues, Big or Small

reflection; something we saw on the street. Anything. While these things may just happen to us, what we do with them can make all the difference in our life. If the inspiration is for some good, normally Satan counters it by suggesting that it is too small to be of any consequence in our life. Why bother. You are not that pious anyway, he assures us. If it is for some vice and we are reluctant to do it, Satan assures us that in light of other vices already in our life, it won't make any big difference. Either way the cornerstone of this Satanic strategy is the trivialization of both vices and virtues.

But the person who listens to this Prophetic teaching will be able to counter this strategy. Small or big, a virtue is a virtue. I need it. I must seize the moment. This person will find that good deeds are connected to each other through an invisible web. Each one is a window to the world of virtue. The goodness generated in the heart by a seemingly small good deed may lead us to a much bigger good deed later. Thus through this regenerative and multiplicative process, even small acts may gradually bring a total change in one's life.

We should certainly go for the big virtues. But we should also remember that no virtue is too small.

Amr-bil-Maroof

IT IS THE MOST common activity in all social settings. Sometimes it is explicit: we argue for or against something. Other times it is implicit: we show interest or lack of interest. More often than we realize we are engaged in persuading others or are being persuaded by them about big and small things in life. It is a very powerful force also. That is why marketers yearn for word of mouth publicity and powerful media machines long for becoming the talk of the town.

Concerned with good as it is, Islam gives this tremendous social force a purpose. It must be used for promoting good, truth and justice and checking evil and injustice. That is the essence of *amr-bil-maroof-wa-nahi-anil-munkar*. And the Qur'an declares it as the defining mission for the Ummah:

كُنتُمْ خَيْرَ أُمَّةٍ أُخْرِجَتْ لِلنَّاسِ تَأْمُرُونَ بِٱلْمَعْرُوفِ وَتَنْهَوْنَ عَنِ ٱلْمُنكَرِ وَتُؤْمِنُونَ بِٱللَّهِ

"You are the best community that has been raised for mankind. You enjoin good and forbid evil and you believe in Allah." [Al-i-'Imran, 3:110]

At another place the Qur'an declares promoting good as an attribute of believers and promoting evil as an attribute of hypocrites:

$$وَٱلْمُؤْمِنُونَ وَٱلْمُؤْمِنَٰتُ بَعْضُهُمْ أَوْلِيَآءُ بَعْضٍ ۚ يَأْمُرُونَ بِٱلْمَعْرُوفِ وَيَنْهَوْنَ عَنِ ٱلْمُنكَرِ$$

"The believers, men and women, are protectors of each other: they enjoin what is good and forbid what is evil…" [At-Tauba, 9:71]

On the other hand,

$$ٱلْمُنَٰفِقُونَ وَٱلْمُنَٰفِقَٰتُ بَعْضُهُم مِّنْ بَعْضٍ ۚ يَأْمُرُونَ بِٱلْمُنكَرِ وَيَنْهَوْنَ عَنِ ٱلْمَعْرُوفِ$$

"The hypocrites, both men and women, proceed from one another. They enjoin the evil and forbid the good…" [At-Tauba, 9:67]

The implications are clear. It is not that a believer will never commit a mistake or be involved in evil. Only that he will never insist on it, justify it, or promote it. He may fail to do some required good. But he will never be a force opposing it. In the Islamic society sin is a private weakness, not a public cause. It is for this reason that repentance for a public sin must also be made in public while we must repent privately for our private sins. A public sin may have encouraged others to do the same. A public repentance will counter that.

Still in this life there will always be tendencies to deviate from the Straight Path. And in the institution of *amr-bil-maroof*, the Community of Believers has a built-in self-correcting mechanism. Consider cruise control in an automobile. Once turned on, it keeps monitoring the car speed and pulling it towards the set point. It does not mean absence of tendency to deviate from the desired speed, only an effective mechanism for monitoring and countering it. What cruise control does for car speed, *amr-bil-maroof* does for the direction of the society.

This mechanism works at two levels. At one level it is the responsibility of every member of the society. When we see a wrong we should correct it. A very famous hadith declares it as an issue of faith.

مَنْ رَأَى مِنْكُمْ مُنْكَرًا فَلْيُغَيِّرْهُ بِيَدِه فَإِنْ لَمْ يَسْتَطِعْ فَبِلِسَانِه فَإِنْ لَمْ يَسْتَطِعْ فَبِقَلْبِه وَذَلِكَ أَضْعَفُ الإِيمَانِ

"Whoever amongst you sees an evil should change it with his hand. If he is unable to do that then with his tongue. If he is unable to do that, then with his heart, and that is the weakest level of *iman*." [*Muslim*, Hadith 70]

So if a person does not even feel bad about an evil, he has no faith whatsoever. Similarly we are encouraged to promote good. One hadith promises that a person who persuades another one to do some good deed will get the same reward as the person he persuaded. At this level the responsibility of every member of the society is for his or her own sphere of influence: family, friends, colleagues, neighbors. When taken together these spheres would encompass the entire society.

At a higher level this is a specialized task. A full time job for a qualified group to always monitor the direction of the society and fight deviations at a collective level.

وَلْتَكُنْ مِنكُمْ أُمَّةٌ يَدْعُونَ إِلَى ٱلْخَيْرِ وَيَأْمُرُونَ بِٱلْمَعْرُوفِ وَيَنْهَوْنَ عَنِ ٱلْمُنكَرِ ۚ وَأُو۟لَٰٓئِكَ هُمُ ٱلْمُفْلِحُونَ ۝

"Let there arise out of you a group inviting to all that is good, enjoining what is right, and forbidding what is wrong. They are the ones to attain success." [Al-i-'Imran, 3:104]

This is the responsibility of the experts, the scholars, those qualified to lead the entire community.

Can we imagine what the Ummah would look like had we followed this one teaching seriously? For today we seem to be doing exactly the opposite. There are Muslim women who have been pressured out of observing *hijab* by friends and relatives. Men and women have been enticed into *riba* transactions. All innovations (*bid'ah*) and false social practices continue under social pressures. Bribery, backbiting, corruption, indecency, and dishonesty flourish under social approval. It is frightening to see how our real life matches the description given for the hypocrites. For we are warned that if we persuade others to commit a wrong we'll add to our burden of sins by the same amount. It is one thing to commit a wrong out of weakness. It is totally different to advocate the wrong and willingly multiply our burden of sins.

Of course for today's secular world *amr-bil-maroof* is an alien concept. This world is driven by interests, not principles. It professes belief in some moral values—like freedom—to be interpreted in the light of perceived interests. Thus defense of a person's obscene attacks on Islam becomes a virtue. Yet it finds nothing wrong in curbing the freedom of those who may challenge its ideas, whether in Algeria or Egypt, in Kashmir or Palestine, because that threatens its interests. No one should be surprised at such contradictions when interests override moral values.

Yet we see many Muslims in the West being influenced by a fierce and misguided individualism. We must remember that the Islamic community is the only community with a declared mission of promoting good and forbidding evil. Its definition of good and evil is not subject to the whims and desires of every generation or the perceived interests of a nation-state. They are permanent concepts as defined in its unalterable sources: the Qur'an and the Sunnah. In a world of moral relativism these permanent values are the hope for the whole mankind. To keep these alive in the society we need the institution of *amr-bil-maroof*.

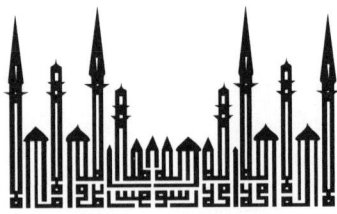

What is Tasawwuf?[51]

﴿قَدْ أَفْلَحَ مَن زَكَّىٰهَا ۝ وَقَدْ خَابَ مَن دَسَّىٰهَا ۝﴾

"Verily, he who has purified the heart is successful and he who has despoiled it has lost." [Ash-Shams, 91:9-10]

MANY PEOPLE HAVE misunderstandings about *tasawwuf*. Many think that it is something beyond the Qur'an and Sunnah. Errant sufis as well as the superficial ulama, although on the opposite ends of the spectrum, are together in holding this mistaken notion. Consequently the first group has shunned the Qur'an and Hadith while the second group has shunned *tasawwuf*. Actually, although the term *tasawwuf*, like many other religious terms in use today, evolved later, the discipline is very much part of the Shariah. The department of the Shariah relating to external deeds like salat and zakat is called *fiqh* while the one dealing with the internal feelings and states of the heart is called *tasawwuf*. Both are commanded in the Qur'an. Thus while commanding salat and zakat, the Qur'an also commands gratefulness to and love of Allah and condemns the evil of pride and vanity. Similarly, in the books of Hadith, along

---

[51] Condensed from writings of Maulana Ashraf Ali Thanvi.

with the chapters on *ibada*, trade and commerce, and marriage and divorce are to be found the chapters on *riya* (showoff) *takabbur, akhlaq,* etc. These commands are as much a mandatory requirement as the ones dealing with external deeds.

On reflection it will be realized that all the external deeds are designed for the reformation of the heart. That is the basis of success in the Hereafter while its despoiling is the cause of total destruction. This is precisely what is known technically as *tasawwuf*. Its focus is *tahzeeb-e-akhlaq* or the adornment of character; its motive is the attainment of Divine pleasure; its method is total obedience to the commands of the Shariah.

Tasawwuf is the soul of Islam. Its function is to purify the heart from the lowly bestial attributes of lust, calamities of the tongue, anger, malice, jealousy, love of the world, love of fame, niggardliness, greed, ostentation, vanity, deception, and so on. At the same time it aims at the adornment of the heart with the lofty attributes of repentance, perseverance, gratefulness, fear of Allah, hope, abstention, *Tauheed*, trust, love, sincerity, truth, contemplation, and so on.

To diagnose and treat the diseases of the heart normally requires the help of an expert mentor or *Shaikh*. Here are the qualities of a good *Shaikh*:

1. He possesses necessary religious knowledge.
2. His beliefs, habits, and practices are in accordance with the Shariah.
3. He does not harbor greed for the worldly wealth.
4. He has himself spent time learning from a good *Shaikh*.
5. The scholars and good *mashaikh* of his time hold good opinion about him.
6. His admirers are mostly from among the people who have good understanding of religion.
7. Most of his followers follow the Shariah and are not the seekers after this world.

8. He sincerely tries to educate and morally train his followers. If he sees anything wrong in them, he corrects it.
9. In his company one can feel a decrease in the love of this world and an increase in the love for Allah.
10. He himself regularly performs *dhikr* and *shughal* (spiritual exercises).

In searching for a *Shaikh*, do not look for his ability to perform *karamat* (miracles) or to foretell the future. A very good *Shaikh* may not be able to show any *karamat*. On the other hand, a person showing *karamat* does not have to be a pious person—or even a Muslim. Prominent Sufi Bayazid Bistami says: "Do not be deceived if you see a performer of supernatural feats flying in the air. Measure him on the standard of the Shariah."

When you find the right *Shaikh*, and you are satisfied with his ability to provide spiritual guidance, you perform *baya* or pledge. This is a two-way commitment; the *Shaikh* pledges to guide you in light of Shariah and you pledge to follow him. Then the *Shaikh* will give his *mureed* (disciple) initial instructions. They include the following:

1. Perform repentance for all the past sins and take steps to make amends, e.g. if any salat has been missed so far in the life, you start making up for it.
2. If you have any unmet financial obligations toward another person make plans to discharge them.
3. Guard your eyes, ears, and tongue.
4. Perform *dhikr* regularly.
5. Start a daily session of self-accounting before going to bed. Review all the good and bad deeds performed during the day. Repent for the bad ones and thank Allah ﷻ for the good ones.
6. Perform *muraqaba-maut* (meditation over death) every night before going to bed. Just visualize that you have died. Reflect upon the pangs of death, the

questioning in the grave, the plain of Resurrection, the Reckoning, the presence in the Court of Allah, etc. This helps bring softness to the heart and break the tendency to commit sins.
7. Develop humility. Even if you observe another individual committing the worst of vices you should not despise him or her, nor should you consider yourself nobler. It is very much possible that the perpetrator of the vice may resort to sincere repentance while the one who despised the sinner become ensnared in the traps of *nafs* and *Shaitan* (Satan). One has no certainty regarding one's end. One therefore has no basis for regarding another with contempt.

The essential idea of *tahzeeb-e-akhlaq* is to bring our natural faculties in a state of balance. The three basic faculties are anger, desires, and intelligence.

ANGER

When in equilibrium it results in valor, forbearance, steadfastness, the ability to restrain anger, and dignity. Excess will result in rashness, boastfulness, pride, inability to restrain anger, and vanity. A deficiency will result in cowardice, disgrace, and feeling of inferiority.

DESIRES

Equilibrium here results in chastity, generosity, *haya* (decency), patience, and contentment. Its excess leads to greed and lust. The other extreme results in narrow-mindedness, and impotence, etc.

INTELLIGENCE

Equilibrium here makes man wise, sharp-witted, and one with great insights. Excess here makes one deceptive and

SELF REFORM

fraudulent. Its lack results in ignorance and stupidity with the consequence that such a person is quickly misled.

A person will be considered as having a beautiful *seerah* (character) only when these faculties are in a state of balance and equilibrium. Internal beauty varies with people just as external beauty does. The possessor of the most beautiful *seerah* was Prophet Muhammad ﷺ. The beauty of our *seerah* is based on its closeness to his *seerah*.

Women and Family

In this section:

- Fair Ladies for the Altar
- Home, Sweet Home
- Gold and Glitter
- For Ever After...
- Motherhood
- Your Heaven, Your Hell
- Parenting Goals and Ideas
- Bonds of Kinship
- Educated, Ignorant, and Feminist
- The Crusade Against Hijab: Then and Now
- Women's Rights: An Islamic Declaration

Fair Ladies for the Altar

IT HAPPENED SOON after Muslims conquered Egypt in 20 AH. A delegation of the local Copts approached the governor Amr ibn al-A'as ﷺ with a pressing matter. "O Amir, our Nile has a habit such that if it is not satisfied it does not flow," they said. "And what is that?" he asked. "On the 12th night of Paona[52] we get a virgin girl with the permission of her parents, dress her in silk and the best clothes available, and then throw her into the Nile. Then it flows." The response of the governor to this bizarre request was immediate. "This cannot happen under Islam. Islam destroys all (superstitions and rites of Ignorance) that preceded it."

Days passed. Then weeks. Then three months. The river remained dry. Caught between a river that "demanded" human sacrifice, and the new rulers who would not permit it, the people prepared to migrate. Seeing this Amr ibn al-A'as ﷺ wrote to Khalifa Sayyidna Umar ﷺ. "You did the right thing," Sayyidna Umar ﷺ wrote back. "Islam does destroy what was before it. I am sending you a note. Drop it into the river." The note was a letter to the river. It read: "From the servant of Allah, Ameerul-Momineen Umar to the Nile of

---

[52] Paona, Epep, and Mesra are months in the Coptic calendar. Paona begins on 8 June, Epep on 8 July, and Mesra on 7 August. The 12th night of Paona thus translates into 20 June.

Egypt. If you were flowing of your own accord then do not flow. But if it is Allah, the One, the Almighty, Who makes you flow then we pray to Him that He makes you flow."

And so it happened, writes historian Ibn Taghri Berdi in *An-Najum uz-Zahira fi Akhbar Muluk Misr wal-Qahira*.[53] Governor Amr ibn al-A'as ﷺ dropped the letter into the river and the next morning the Nile not only had started flowing, but its level also had risen 16 cubits (24 feet) in one night. Islam had liberated the women in Egypt from the tyranny of a terrible pagan practice.

Human sacrifice in one form or another was common to all pagan societies. A very large number of these sacrifices involved women. They were thrown into rivers or lakes (to appease these vital sources of life), buried alive in the foundations of bridges (to make the bridge strong), or just offered as sacrifice to the gods for the protection of the community.

The game "London Bridge Is Broken Down," and the accompanying rhyme are reminders of the practice of human sacrifice at the building of a bridge. The bridge has fallen down, and all rebuilding attempts will fail. Then suddenly a solution pops up in the form of the arrest of a woman prisoner.

> London Bridge has fallen down, fallen down, fallen down,
> Build it up with lime and stone ...
> Stone and lime would wash away ...
> Build it up with iron bars ...
> Iron bars would bend and break ... etc., etc.
>
> What has this poor prisoner done? ...
> Off to prison she must go.
> My fair lady!

Ibn Battuta gives an account of the practice in pagan Maldive Islands. Every month a young virgin girl was dressed up then

---

[53] Vol. 1, p. 45-46.

left overnight in a temple on the shore to appease a jinni. In the morning they would find the girl dead and violated. A Muslim visitor Abul Barkat Berberi learned about it from his host, an old woman whose only daughter had been drafted for the next sacrifice. Abul Barkat, who was a hafiz, offered to go in her place. In the temple he kept reciting the Qur'an all night. When they found him alive and well next morning, the news spread throughout the island and within a month the entire population had accepted Islam. The woman of another land had been liberated from the pagan tyranny.

The record of Christianity is less clear. First, it endorsed the basic idea of human sacrifice by suggesting that Jesus, peace be upon him, had died on the cross to atone for the sins of humanity. Second, it was content to merely change the pagan rites into more benign forms. The earlier offerings of human sacrifices of Saturnalia were replaced by offerings of Christmas gifts. The same with Halloween, which started in Great Britain with the ancient Druid culture. The Druids believed that the witches, ghosts, and evil spirits walked on earth on the night of October 31. They would light huge bonfires to ward off these spirits. They would then go from door to door asking for treats. These "treats" were not candy. They were victims—young virgins—for human sacrifices. If the Druids received their "treat" they would leave a lighted jack-o'-lantern at that house as a sign that a sacrifice had been obtained there.

That most of these symbols survive (and thrive) today reminds us that the post-Christian western civilization remains at heart a pagan civilization, albeit a more polished one. The drastic rituals have been replaced but the crooked ideas behind them survive. What was the idea behind throwing a virgin into the Nile? That a woman must sacrifice her life for the economic prosperity of the society. In forcing the women outside the home and herding them into offices and factories, the Industrial Revolution preserved the same idea. In putting them on display to attract customers, the "marketing revolution" preserved the same idea. The women must sacrifice their lives, dignity, and security for the economic prosperity of the society. If it leaves them prey to an avalanche of advances and assaults, so be it. If it destroys the home and family life, so be it. The goddess of "economic progress" demands their sacrifice, and they must submit. Today the woman has been uprooted from her home, separated from her family, violated, left to tend for herself, and expected to be grateful for this "emancipation"!

How can we explain what was going on with the Nile? Perhaps the answer lies in that when a people choose to reject Allah's clear Signs and Commands, then their own chosen path of destruction is made easy for them.

وَٱلَّذِينَ كَذَّبُواْ بِـَٔايَٰتِنَا سَنَسْتَدْرِجُهُم مِّنْ حَيْثُ لَا يَعْلَمُونَ

"Those who reject Our Signs, We will lead them step by step to ruin while they know not." [Al-A'raf, 7:182]

As the Nile remained dry, it was a test for the believers. Would they hold fast to the rejection of all pagan rites or would they waver in the face of an apparent calamity? The letter to the river was a marvelous act. It radiated unwavering faith in Allah ﷻ and unremitting disdain for pagan beliefs and practices. Only such faith could free humanity from the cruelty of pagan ignorance.

The test continues. For the women today need to be liberated from the tyranny of modern paganism, just like they needed to be liberated from the tyranny of ancient paganism.

Home, Sweet Home

"MY OWN FEELING IS that we've pushed women too far," said Dr. T. Berry Brazelton, the then 80 year old Harvard University doctor, also known as "America's Pediatrician," in an interview in the *Los Angeles Times*.[54] "We've split them in two, and we have not given them back anything to support themselves on either end." He had witnessed what forcing the women into the workforce and the breakdown of the family had done to the American children. "I just think our country is in deep, deep trouble," he agonized.

Opinion leaders of all persuasions agree. Ask America's former first lady Hillary Clinton, who considers herself a champion of women's and children's causes. In her 1996 book *It Takes a Village*[55] she offers this assessment: "...children's potential lost to spirit-crushing poverty, children's health lost to unaffordable care, children's hearts lost in divorce and custody fights, children's futures lost in an overburdened foster care system, children's lives lost to abuse and violence, our society lost to itself as we fail our children."

---

[54] Dr. T. Berry Brazelton, "Explaining the Needs of Children to Parents—and Lawmakers." By Melissa A. Healy. *The Los Angeles Times*, April 5, 1998

[55] Hillary Clinton, *It Takes a Village: and Other Lessons Children Teach Us*. (New York: Simon & Schuster, 1996).

WOMEN AND FAMILY

This is a society in which by her account: "homicide and suicide kill almost seven thousand children every year; one in four of all children are born to unmarried mothers, many of whom are children themselves; and 135,000 children bring guns to school each day. Children in every social stratum suffer from abuse, neglect, and preventable emotional problems." She also approvingly quotes: "If you bungle raising your children, I don't think whatever else you do matters very much." It is obvious that America as a nation, has bungled this thoroughly.

Welcome to the dark side of "Women's Emancipation." Today women are free in America. Free from the protection of a home and the support of a husband who would be responsible to provide for them. They are on their own. In turn, the children have been freed from the rigidities of the traditional home, where father and mother provide for them, take care of them, and guide them. The children are also on their own. Just in case they do not like it, the society has been experimenting with all kinds of poultry farms—day care they call them—to take care of them.

Things have gone so wrong for so long that everyone has lost all hope that the society can rectify it completely and retrace its steps. Hillary Clinton admits: "My personal wish, that every child have an intact, dependable family, will likely remain a wish." So, she is just trying to build a better poultry farm with the help of the whole village. Dr. Brazelton knew that the children need the mother at home. "I think you are giving a gift to the child when you stay home with him as long as you can." However, he knew that it cannot be very long, as, to stay home, "being just a mother," was not good enough any more. He knew the psychological crisis faced by the stay-at-home mothers, so he pleaded with everyone to do as much as they could.

Now contrast this with the UN edict that the women in the rest of the world, especially the Muslim world, must take up all kinds of jobs outside the home; that the goal should be their total economic independence. In other words, women must be forced outside the home so they are no longer available to take care of the children within the home. They must be "liberated" from the home, so they can enjoy the same fruits of "emancipation" as the women are "enjoying" in the West.

The destruction of the family in the West was not planned. It just happened as a logical result of the materialistic, hedonistic, Godless civilizational values that have gripped these societies. But the UN decree that the rest of the world must follow the same disastrous path, is something else. It is as if a person lost an eye to horseplay, and now wants everyone else to voluntarily have an eye removed!

It is unconscionable that we should be answering such chicanery with apologetics of the kind that normally begin with, "Islam also allows women to," as in, "Islam also allows women to work outside the home." Yes, it does in case of necessity and with important safeguards, but that is beside the point. The real issue is that Islam frees a wife from the burden to provide for the family. It is solely the husband's responsibility. In return, the wife's main responsibility is to stay home and take care of the children. The primary field of women's endeavor is the home, sweet home. And this has to be stated without hesitation or apology. The Qur'an says:

$$وَقَرْنَ فِي بُيُوتِكُنَّ$$

"And stay quietly in your homes." [Al-Ahzab, 33:33]

And the Prophet ﷺ said:

$$كُلُّكُمْ رَاعٍ وَكُلُّكُمْ مَسْئُولٌ عَنْ رَعِيَّتِهِ... وَالْمَرْأَةُ رَاعِيَةٌ عَلَى بَيْتِ بَعْلِهَا وَوَلَدِهِ وَهِيَ مَسْئُولَةٌ عَنْهُمْ$$

"Everyone of you is in charge and everyone will be accountable for those given in his charge...The wife is responsible for taking care of the home of her husband

and his children, and she will be accountable for them."
[*Bukhari*, Hadith 2368]

This is also the most rewarding job that anyone can think of. The Prophet ﷺ assured the woman who stays home to take care of the children that she would be with him in Paradise. According to another hadith, during pregnancy and nursing the believing mother is like the soldier on active duty. If she dies, she gets the reward reserved for a martyr. Yet another hadith says to the women:

$$\text{عَلَيْكُنَّ بِالْبَيْتِ فَإِنَّهُ جِهَادُكُنَّ}$$

"Take care of the home. That is your jihad." [*Musnad Ahmed*, Hadith 23257]

All of these clearly establish the basic division of labor between men and women according to Islam: men are responsible for the affairs outside the home and the women are responsible for taking care of the home. This division is not a relic of some dark past; it is the only basis on which a healthy society has ever been built and can be built today. The nations that have tried to alter this natural arrangement long enough have nothing but grief and trouble to show for their efforts. And they seem to be groping in the dark, unable to undo the damage and get out of the quagmire. Is there any sane reason that those who have the Light should follow them on the dark highway to disaster?

Gold and Glitter

وَمِنْ ءَايَـٰتِهِۦٓ أَنْ خَلَقَ لَكُم مِّنْ أَنفُسِكُمْ أَزْوَٰجًا لِّتَسْكُنُوٓا۟ إِلَيْهَا وَجَعَلَ بَيْنَكُم مَّوَدَّةً وَرَحْمَةً ۚ إِنَّ فِى ذَٰلِكَ لَءَايَـٰتٍ لِّقَوْمٍ يَتَفَكَّرُونَ ۝

"And among His signs is that He created for you mates from among yourselves, that you may dwell in tranquility with them and He has put love and mercy between your hearts: verily in that are signs for those who reflect." [Ar-Rum, 30:21]

"Blessed be God King of the Universe that Thou has not made me a woman." – Jewish Man's Prayer

"What is the difference whether it is in a wife or mother, it is still Eve the temptress that we must be aware of in any woman." – St. Augustine

AMONG THE FAVORITE topics of the media machine to show Islam's "despicable" treatment of women is the "plight" of women in Saudi Arabia: women are not allowed to drive there. Every time it is mentioned embarrassed Muslims rush

WOMEN AND FAMILY

to point out the fact that in the rest of the Muslim world women can indeed drive.

It is true that in most of the Muslim world women can drive and it is debatable whether the Saudi policy is good or bad. There are even indications that the Saudi government may be contemplating a U-turn on the issue. But the encounter misses the central issue. Is driving a *right* or a *privilege*? Rights are inalienable. They can be demanded. Not privileges; they are granted or refused at the discretion of authorities everywhere. And before you can blame someone for usurping a right, you must first establish that what you are complaining about is indeed a right. Now one does not need to search beyond his or her driving license to realize that throughout the world driving is considered a *privilege. For one does not need any licenses for the exercise of a right but one may need it for enjoying a privilege.* And everywhere this privilege can be granted or revoked by a state agency at its discretion. In the United States, for example, one's driving license can be revoked, for no fault of his own, if someone else hits him and he did not carry insurance when hit. The rule punishes you when you are not at fault but it cannot be challenged because driving is not a right. It is a privilege. Case dismissed.

The exchange highlights the difficulty of objectively discussing the issue of status of women in today's highly charged atmosphere, produced in large part by a very powerful media machine. And expectedly so, for on probably no other issue is the evangelism of the western civilization more self-assured. The *gold standard* for the women's status in the society has been developed by the West. And everyone must now comply. The history of women's struggle and eventual victory in the West has to be the guiding light for the entire humanity.

It is true that there has been a lot in the history of the West for the women to revolt against. As late as the 1860s, a married Englishwoman did not exist as a legal person. Upon marriage she entered a condition called "converture," effectively making her a possession of her husband. Her last name was changed to indicate the new ownership, a practice that continues to date. She could not own property, make a contract or will, or get custody rights for her own children. The 1632 English law declared: "That which the husband hath is his own. That which the wife hath is the husband's." Worse, she had no rights to get out of a miserable marriage. Until 1857, divorce was obtainable through the passage of an Act of Parliament.

Her second-class status was widely believed: "[Man] is the image and glory of God; but woman is the glory of man".[56] So we see no respectable leader in the West in the 15th through the 18th centuries challenging these ideas. Here, for example, is the great reformer Martin Luther: "If they become tired or even die, that does not matter. Let them die in childbirth, that's why they are there."

The works of Mary Wollstonecroft (1792) and John Staurt Mill (1869) are presented as the first voices of revolt. But these were controversial people who were rejected and ignored by their contemporaries. Both would be rediscovered in the second half of the 20th century because they provided a justification for the later developments.

The scene begins to change in the 19th century, not under the force of any moral argument, but because of pressures generated by the Industrial Revolution. The juggernaut of Industrial Revolution destroyed the old handicraft based economy and forced the workers to move to the sweatshops in big cities. They demanded, in vain, "family wages" so a man could support his family on his income. The capitalists would rather have the family also come to his service if it wanted to eat. There was no option but to send the women (and children) to the factory to make ends meet.

Later, the opening of clerical jobs needed millions of other women to come out of their homes and become salesgirls, typists, secretaries, waitresses. Cheap labor. The

---

[56] I Cor. 11:7

process was given a moral purpose by the language of the feminist movement. It measured their "progress" by how many had been driven out of their homes. It labeled the social upheavals caused by the Industrial Revolution as women's emancipation. According to its convoluted logic if a woman serves food to her husband and children, it is slavery. If she provides the same service to total strangers in a restaurant or aircraft, risking their never ending advances, that is emancipation!

The ancient Greek philosophers argued whether or not woman had a soul. But the civilized West has settled the question once for all. Its answer: the woman is nothing but body. That is why we see her semi-clad and nude pictures on every square inch of available space at a time when the West is busy congratulating itself for the remarkable progress of its women.

A *Los Angeles Times* report on pornography on the Internet highlights the moral abyss this value system creates. The nudity may be degrading, it says, but the positive side is that "the Web has allowed some of these women to become entrepreneurs by marketing their own physical assets."[57] Is it any wonder that despite the fact that he had been accused and generally believed to have performed indecent acts against women, Bill Clinton received more votes from the women? Probably nobody cared as sexual harassment in all segments of society has become everyday news.

The destruction of the home is a direct result of this progress. In 1994, 1.2 million divorces took place in the United States. And experts predicted that half of all new marriages would end in divorce. An unjust system has only changed the forms of exploitation. They could not improve things at home. So they "freed" the woman from it.

Islam, on the other hand, gives her her God-given rights without forcing her out of the home. She has rights of

---

[57] Michelle V. Rafter, "The Internet's Burgeoning Sex Industry Helped Spur Passage of Controversial Decency Law Series: Indecency in Cyberspace," *The Los Angeles Times*, March 17, 1997, 1.

property ownership, and inheritance; she has rights in her marriage similar to the rights of the husband. Far from the non-adult she is depicted to be, she is responsible for effective management of the home and the upbringing of the children, a most challenging job.

The paradise of her children lies at her feet. The righteousness of her husband is to be judged by his kind treatment to her. To bring her up in a loving caring manner assures her father protection from Hell-fire. While the feminist model depends on friction, here the relationship is one of love and respect, leading to peace and harmony.

This is *real gold*. Why should anybody trade it for glitter?

For Ever After...

IN ALL SOCIETIES and at all times marriage has been considered an occasion for great joy. The word most used with "wedding" is "celebration." In fiction, which reflects our inner desires, they "lived happily ever after." Obviously seeking success in marriage has been a preoccupation of all societies.

Today in the United States—a society as advanced as human endeavor alone without Divine Guidance can make it—the average length of "ever after" is about seven years. That is the average period a new marriage lasts today. But even this period is not entirely a period of happiness. As the Surgeon General report indicated a few years ago, home had become the most dangerous place for the American woman. The leading cause of injuries to them was beatings by husbands and boyfriends.

Obviously Science and the Age of Reason have not exactly delivered the happiest homes on earth. The secret to marital bliss eludes the western civilization, although arrogance and conceit keep it from admitting fundamental flaws and looking elsewhere for solutions. Otherwise it would have found the solution in Islam.

Islamic prescription for success in married life is based on *taqwa*, fear and consciousness of Allah ﷻ. Taqwa—the basis for all aspects of Islamic life—is especially relevant to the household. That is why Surah An-Nisa, where many commands regarding rights and responsibilities of spouses are given, begins with repeated reminders of taqwa.

A hadith explains why. It describes a scene from the court of Satan where his assistants are reporting their achievements but he is not pleased. Then comes an assistant who says: "I did not spare any effort until I sowed the seed of discord between a husband and his wife." Satan embraces him in joy saying, "Well done."[58]

To fight Satan, one needs Allah's help and it comes with taqwa, that is living with the awareness that Allah ﷻ is watching us and will hold us accountable for our actions. A direct and far reaching consequence of this awareness is that a fight for rights is replaced by a concern for responsibilities. One's rights are another's responsibilities. A Muslim husband and wife will be concerned with discharging their duties toward each other. Not a very attractive prospect for those itching to start a fight for rights. But it provides for a home that is a model of peace, love, and harmony.

Islam emphasizes organization and discipline, the five daily congregational prayers being a good reminder of that concern. If two Muslims travel together, they are required to choose one as the leader. Quite naturally the principle extends to the home as well, and the husband is the head of the household. He is responsible for handling all outside affairs and providing finances, protection, and overall direction. The wife is his assistant in the home, responsible for taking care of the home and the children. A very famous hadith explains it:

كُلُّكُمْ رَاعٍ وَكُلُّكُمْ مَسْئُولٌ عَنْ رَعِيَّتِهِ...وَالرَّجُلُ رَاعٍ عَلَى أَهْلِ بَيْتِهِ وَالْمَرْأَةُ رَاعِيَةٌ عَلَى بَيْتِ زَوْجِهَا وَوَلَدِه

---

[58] *Muslim*, Hadith 5032

> "Everyone of you is in charge and everyone will be accountable for those given in his charge...The man is in charge of the household and the woman is in charge of the home of her husband and his children." [*Bukhari*, Hadith 4801]

This hierarchy of authority and responsibility is key to the stability and proper functioning of the society.

Authority does carry risk of misuse. The solution does not lie in eliminating authority but in including suitable protections against the possible abuse. On the legal level this is achieved by delineating the boundaries of this authority. The basic ground rule in the Islamic society is that no one can ever ask for anything against the Shariah. Additionally, a wife's legal obligation is very limited. In fact her only legal obligation is to stay in the home of her husband. She is not legally bound even to cook food, much less serve the parents or other relatives of her husband. The delicate balance between the legal and the moral here is very illuminating. On the moral plane she is expected to take care of household chores, but this is to be taken as a favor by the husband.

Too many husbands take these services for granted. Realizing this necessary function as kindness would call for greater kindness in return. And a heavy emphasis on kindness keeps the husband's authority in check:

> خَيْرُكُمْ خَيْرُكُمْ لِأَهْلِهِ وَأَنَا خَيْرُكُمْ لِأَهْلِي
>
> "The best of you are those who are best in dealing with their wives and I am the best in dealing with my wives." [*Tirmidhi*, Hadith 3830]

A problem may still arise between the husband and wife. No two human beings can always meet the expectations of the other. Human beings are neither perfect nor perfectly matched. What is a husband to do if he sees something in his wife that he does not like? Unless the issue of concern is an unacceptable behavior according to Shariah—in which case he should use appropriate persuasion to change it—the husband is asked to ignore the negative and focus on the positive.

$$\text{لَا يَفْرَكْ مُؤْمِنٌ مُؤْمِنَةً إِنْ كَرِهَ مِنْهَا خُلُقًا رَضِيَ مِنْهَا آخَرَ}$$

"No believing man should totally detest a believing woman [who is his wife]. If he dislikes something in her, there would be something else in her that he would like."
[*Muslim*, Hadith 2672]

Most problems in domestic life begin as minor incidents that become magnified by taking exactly the opposite approach. On the other hand even the most trying moments in marital relations can be overcome by following this one piece of Prophetic advice.

Easier said than done? Well, what protects us from succumbing to our anger or frustrations in trying real-life situations is taqwa and remembrance of Allah ﷻ. He has more power over us than we have over those given in our charge. We remember His Authority and seek His Mercy. The success of our married life depends upon His Mercy and not on our power or ability to fight or manipulate. This search for His Mercy brings the best in us. As one hadith says: "When a husband and wife look at each other with love, Allah looks at both of them with mercy." And that is the real secret to marital bliss!

Critics will point out the many domestic problems in Muslim societies today similar to (but on a smaller scale than) the problems in the West. True. But that should not blind us to the key difference between the two. The problems in the West are a result of the value system adopted by it; those in Muslim homes result from deviating from their values. One is suffering by choosing the wrong medicine; the other has the right medicine but is failing to take it.

Motherhood

IN APRIL 1997 the then President Clinton gathered an army of former presidents, state governors, city mayors, and hundreds of prominent people from all 50 states to address one of the most pressing problems facing America today. He brought former chairman of the Joint Chiefs of Staff, Colin Powell, to lead this army. Their task: solve the problem of 15 million young Americans considered at-risk youth. "They are at risk of growing up unskilled, unlearned, or, even worse, unloved," said Powell, who was appointed chairman of President's Summit for America's Future. The problem has "the potential to explode our society," he warned.

He was not exaggerating. Fifteen million in a total population of about sixty million youth is a huge number. Mostly they come from dysfunctional families and fall victims to the "pathologies and poisons of the street." Every year 3.4 million of them try drugs. Half a million attempt suicide. A lot of them will drop out of high school and will be functionally illiterate in a country with free universal education. Their sexual mores differ little from those of breeding horses (70% have done it before the age of 17). Some time before this a prominent lawyer and writer, Alan Dershowitz, suggested reducing the age of consent to 15. (Marriage at that age will, of course, remain illegal!) Violent crimes committed by these youngsters have become such a problem that in May 1997 the Congress passed the Juvenile Crime Bill that allows people as young as 13 to be treated as adults in the criminal justice system.

What was Powell's solution for this daunting problem? He would find mentors—adult volunteers who would take care of these children. But what happened to their parents? They were not killed in a war, or by a plague, or some other natural disaster. Their problem is self-inflicted. Mothers left the home to "realize their full potential" on the factory floor, in the show room, or in the office. A society that belittled the task of homemaking lost the homemakers. With the free mixing of men and women in the work place, one thing led to another. The home was destroyed from both ends.

Life is fun. Homemaking is dull. Children are a burden. Now 15 million of them are a burden on the society. It remains to be seen how a society, whose members could not take care of their own children, will make them take care of other's children. But the elite team of American leaders could not bring itself to admitting that the root of the problem has been in the forcing of the women out of the home.

Former Soviet leader Mikhail Gorbachev was a little more candid. In his 1987 book *Perestroika*, he mentions the "paradoxical result of our sincere and politically justified desire to make women equal with men in everything." He notes: "But over the years of our difficult and heroic history, we failed to pay attention to women's specific rights and needs arising from their role as mother and homemaker, and their indispensable educational function as regards children. Engaged in scientific research, working on construction sites, in production and in the services, and involved in creative activities, women no longer have enough time to perform their everyday duties at home—housework, the upbringing of children and the creation of a family atmosphere. We have discovered that many of our problems—in children's and young people's behavior, in our morals, culture, and in production—are partially caused by the weakening of family ties and slack attitude to family responsibilities… That is why we are now holding heated debates in the press, in public organizations, at work and at home, about the question of what we should do to make it possible for women to return to their purely womanly mission."[59]

Well, Gorbachev (and the world), listen to the best teacher and guide for humanity, Prophet Muhammad ﷺ. He elevated the women from their status as chattel to the dignity of being equal servants of Allah ﷻ with men. Yet their status in society was not conditioned upon entering man's world. Their most important task is to take care of the home and children. "Take care of your home for *that* is your jihad."[60] Jihad is the epitome of Islamic life. Declaring homemaking as jihad for women is giving it the highest possible status in an Islamic society.

Not only is it an all-important task, only women are uniquely qualified to do it. It is not by accident that pregnancy and nursing are purely feminine tasks. Allah ﷻ has given women the special talents and psychological makeup needed to take care of the children. There is no substitute for mother's milk or mother's love. No one can extract and bottle motherly compassion. Her patience, kindness, willingness to sacrifice her own comforts, and her natural affinity for children—and the children's natural affinity for the mother—are the key to successful upbringing of children. A mother understands the children's problem even when they cannot express it. She can uniquely sense their needs, both physical and emotional. She can satisfy some of these herself. For others, children need the father. But even he needs her insights in discharging his responsibilities in this area. No day care center or nursery can make up for the absence of the mother and father. "What the children need for their upbringing is not a poultry farm," says Mufti Taqi Usmani.

---

[59] Mikhail Sergeyevich Gorbachev, *Perestroika: New Thinking for Our Country and the World.* (New York: Harper & Row, Publishers, 1987), 117.
[60] *Musnad Ahmed*, Hadith 23257

Mothers are the silent workers who are indispensable for building character of the next generation. A believing mother, who understands the crucial nature of her responsibility, will imbue her children with faith and moral values, as only she can. She will raise children with courage, honesty, truthfulness, patience and perseverance, love and kindness, faith, and self-confidence. On the other hand, a society without mothers and homemakers will produce at-risk youth.

In a way their role is like that of the archer's in the battle of *Uhud*. It looked less important, but was the key to the fate of the entire army. If women hold on to their front, the entire army will succeed. If they leave it for "greater action" elsewhere, everyone will lose.

Your Heaven, Your Hell

A PERSON ONCE ASKED Prophet Muhammad ﷺ, "What is the right of the parents over their children?" He answered:

هُمَا جَنَّتُكَ وَنَارُكَ

"They are your Heaven and Hell." [*Ibn Majah*, Hadith 3652]

This beautiful hadith answers in just three words (in the original Arabic) not only what but also why. We are to honor them, serve them, and take care of them in such a way that pleases them. For we will find the pleasure of Allah ﷻ in the pleasure of our parents. On the other hand, if a person is disrespectful, disobedient, or careless toward his parents, he has just opened his door to Hell through this behavior.

It is a sign of the importance of this issue that in the Qur'an, the command about our duties to the parents always occurs next to the command reminding us of our duties to Allah ﷻ.

$$\text{أَنِ ٱشْكُرْ لِي وَلِوَٰلِدَيْكَ إِلَيَّ ٱلْمَصِيرُ}$$

"Show gratitude to Me and to your parents. To Me is your return." [Luqman, 31:14]

$$\text{أَلَّا تُشْرِكُوا۟ بِهِۦ شَيْـًٔا ۖ وَبِٱلْوَٰلِدَيْنِ إِحْسَٰنًا}$$

"Join not anything with Him and be good to your parents." [Al-An'am, 6:151]

$$\text{وَقَضَىٰ رَبُّكَ أَلَّا تَعْبُدُوٓا۟ إِلَّآ إِيَّاهُ وَبِٱلْوَٰلِدَيْنِ إِحْسَٰنًا ۚ إِمَّا يَبْلُغَنَّ عِندَكَ ٱلْكِبَرَ أَحَدُهُمَآ أَوْ كِلَاهُمَا فَلَا تَقُل لَّهُمَآ أُفٍّ وَلَا تَنْهَرْهُمَا وَقُل لَّهُمَا قَوْلًا كَرِيمًا ۞ وَٱخْفِضْ لَهُمَا جَنَاحَ ٱلذُّلِّ مِنَ ٱلرَّحْمَةِ وَقُل رَّبِّ ٱرْحَمْهُمَا كَمَا رَبَّيَانِي صَغِيرًا}$$

"Your Lord has decreed that you worship none but Him and that you be kind to parents. Whether one or both of them attain old age in your life, say not to them a word of contempt, nor repel them, but address them in terms of honor. And, out of kindness, lower to them the wing of humility, and say: 'My Lord! Bestow on them Your Mercy even as they cherished me in childhood.'" [Al-Israa, 17:23-24]

This bracketing of the two obligations calls for reflection. The fact is that the relationship of parents and children is unique among all human relationships. Parents sacrifice everything for their children and genuinely want them to be better off than themselves, without any calculations or expectation of returns. Parental love is indeed part of Divine love.

While parental love is mostly instinctive, the way we treat our parents has been left to us. We can choose to honor and obey them or we can choose to do otherwise. Hence the reference to Heaven and Hell. For it is through exercise of our free will that we choose the path of Heaven or Hell. There is another important reminder here: we should never think that we have done all we had to do.

This is a very different concept of the family then one finds in today's society. In English the common metaphor used to describe the family is that of the bird's nest. Little birds stay in the nest and are taken care of by the parents. A soon as they grow up they leave the nest to enjoy their own life. Of course, grown up birds do not know or care about parents (or grandparents or uncles or aunts or other relatives). For their low level animal existence this is okay because they don't have to build a civilization or develop human society. Unfortunately, this metaphor too closely reflects real life in the West, which has descended to the level of birds and animals. In this society, father is the "old man," and the battle cry of the young man is, "this is my life, leave me alone." The legal structure also supports this view as do literature and media and experts of every persuasion.

The resulting devastation is now well known. Family has been disintegrated beyond recognition and human relations have been decimated. Old people live a sad existence in retirement homes. Sacrifice, commitment, and deference to parental authority are as alien as the extended family, and increasingly, even the normal family. "In the West most persons do not have a single individual in their life that they can trust," says an American convert to Islam. Compared to this despicable situation the family life in the Muslim countries is a great blessing—despite the general decline there.

Today this institution of the family is under attack from all directions. A central line of attack incites children in rebellion against parents and targets parental authority in the name of—what else—children's rights. Those who are living and growing up in this environment, and who have absorbed its cultural symbols and its metaphors may find Islam's teachings as strange as does a sick person when tasting normal, healthy, and good-tasting food. Nevertheless, it is important that we remind ourselves and our children of Islam's teachings regarding parents. Here is a summary:

We must honor and respect out parents under all circumstances. It does not depend on their having "earned" this honor in our eyes. It is a right granted to them even if they are non-Muslim.

The most important thing in this regard is our conduct toward them. We are not to say a word of contempt or even one showing the slightest level of irritation; rather we must show great humility toward them.

We must obey them within the bounds of the Shariah. In Islam, there is no absolute obedience to anyone. All obedience—of subordinates to the bosses, of the children to the parents, of the ruled to the rulers, of the wife to the husband—are constrained by an overriding principal described in a hadith:

أَلاَ لاَ طَاعَةَ لِمَخْلُوقٍ فِي مَعْصِيَةِ الْخَالِقِ

"Beware! There is no obedience to a creation if it means disobedience to the Creator." [*Kanzul Ummal*, Hadith 6225]

Within the bounds of the Shariah a person should obey the parents even if they had been unjust to him in the past. In one hadith the Prophet ﷺ repeated the statement three times "even if the parents had been unjust to him."

While mandatory acts under the Shariah are not subject to parental approval, the voluntary acts are. As an example, scholars say that leaving home to invite people to Islam, though a very meritorious act, is a voluntary good deed and therefore subject to approval by the Muslim parents. It is their right that we should also pray for them, both while they are alive and after their death. It is doubtful that anyone praying for his parents will then turn around and intentionally do things to hurt them.

Good conduct toward the parents should also be extended to their friends and relatives.

While we do all this with a deep sense of gratitude and with an eye toward the rewards in the Hereafter, it is also important to remember that good or bad behavior toward the parents also brings its rewards and punishments in this world. Those who bring sorrow to their parents will see sorrow themselves and those who bring joy to them will see joy themselves in this life.

Parenting Goals and Ideas

يَـٰٓأَيُّهَا ٱلَّذِينَ ءَامَنُواْ قُوٓاْ أَنفُسَكُمْ وَأَهْلِيكُمْ نَارًا وَقُودُهَا ٱلنَّاسُ وَٱلْحِجَارَةُ

"O you who believe! Save yourself and your families from a Fire whose fuel is men and stones." [At-Tahreem, 66:6]

THIS VERSE POINTS to the goal as well as the required seriousness of our efforts in bringing up our children. The central goal of their education and upbringing must be to prepare them for the future—the Ultimate and Everlasting Future. One path leads to success there. It is the path of obedience to our Creator. We must protect them from taking any other path for all other paths lead to the blazing Hellfire. Our efforts must have the urgency they would have if we saw flames engulfing our children here.

While this is a universal command to believing parents everywhere, it assumes special importance for those living in non-Muslim societies for two principal reasons:

The pressures to assimilate from all societal organizations are just overwhelming. While schools and television remain the two most potent instruments for corrupting both the intellectual as well as the emotional space of the young minds, the popular culture and secular ideas invade from all possible directions.

The institutions that have been built so far to counter this tremendous force miss the target by a huge margin in numbers as well as quality. In the United States, for example, the full time Islamic schools can only accommodate about five percent of the Muslim student population. More than 95% will go to the government run secular schools. Moreover, even those going to the Islamic schools are taught the same secular-humanist values and ideas that are dispensed by the public school system as no integrated Islamic curriculum exists today. The Islamic schools merely add Islamic studies, Arabic, and Qur'an to a secular curriculum that remains intact.

The results are devastating. Despite all the noise about Islam being the fastest growing religion (in the USA/West/World), the Muslim children in western countries are succumbing to the pressures at an alarming rate. Some openly renounce Islam. A large number develop doubts and misunderstandings about their religion. They seek compromises between Islam and un-Islam, or quietly develop those compromises in their lives without telling their parents. The result is an epidemic of confusion, split personalities, arguments with parents, or rebellion.

While that should be the impetus for developing better Islamic schools and other institutions, we should never lose sight of the fact that the biggest role in the upbringing of the children belongs to the parents. This verse says clearly that the responsibility for proper education and upbringing of the children lies squarely with the parents. This is a duty assigned to them by Allah ﷻ and they will be held accountable for it.

As parents are we up to the task? Are we even clear about where we want to go and how to get there? Do we understand Islamic teachings about parenting and our responsibilities according to the Shariah? Sadly, the answer is no. Our goals as well as ideas about parenting show the same confusions that we are finding in the next generation about Islam. Here is a look at some commonly held ideas and "truths" about parenting.

"Outside influences do not matter if the home is good."
A good home is essential to proper upbringing. At the same time, we cannot be complacent about outside influences. Children, like budding plants, have to be protected from the harmful environment, whether it is friends, media, books, or whatever. It is not healthy to let the children be pulled in all different directions in the fallacious hopes that they will ultimately sort out things for themselves.

"It makes no difference if the mother stays home or works outside."
Children everywhere need the loving, nurturing presence of the mother. But, in immigrant Muslim communities, where other support facilities are often missing or woefully inadequate, it makes a huge difference. Unfortunately, most mothers are reluctant to step up to their responsibility here. First, their own education did not prepare them for it, physically or psychologically. Second, there is a lot of self-generated economic pressure forcing women into the work force. Third, and most distressing, in many Muslim communities the working women enjoy a higher social status than the "mere housewives." Mothers should remember the hadith, that the wife is responsible for the children of her husband and will be held accountable for them. Those who belittle the task of homemaking are putting our next generations at extreme risk.

"Good scores mean good upbringing."
Good scores only mean that the student has absorbed the material that he was tested on very well. Whether that is good or bad depends upon the material itself. If a student

obtained top grades in world history, for example, it does indicate a high probability that he also swallowed—hook, line, and sinker—all the lies and distortions in world history and history of Islam that were part of his history text and lectures. Do not be surprised then, when he grows up a living question mark about Islam. As long as they are not being taught from an integrated Islamic curriculum, our blind emphasis on high scores in all subjects may be misplaced.

"Too much discipline will cause rebellion."
Too much discipline can certainly cause rebellion. So can too little. Muslim homes should be loving, caring homes where persuasion works most of the time. But when there is need for discipline, shying away from it can only exacerbate the problem. In the USA, spanking a child by the parents is a no-no. Yet laws allow a thirteen year old to be treated as an adult (and held with adult criminals) in violent crime cases. Islam asks us to avoid both extremes. Insufficient parental control can be as damaging as too much parental control.

"Daughters and Sons: Islam demands equality."
Most certainly, Islam strictly forbids preferential treatment of boys or girls. But it is a gross misinterpretation of this command that Islam favors a unisex world. Men and women have different roles in life and our sons and daughters must be prepared for their respective roles.

Bonds of Kinship

مَنْ كَانَ يُؤْمِنُ بِاللَّهِ وَالْيَوْمِ الآخِرِ فَلْيَصِلْ رَحِمَهُ

"Whoever believes in Allah and the Last Day, let him maintain the bonds of kinship." [*Bukhari*, Hadith 5673]

THE YOUNG MAN WENT to attend the weekly hadith lecture of Sayyidna Abu Hurairah ﷺ but the routine opening announcement stopped him. "If anyone sitting here has severed any ties of kinship (*qata-ur-rahim*), he should leave." He recalled that an aunt lived in the town with whom he had not been on speaking terms. The young man quietly left the gathering and went straight to his aunt's home. He asked for forgiveness for his past behavior and sought rapprochement. When the aunt inquired about the reason for this change of heart, he narrated the entire incident. She accepted the apology but asked him to inquire from Abu Hurairah ﷺ the reason for this unusual announcement. Why did he leave all the other major sins and focus only on this? What was so special about ties of kinship? Sayyidna Abu Hurairah ﷺ replied that he had heard from the Prophet ﷺ that our deeds are presented to Allah ﷻ every Thursday night and anyone who has severed family ties has all his good deeds rejected. He did not want any such person sitting in his gathering, which was held on the same night, for fear that it could deprive the entire gathering of blessings. Another hadith explains further the reason for this fear: "Allah's mercy will not descend on people among whom there is one who severs ties of kinship."[61]

Maintaining the bonds of kinship (*silat-ur-rahim*) indeed enjoys extraordinary importance in Islam. Conversely, severing the ties (*qata-ur-rahim*), is very high on the list of enormities. At two places in the Qur'an, Allah ﷻ has cursed the one severing family ties.

وَٱلَّذِينَ يَنقُضُونَ عَهْدَ ٱللَّهِ مِنۢ بَعْدِ مِيثَٰقِهِۦ وَيَقْطَعُونَ مَآ أَمَرَ ٱللَّهُ بِهِۦٓ أَن يُوصَلَ وَيُفْسِدُونَ فِى ٱلْأَرْضِ أُو۟لَٰٓئِكَ لَهُمُ ٱللَّعْنَةُ وَلَهُمْ سُوٓءُ ٱلدَّارِ ۝

"And those who break the covenant of Allah, after its ratification, and sever that which Allah has commanded to be joined (i.e. they sever the bond of kinship and are not good to their relatives), and work mischief in the land, on them is the curse, and for them is the unhappy home (i.e. Hell)." [Ar-Ra'd, 13:25. See also Muhammad, 47:22-23]

A cursed person is one who is deprived of the Mercy of Allah ﷻ. It is an indication of this deprivation that this sin is punished in this world as well as in the Hereafter. "There is no sin more deserving of having punishment meted out by Allah to its perpetrator in advance in this world along with what He stores up for him in the next world than oppression and severing family ties."[62]

Another hadith highlights the high stakes involved here in a compelling way: "*Rahim* (family ties) is a word derived from *Ar-Rahman* (The Compassionate One). And Allah says:

---

[61] Imam Baihaqi's *Shuab Al-Iman*
[62] *Tirmidhi*

'I shall keep connection with him who maintains you and sever connection with him who severs you.'"[63]

Silat-ur-rahim has been defined as politeness, kind treatment, and concern for all one's relatives even if distantly related, corrupt, non-Muslim, or unappreciative.[64] While nearly every religion has emphasized good family relations, Islam has taken it to unprecedented heights. It is a duty to be discharged without an eye for reciprocity. A Muslim is required to be kind even to his non-Muslim relatives. Similarly he is required to be kind to even those relatives who are harsh to him.

The most telling example in this regard is that of Sayyidna Abu Bakr ﷺ. Among the many people who benefited from his generosity was a relative Mistah ﷺ. The latter, unfortunately became involved in the scandal about the Mother of Believers Sayyida Aisha ﷺ that was started by the leader of the hypocrites. It was a whole month of torment and torture for all involved, after which verses of Surah Noor were revealed exonerating her and prescribing punishment for those involved in the false accusation. Feeling hurt and betrayed, Sayyidna Abu Bakr ﷺ vowed never to help Mistah again. Yet the Qur'an asked him to forget and forgive and continue helping his relative, which he did. Is there another society that can even come close to this standard in maintaining family ties?

Islam came to set all our relationships right. This includes our relations with Allah ﷻ as well as with other human beings. *Silat-ur-Rahim* is a very important part of the latter.

Today, unfortunately, these teachings are not normally followed in Muslim societies. The best we do today is reciprocate; more commonly we backbite, cheat, and hurt our relatives and continue the spiral of hurt and humiliation as they respond. And we just abandon those of our relatives who are economically unfortunate.

---

[63] *Bukhari*
[64] Shaikh Abdul Wakil Durubi in *Reliance of the Traveller*

There are three reasons for this sad situation. First is the widespread ignorance about Islamic teachings in this regard. Even in various Islamic groups the subject hardly gets the attention it deserves. Second is the rampant materialism. While materialism hurts all aspects of our life, it is especially damaging to family ties for they require sacrifice of time, money, and personal comfort. The third reason has to do with recent history. It is a "gift" of the transformation of Muslim societies under colonialism.

Industrial Revolution came at a time when Muslim civilization was in doldrums. Muslim historians point out very accurately that the genesis of European Renaissance and the Industrial Revolution was in the Golden Age of Muslim Spain. Yet it is also true that it progressed at a time of Muslim decline. And that explains the form it took and the devastation it caused to the family life. Everywhere it disrupted human relations. Poet Iqbal pointed to this when he said in his famous line: "The rule of machines is death for the heart. Machine tools crush compassion." Later, under the influence of colonialism, urban centers throughout the Muslim world faithfully duplicated all of these problems. This was just what a blind following of the West promised. Relations between husband and wife, between parents and children, between workers and managers, between neighbors, between relatives, in other words between all segments of society were dealt a devastating blow.

The process continues in the post industrial, neo-colonial period. To quote one example, television is rapidly destroying what was left of human relations, cutting off even members of the same family from each other and engulfing everyone within his or her own pleasure cocoon, oblivious to the world without. It is just one, but probably the most subversive and intrusive tool of our so-called postmodern global village. Village of distant neighbors without love and kinship.

Book Review:
Educated, Ignorant, and Feminist

Title: Feminism and Islam, Legal and Literary Perspectives
Editor: Mai Yamani
Publisher: School of Oriental and African Studies, University of London.
Year: 1996
385 pages.

REMEMBER WHEN THE SOVIET UNION was a superpower, and reading Lenin and Marx (or at least pretending to have read them) was a sign of intellectual achievement? In those "glorious" days claims that Islam also espoused its own brand of socialism, and that Islamic Socialism was the need of the hour had gripped the intellectual landscape of the Muslim world. As Soviet Union disappeared the mental slaves and their arguments also found their way to the trash heap of history.

However, real mental slaves do not die. They just reappear in another guise, always submitting to whatever seems to be the dominant ideology of the time. Enter Feminism: women of the world unite. And sure there are already a lot of "experts" on Islamic Feminism. Fifteen of them have contributed chapters to this book, which is an intellectual attempt to serve the cause of this fancy new ism. It differs from the previous ism only in the chutzpah of its proponents. For note that the book is titled "Feminism and Islam" and not "Islam and Feminism." For these pundits feminism (whatever it means) is the self-evident and absolute Truth. Islam, on the other hand, is a "man-made" religion, to be examined and reformed according to the dictates of the former! After all, the great Islamic jurists were all men, "moved by thirst for power" who, acting like "privileged oppressors," gave their gender more and more privileges, usurping the rights of women [p 331]. Those who wrote the tafsir (exegeses) of Qur'an were men, as were the people like Bukhari and Muslim who compiled quotes "allegedly said by the Prophet [☪]." [p 35].

Things get a lot more sinister. The early Islamic scholars, *muhadditheen, mufassireen*, as well as historians, were not only men bent upon usurping the rights of women, they were also liars who deliberately distorted history to throw a bad light on everything that preceded Islam [p 77]. It is because of their distortion that people generally believe that Islam had significantly improved the lives of women. Despite the elaborate "cover up," a dedicated researcher Ghada Karmi, Senior Research Fellow, Center for Middle Eastern and Islamic Studies, Durham University, through her sheer brilliance has found that actually women were better off before Islam! The existence of goddesses like al-Uzza, Manat, and al-Lat is proof that "society was originally organized on a matriarchal and/or matrilineal basis." In addition in the *Jahiliya* society a woman could have many husbands just like the man could have many wives, thus producing balance, which was destroyed by Islam! Moreover, when she bore a child, she would call all the "husbands" and decide who she thought was the father. "And her word was law." What a position of power!

To respond to any of the above arguments is to dignify unadulterated nonsense, but it is important to note that in this "scholarly" book, she has as much claim to the crown of *ijtihad-dom* as the next expert. Her *ijtihad* holds that the Qur'an should be stripped of those verses dealing with legislation, as they are the variable part. We should leave other verses that deal with the spiritual content, for that is the constant part.

Afraid that this "bold" suggestion may not be accepted, other "experts" offer new interpretations of the Qur'anic verses toward the same goal. One suggestion that occurs repeatedly is that Islam does not require Muslim women to observe *hijab* or veil. There is nothing new about the argument that the injunction about veil applies only to the wives of the Prophet ﷺ. But it is interesting and instructive to look at their treatment of the subject. This argument is based on this verse:

يَٰنِسَآءَ ٱلنَّبِيِّ لَسْتُنَّ كَأَحَدٍ مِّنَ ٱلنِّسَآءِ إِنِ ٱتَّقَيْتُنَّ فَلَا تَخْضَعْنَ بِٱلْقَوْلِ فَيَطْمَعَ ٱلَّذِى فِى قَلْبِهِۦ مَرَضٌ وَقُلْنَ قَوْلًا مَّعْرُوفًا ۝ وَقَرْنَ فِى بُيُوتِكُنَّ وَلَا تَبَرَّجْنَ تَبَرُّجَ ٱلْجَٰهِلِيَّةِ ٱلْأُولَىٰ ۖ وَأَقِمْنَ ٱلصَّلَوٰةَ وَءَاتِينَ ٱلزَّكَوٰةَ وَأَطِعْنَ ٱللَّهَ وَرَسُولَهُۥٓ

"O Wives of the Prophet! You are not like any of the other women: If you do fear Allah, be not too complaisant of speech, lest one in whose heart is a disease should be moved with desire: but speak a speech that is just. And stay quietly in your houses, and make not a dazzling display, like that of the former times of Ignorance; and establish regular prayer, and give zakat and obey Allah and His Messenger." [Al-Ahzab, 33:32-33]

The interpretation given by all the scholars has been that these commands apply to all the believing women and that the reference to the Prophet's wives is only aimed at emphasizing their greater responsibility as they are the role models for all other believers. But the feminists cannot resist the temptation for a strictly literal interpretation as a way out of the first two commands. The problem is that here five commands are given in the same tone, and it is obvious that the last three apply to all the believing women. If there is a basis for selectively restricting the first two to the Prophet's wives no one has shown that. In fact the reasoning given a few verses later demolishes the feminist's argument completely.

وَإِذَا سَأَلْتُمُوهُنَّ مَتَاعًا فَسْأَلُوهُنَّ مِن وَرَآءِ حِجَابٍ ذَٰلِكُمْ أَطْهَرُ لِقُلُوبِكُمْ وَقُلُوبِهِنَّ

"And when you ask (his ladies) for anything you want, ask them from behind a curtain: that makes for greater purity for your hearts and for theirs." [Al-Ahzab, 33:53]

To say that veil was required only of the wives of the Prophet ﷺ is to claim that either the rest of the believing women have purer hearts that do not need the protection of veil or that for them purity of heart is not required!

Unaware of this problem, but happy with her literal interpretation, A. L. Marsot gives away her real reason for opposing the veil at the end of her article. Veil to her implies an inferior role for the women [p 46]. Let's ignore whether this observation is justified or not but it is impossible to ignore the sentiments expressed here: veil is a sign of inferiority, so let us restrict it to the Mothers of the Believers!

The article by Mona Siddiqui, Lecturer in Islamic Studies, Faculty of Divinity, University of Glasgow, examines the law of *Kafa'a* (compatibility) in Hanafi school to demonstrate the "tensions" between legal rights and social norms. The basic principle underlying *Kafa'a* is that a Muslim woman should not marry a Muslim man below her status and that of her family. Such a marriage would be allowed only if not only the woman but also her guardian approves of it. The law prevents a woman from contracting herself in an incompatible and therefore potentially disastrous marriage and it defines compatibility in precise detail. Thus there are two possible situations. A marriage within *Kafa'a* and one outside it. In the first case the woman can legally contract herself in marriage but it is still desirable for her to have a *wali* or guardian to marry her off so as not to be associated with shamelessness. In the second, marriage is not valid if the *wali* disapproves of it. Mona Siddiqui sees problems with both: "The taint of shamelessness that is associated with a woman who acts within the legal parameters reflects a society reluctant to equate the observance of a legal right with approved behavior." The tension she sees is a result of a failure to understand the complementary relationship between law and moral teachings. For example, legally divorce is permissible, but it is the most abhorrent of all the permissible things. Is there a conflict? Not at all. Divorce is legally permissible because the safety valve has to be there for the rare situation when it may be needed. At the same time, moral teachings and societal norms aim at reducing as much as possible the need for this valve. Should we complain that the exercise of a legal right is being compromised under societal pressures? Similarly modesty and *haya* are the most important qualities of a believing woman and anyone who is not totally deprived of these attributes can see the need for a *wali* to marry her off. Why is there a conflict between this norm and the right to accept or reject a marriage proposal?

She also notes that "In Islamic law texts the abstractions of romantic love do not figure and thus, in the socio-structural patterns that are discussed, the potential importance of love as affecting mate choice is denied any juristic reckoning." The suggestion is that as intermixing of men and women in schools and places of employment increases, thereby leading to increasing episodes of "romantic love," the law should be changed to accommodate the new realities. Interesting. And you thought that she understood that the whole doctrine of *Kafa'a* and of rights of *wali* is aimed at making sure that romantic love does not run amuck!

World Bank adviser Lama Abu-Odeh also emphasizes the need for this kind of adjustment. She calls for an end to the crimes of honor for their obvious cruelty. If a woman commits fornication or adultery and her father, brother, or husband finds out about it and kills her in a fit of rage, the laws in many Muslim countries consider it a special situation, thereby reducing the sentence for murder. That is a crime of honor. The development of these laws, many of which came from European sources, is a result of three factors. 1) Abrogating Islamic *hudood* laws, 2) development of pressures that lead to illicit acts, and 3) the desire to keep the resulting mess under control. The article notes correctly that "[the new sexual practices] are the nationalist's nightmare: they are the product of the nationalists' own policies, yet ones that nationalist ideology consciously rejects." The sensible remedy would be to fix the problem at the root by relieving the pressures (television, films, radio, magazines, newspapers features and ads that excite the senses) and removing the opportunities (free mixing in schools and businesses, easy availability of contraceptives) for indecent acts that later lead to the crimes of honor. It would also include the introduction of *hudood* laws according to Shariah to act as deterrent. What she suggests instead is simply to abrogate the provisions for the crimes of honor and let the chips fall where they may. The author is intelligent enough to recognize that this unilateral suggestion would face opposition on the grounds that it will promote promiscuity. For that she suggests several rhetorical responses, thus giving us a glimpse of the internal strategy session of the feminists: 1) Only poor women are the victims of crimes of honor. 2) Arab women will never become like western women. 3) It does not look good abroad. 4) Proper sexual behavior should be promoted through ethical teachings rather than violence. 5) There is nothing wrong with romance. Clever propaganda points!

This leads us to the question of the real agenda behind this book. Except for one article by Raga El-Nimr, which may have been included to maintain the façade of objectivity, the contents of this book contains gems like the ones mentioned above. It is obvious that the book has nothing to do with the real problems facing Muslim women. Isn't it intriguing that it talks about the discrimination against women in Lebanon who are not allowed to undertake mining, foundry work, brewing and distilling, and driving heavy equipment [p 328] yet says not a word about the plight of Muslim women in Bosnia, Kashmir, or Palestine?

Actually, as in all feminists' works, the real issues of Muslim women are not touched here at all. The foremost issue for Muslim women is the protection of their dignity and prevention of their degrading and demeaning portrayal in the media, which in turn leads to all sorts of abuses. There needs to be a total ban on displaying the pictures of their bodies for commercial gain. They also need protection from un-Islamic practices forced on them. Sometimes there are husbands who force their wives to unveil in public or attend to their friends or even discourage them from praying. A Muslim women must have legal recourse against such coercion no matter where it comes from. Similarly there are regimes that force women to unveil in public. This is state-sponsored religious persecution and she needs her rights restored through a total stop to it. A Muslim woman also needs an educational system that caters to her needs, instead of forcing her to become a man in a blind quest for equality. She needs healthcare facilities that respect her dignity and her need for privacy. Today in many countries a women is totally helpless and a potential victim of all kinds of assaults once she enters a hospital. A Muslim woman also needs a legal and justice system that assures her that she can get her rights in case of disputes according to the Shariah. She needs an economic system in which she is not forced to leave home to share the burden of earning a living. She needs an environment in which her natural instincts for motherhood and homemaking are respected not crushed. And yet on all of these issues there is a deafening silence in the feminists' quarters.

Of course one should not expect any of that from a book that mentions the notorious Cairo Conference with respect and quotes such "notables" as Benazir Bhutto on the need for following the "correct form of Islam" or Suzanne Mubarak on the "importance of democracy." There is an additional problem here—for the telltale signs are all over—that this book may actually be a covert operation of the UN. Any doubts in this regard should be removed by reading chapter 16 by Jane Connor's about Women's Convention on the Elimination of All Forms of Discrimination Against Women. What lurks behind those unwieldy but innocent-sounding words is a complete "Shariah" of the UN that aims at overriding Islamic Shariah. It calls for ending segregation in workplace, and ending Islam's laws of evidence, marriage, divorce, custody of children, paternity, and alimony payment. Further in case of any disputes, it gives jurisdiction to the International Court. The Convention went into force in 1981 while a non-binding Declaration was adopted in 1963. This has been going on quietly, without any debate or awareness in Muslim countries. What the Muslim countries have been doing, working individually instead of as a common block, has been to make reservations against some of the objectionable provisions. The UN, to get its foot in the door ignored these reservations, a right of sovereign UN members. Now in the unipolar world, the UN is making the move to end those reservations. The article by Jane Connors, the "Islamic expert," assures us that most of the reservations were not based on Islamic Shariah, which has nothing to do with these mundane matters! Sure.

Her report should be an eye-opener for the Muslim leaders who had briefly turned their attention to these matters during the Cairo Conference, and have since seemed to have gone back to slumber. The UN has been acting on this thing for several decades now and there is no let up in its efforts. At one time the Convention requested the UN "to promote or undertake studies on the status of women under Islamic laws and customs and in particular on the status and equality of women in the family... taking into consideration the principle of *El Ijtihad* in Islam." According to Connors that plan was shelved under protest by some Muslim countries including Bangladesh and Egypt. However "Feminism and Islam" fits the bill precisely. Its publication from University of London, instead of the UN press, gives it additional cover of objectivity and respectability. If only it can act as another wake-up call for the Muslim leaders.

The Crusade Against Hijab: Then and Now

IN THE EARLY 20TH century the Rockfeller Foundation sent Ruth Frances Woodsmall on an eighteen month trip to the Muslim World to study the changing state of Muslim women under the influence of colonial rule. Her voluminous report was published by the American University of Beirut[65] in 1936. She traveled to Turkey, Syria, Egypt, Palestine, Trans-Jordan, Iraq, Iran, and India. At each place she put the subjects of her study under the microscope, looking at all signs of westernization, which she called advancement and progress. "Undoubtedly the barometer of social change in the Moslem World is the veil," she wrote. So she studied it in great detail noting the designs, material and sizes, and practices regarding it. She wrote passionately, cheering those who were fighting to eradicate the "evil of the veil."

---

[65] Ruth Frances Woodsmall, *Moslem Women Enter A New World*. (London George Allen & Unwin, 1936). It is interesting to note that Bayard Dodge of the American University of Beruit introduced Woodsmall in the preface to this book as "an understanding friend of the East."

The Crusade Against Hijab: Then and Now

Mustafa Kamal Pasha (1881-1938), the despotic dictator of Turkey from a crypto-Jewish *donmeh* family in Salonika, had banned and banished the veil along with several other Islamic obligations and was, therefore, a hero in the eyes of Miss Woodsmall. He received glowing tributes from her. Everything he did in this regard was, of course, logical and just. "When Turkish women were granted suffrage, women wearing veils were debarred from voting, a regulation which was accepted as entirely logical."

In Iran the puppet His Majesty Shah Riza Pahlvi declared 8 January 1936 as the day of "emancipation" forcing women's "advance." Along with the compulsory unveiling in schools and elsewhere, it brought the oppressive measure that no veiled woman could receive treatment in Iran at a public clinic or ride in a public conveyance. What did Woodsmall think about this gross denial of a basic human right, the right to observe one's religious obligations? "These two regulations will doubtless for a time work genuine hardship on conservative Moslem women but eventually their conservatism will doubtless be overcome." She also happily reported, "In the spring of 1935 the Ministry [of education in Iran] made unveiling practically compulsory through the regulation that no girls wearing the veil could receive school prizes or diplomas."

Another self-appointed "civilizing" potent, King Amanullah (d. 1960) unveiled his Queen Surraiya and set about promulgating the same "spectacular change" in Afghanistan. But his "tragic fall" delayed women's "advance" in Afghanistan and slowed it in Iran, forcing George W. Bush, forty-one years later, to rain missiles and daisy cutters on the Afghans to bring civilization and liberate their women.

The book is full of condescending comments that betray a typical ethno-centric mindset. One entry in her book reports: "A former young Moslem leader of Beirut who was taking an advanced position there in regard to the veil, after her marriage in Jerusalem has followed the prevailing convention of the veil." Another gives the good news: "Madame Sharawi Pasha, the leading Moslem woman in Egypt, head of the Feminist Movement, with her niece Mlle Ceza Nebaraoui, the Editor of L'Egyptienne, unveiled in 1923, giving prestige to the whole movement."

The colonial rulers used all of their powers in this crusade against the hijab from ridicule to fierce propaganda to coercion. Hijab was a relic of the dark ages, a sign of oppression, an impediment to economic progress, and an infringement on women's rights. The campaign has continued in the post-colonial period through a vastly improved propaganda machine as well as through myriad agencies of that surrogate of the colonial powers known as the UN.

There have also been cases of aggressive actions by European officials in Muslim countries. In October 2000 it was revealed that a French run school in Alexandria, Egypt banned hijab for its students. When a lawsuit was brought against the school administration, the French embassy tried to shield them by claiming diplomatic immunity[66]. In January 2003 it was reported that the Jeddah Prep and Grammar School, operated by the British and Dutch embassies, did not permit its students to wear hijab. Girls wearing hijab were forced to remove it every morning before entering the school. It was only the refusal of one Egyptian girl, Lujain, to take off her hijab and subsequent refusal of the school to let her attend classes that brought the issue to the surface. When contacted by an Arab News reporter, the school administrative secretary said the school policy was a total ban on head scarves. She added, "Any girl wearing a head scarf will *not* be allowed to enter school." The resulting public outcry and pressure from the Saudi Ministry of Education finally persuaded the school to change its policy.

And yet for all the sustained propaganda and the putting of impediments against observing hijab, the tide has been

---

[66] For further details see "Secularism in France," which begins on page 394.

turning back. More and more Muslim women, from all social groups, rich and poor, highly educated and not so educated, and from the academies and professions, are coming back to Islam. Now the hijab is being observed by even a greater number of women all over the world, including, naturally, in Europe and America.

A century ago hijab seemed to be on the way out in the Muslim world; today it can be seen in increasing numbers even in London, Brussels, and New York. Further, despite the incessant propaganda about the oppression of women by Islam, western women are coming to Islam in even greater numbers than western men. They have found through personal experience and observation that Islam—hijab and all—is the true liberator for all humanity that brings peace to the mind, contentment to the heart, and dignity to life.

These old and new Muslims in the West represent a change that some narrow-minded and bigoted people view with a certain irrational fear. Phobia and ethno-centric arrogance were two sides of the same coin. If Muslims were not toeing and imitating post-Christian and postmodern cultural norms, then they were a threat to their civilization. Perhaps, there was also a subconscious sense of envy or inferiority; while they had long given up their Abrahamic habits and culture of modesty and dignity, Muslims were sticking to theirs. The Muslim girl wearing hijab engendered so much anger in them because she was a reminder that the Emperor had no clothes.

Banning hijab is banning modesty and decency. Those engaged in this crusade out of a feeling of injury may be better advised to simply get dressed up, instead of wasting their time and effort in trying to snatch scarves from the heads of schoolgirls.

Women's Rights: An Islamic Declaration

كُنتُمْ خَيْرَ أُمَّةٍ أُخْرِجَتْ لِلنَّاسِ تَأْمُرُونَ بِٱلْمَعْرُوفِ وَتَنْهَوْنَ عَنِ ٱلْمُنكَرِ وَتُؤْمِنُونَ بِٱللَّهِ

"You are the best of peoples evolved for mankind, enjoining what is right, forbidding what is wrong, and believing in Allah." [Al-i-'Imran, 3:110]

MUSLIMS HAVE BEEN given the task to be the witnesses to Truth for the entire mankind and to stand up for what is right. This is a logical consequence of one's belief and one's love for humanity. If you know that there is a right path that will lead to eternal success and that all others will lead to the exact opposite, it is natural to let others know about it. But it is also needed for one's own protection. For we live in a world where each person's thoughts and actions influence others; when a people stop calling others to the right path, they themselves become the target of their calls to the other paths.

The results of our collective dereliction of responsibility in this matter are all around us to see today. The campaign launched internationally in the name of women's rights and gender equality, which has recently gained lot of momentum, is one example of this.

Equality is a slick and catchy slogan. But what does equality actually mean? In mathematics if two variables are equal, one can be substituted for the other without changing the result in any way at all. If men and women are equal in this sense, then a woman can do anything a man can do and vice versa. You can substitute one for the other everywhere. Thus a woman can be a truck driver, a coal miner, a prison guard, or what have you. Similarly a man can become Mr. Mom, replacing the mother in taking care of the children.

That such mathematical equality is absurd is manifest to anyone who knows the biological and psychological differences between men and women. Yet this is precisely the direction that the so-called gender equality campaign has blindly taken. It aims at replacing the complementary relationship between men and women with a competitive one. The result can only be a social upheaval of unprecedented scale.

Some people in the societies that for centuries refused to consider women as human beings or to give them any rights have gone to one extreme from the other. Islam has nothing to do with such nonsense. When women had no rights in the world, it declared:

$$\text{وَهُنَّ مِثْلُ ٱلَّذِى عَلَيْهِنَّ بِٱلْمَعْرُوفِ}$$

"And women shall have rights, similar to the rights against them, according to what is equitable." [Al-Baqarah, 2:228]

That remains its command today and forever. Similar rights, not same rights. Equity, not a blind equality. Both men and women are equal in their humanity, in their accountability before Allah ﷻ, in their responsibility to perform their assigned tasks and be judged based on their performance. But their assigned tasks are not the same. They have been given different capabilities—and the tasks based on those capabilities—by their Creator. This differentiation is not an error that needs to be corrected. It is the only basis for building a healthy and prosperous society. Islam liberates a woman from the modern tyranny of having to become a man in order to get a sense of self worth and achievement.

If Muslims had done their job, they would be asking for universal rights for women as given by Islam and generally ignored in the world today. That would be quite a revolutionary—and liberating—act. Islam's universal declaration of women's rights would include the following:

1. Men and women have been given dignity by their Creator, but forces of immorality and darkness attack it in many ways. A prevalent form of this attack on women is pornography. Pornography is an affront to the respect and honor of women and produces an atmosphere where other crimes against them become possible. In many countries it has become an "industry" and they are exporting this filth to all parts of the world. Newer technologies—especially the Internet—have also become mediums of choice for the purveyors of filth, posing a serious threat to morality everywhere. Pornography must be condemned and all trade in porn banned universally in the same way that dangerous drugs are banned.
2. Prostitution must be recognized as a despicable act of exploitation of women. No one who condones it can be taken seriously in their claims to respect women's rights.
3. It is the responsibility of the husband to provide for the family. Islam has freed the woman from this responsibility so she can take care of the home. All efforts to snatch this freedom and economic security from the women and forcing them out of the home into the labor force must be resisted.
4. Homemaking is a very honorable job and a serious responsibility; it is the foundation on which healthy societies can be built. The societies that disrespect homemaking lose the homemakers and result in broken homes as can easily be witnessed in many parts of the world. It should be recognized

that the trend to belittle the task of homemaking is anti-family and anti-society and must be curbed.

5. It is a Muslim woman's right to dress modestly, wear *hijab*, and refuse to be put on display. This right must be accepted universally and any effort to restrict this right must be recognized for what it is: religious discrimination and persecution.[67]

6. There is only one legitimate form of the family, that created by the union between a man and woman as provided in all revealed religions. Any other form is not only immoral; it poses a serious threat to humanity.

7. Families should be protected from outside intrusion, especially intrusion by governments as much as possible. This also includes intrusion in the name of help. For resolution of family disputes, Islam suggests a three-phase procedure.

A) Resolve the conflict within the home.
B) Resolve it within the family by involving elders from the families of husband and wife.
C) As a last resort resolve it through courts of law.

There is great wisdom in this approach. Sayyidna Umar ؓ said in a directive to the *qadis*: "Refer the family disputes to the families (so they can resolve them within the family with the help of elders), for the judge's verdicts create hatred and malice." Ignoring this scheme can only hurt the families that the perpetrators of intervention by outsiders in family affairs claim to help.

---

[67] With the ban on hijab in public schools in France and similar moves in Germany and other European countries, this declaration has become most urgent.

Education

In this section:

- Seeking Knowledge
- The Real Purpose of Education
- What is Wrong with Our Education System?

Seeking Knowledge

وَمَا كَانَ ٱلْمُؤْمِنُونَ لِيَنفِرُواْ كَآفَّةً ۚ فَلَوْلَا نَفَرَ مِن كُلِّ فِرْقَةٍ مِّنْهُمْ طَآئِفَةٌ لِّيَتَفَقَّهُواْ فِى ٱلدِّينِ وَلِيُنذِرُواْ قَوْمَهُمْ إِذَا رَجَعُوٓاْ إِلَيْهِمْ لَعَلَّهُمْ يَحْذَرُونَ ۝

"And the believers should not all go out to fight. Of every troop of them, a party only should go forth, that they (who are left behind) may gain sound knowledge in religion, and that they may warn their folk when they return to them, so that they may guard themselves (against evil)." [At-Tauba, 9:122]

ACCORDING TO THE renowned Qur'anic scholar, Abu Abdullah Al-Qurtubi (d. 671 AH), this verse lays the foundation of Islam's education policy. The goal of that education is described as seeking '*tafaqquh fid deen*', translated above (by Pickthall) as sound knowledge in religion. It can also be translated as sound understanding of religion. The choice of *fiqh* (understanding) over *ilm* (knowledge) here points out that what is required is not mere literacy, but insight. And it has to be of such a level that it can be a force against evil. A purely intellectual exercise bereft of that practical utility does not qualify.

This message itself is very important but what is even more important is the context in which this verse was revealed. For it happened after the Tabuk expedition, which saw the largest mobilization of the Islamic State under the leadership of Prophet Muhammad ﷺ himself. To face up to one of the two super powers of that time, every able-bodied Muslim was called upon to join the jihad. Despite the most adverse circumstances everyone responded, except ten Companions who were reprimanded and later forgiven. Surah At-Tauba contains a detailed account of all this, emphasizing the importance of responding to the call for jihad when that call is made by a competent authority. Then this verse explains that jihad should not be the only preoccupation of the Islamic State. Seeking knowledge is so important that even during the prosecution of a war, a segment of the society must be engaged in it.

Most of us are familiar with the hadith, reported by Anas ﷺ:

طَلَبُ الْعِلْمِ فَرِيضَةٌ عَلَى كُلِّ مُسْلِمٍ

"Seeking knowledge is the duty of every Muslim." [*Ibn Majah*, Hadith 220]

What kind of knowledge does this hadith refer to? The same as is meant in this hadith:

إِنَّ الْعُلَمَاءَ وَرَثَةُ الْأَنْبِيَاءِ إِنَّ الْأَنْبِيَاءَ لَمْ يُوَرِّثُوا دِينَارًا وَلَا دِرْهَمًا إِنَّمَا وَرَّثُوا الْعِلْمَ فَمَنْ أَخَذَ بِهِ أَخَذَ بِحَظٍّ وَافِرٍ

"The scholars are heirs of the Prophets. The Prophets do not leave behind an inheritance of gold and silver; they leave behind the inheritance of knowledge. Whoever acquired knowledge, acquired a lot of wealth." [*Tirmidhi*, Hadith 2606]

Does it mean that every individual Muslim must also become a religious scholar? Not at all. What is required of an individual is only sufficient knowledge that can enable him or her to carry out their religious obligations. As a minimum every Muslim must learn the articles of faith and what they really mean. He or she must also learn the laws and teachings of Shariah as they relate to their life. The basic rule is that accompanying every religious duty is another duty to learn about the requirements of that duty. Thus it is our duty to learn the Shariah teachings about salat, fasting, zakat, and Hajj. For a businessman, it is a religious duty to learn Islam's teachings about economics and *halal* and *haram* transactions. For a person getting ready to get married, it is a religious duty to learn Islamic teachings about marriage and spousal rights and responsibilities. And so on.

Similarly some spiritual knowledge is part of this required Islamic course. One must learn about the nature and forms of arrogance so it could be avoided. Similarly rage, jealousy, and malice. One must learn about desirable spiritual qualities like humbleness, patience, and gratitude. There is a surprising depth of knowledge about such subjects in Islamic literature. And although they may not seem to be important subjects for serious study to some, one can recount innumerable cases where Islamic communities have been damaged beyond repair by "highly educated" people, who were uneducated in these subjects.

Such knowledge would not make us experts. The expert knowledge belongs to the scholars who pursue in-depth study of the Qur'an, Hadith, exegeses (*tafsir*), jurisprudence (*fiqh*), history, and myriad other subjects in Islamic sciences. There must be some people in each community who devote their lives to the pursuit of such expertise, and as long as some do, others are relieved of the responsibility. That is why it is called as *fard-kifayah* or collective responsibility.

The acquisition of skills that may help one earn a living—the real focus of nearly all education that goes on these days—falls in the category of *mubah* or permissible.

Here one has wide latitude from a religious point of view. One can choose any profession, as long as it does not fall in the category of prohibited activities, and get needed education to earn a living from that profession.

Similarly one may pursue studies to satisfy one's curiosity. It is obvious that people will differ greatly in their abilities and inclinations in this area, and that is accommodated by the Shariah. It generally does not force or restrict this pursuit.

Of course there is a problem when social or even physical sciences are taught with a secular perspective. In that case social studies, history, or biology all become camouflages for teaching secular philosophy. Islam, of course, cannot permit that. A believer cannot teach that man evolved from apes. This is certainly a big problem and it requires a separate discussion.

A bigger problem occurs when the different categories of *fard* and *mubah* are confused, leading to a tremendous imbalance. A person obtaining a college degree has fulfilled his duty as required by this hadith. Right? Not quite. A person may become the best scientist, engineer, or whatever, but if he has not acquired the basic knowledge about his religious obligations, he simply has not discharged his duty to acquire knowledge. In the eyes of Islam, he remains an uneducated person.

Today we have millions of people in the Muslim world who may have obtained many degrees but who have not learned how to read the Qur'an or offer the salat or even perform *wudu*. They may have no idea about Islamic teachings about the situations they encounter in their daily life, home life, business life, or social life. How many MBAs have learned Islam's teachings about business and commerce? How many Muslim doctors have learned the Islamic medical ethics? We are the educated-illiterate class—the product of colonial education systems. Our "education" keeps us from acknowledging our ignorance. Do we know?

The Real Purpose of Education

EDUCATION—LIKE DEMOCRACY, free markets, freedom of the press, and "universal human rights"—is one of those subjects whose virtue is considered self-evident. So is the superiority of the industrially advanced countries in attaining them. Consequently, any package that arrives with one of these magic labels on it automatically qualifies for the "green channel" at the entry ports of the Muslim world. No questions asked. This uncritical acceptance has severely crippled their discussion of all these vital topics. For example in education most of their discussion centers around literacy statistics and the need to have so many graduates, masters, PhD's, and so many professionals—engineers, doctors, etc.—in a given country based on the standards in the industrially advanced countries. The central issue of curriculum, and even more fundamental issue of the purpose of education, normally do not attract their attention; they have already been decided by the "advanced" countries for them and their job is only to follow in their footsteps to achieve their level of progress.

In the "first" world, education has become an extension of the capitalist system. Its purpose is to provide qualified workforce for its machinery of production and eager consumers for its products. Stated in a more polished form, the purpose of education is to provide for the economic prosperity of a country. Similarly on a personal level today the purpose of education is to be able to earn a respectable living.

While earning *halal* living and providing for the economic well-being of a country are certainly important Islamic goals as well, the linking of education to financial goals is extremely unfortunate. It turns the centers of learning into mere vocational centers in their outlook and spirit. It degrades education and through it the society.

There is a fundamental difference between human beings and animals. Instincts and physical needs alone can bring ants, bees, or herds of beasts together to live in a perfectly functioning animal society. Human beings do not function that way. They are not constrained by nature to follow only those ways that are necessary for the harmonious operation of their society. If they are to form a viable, thriving society, they must choose to do so. What drives that choice is the sharing of common goals, beliefs, values, and outlook on life. Without a common framework binding its members, a human society cannot continue to exist; it will disintegrate and be absorbed by other societies. Further, the society must ensure that the common ground will continue to hold from generation to generation. This is the *real* purpose of education. The education system of a society produces the citizens and leaders needed for the smooth operation of that society, now and into the future. Its state of health or sickness translates directly into the health or sickness of the society that it is meant to serve.

Today we find many internal problems—corruption, injustice, oppression, and crippling poverty to name a few—everywhere we turn in the Muslim world. If we think about it, we may realize that most of these problems are man-made. Which is another way of saying that they are largely traceable, directly or indirectly, to the education system that produced the people who perpetuate the problems. The rulers who sell out to foreign powers and subjugate their people; the bureaucrats who enforce laws based on injustice; the generals who wage war against their own people; the businessmen who exploit and cheat; the journalists who lie, sensationalize, and promote indecencies, they are all educated people, in many cases "highly" educated people. Their education was meant to prepare them for the roles they are playing in real life. And see what it has done!

The problem plagues all layers of society. Why are Muslim communities in the grip of so much materialism today? What should we expect when our entire education system is preaching the gospel of materialism? Why have we effectively relegated Islam to a small inconsequential quarter in our public life? Because that is precisely where our secular education system has put it. Why in our behavior toward each other we see so little display of Islamic manners and morals? Because our imported education system is devoid of all moral training. Why our societies are sick? Because our education system is sick.

This *is* the real *crisis* of education. Before we got into this mess by importing from the colonial powers what was current and popular, education in our societies was always the means of nurturing the human being. Moral training, *tarbiya*, was always an inalienable part of it. The *ustaz* (teacher), was not just a lecturer or mere professional, but a mentor and moral guide. We remembered the hadith then,

مَا نَحَلَ وَالِدٌ وَلَدًا مِنْ نَحْلٍ أَفْضَلَ مِنْ أَدَبٍ حَسَنٍ

"No father has given a greater gift to his children than good moral training." [*Tirmidhi*, Hadith 1875]

Our education system was informed by this hadith. Our darul-ulooms still maintain that tradition but the number of students who pass through their gates is minuscule compared to the secular schools.

In the United States and Europe, schools were started by the church. Later as forces of capitalism overtook them, they molded them into their image. Moral training was a casualty of that takeover. But capitalism and their political economy did need people trained to work under these systems. So citizenship training was retained as an important, though diminishing, component of the curriculum—a religion-free subset of the moral training it displaced. Whatever civility we see here is largely a result of that leftover component. The imported versions in the Muslim countries, though, had even that component filtered out. And the results are visible.

We can solve our problem once we realize our mistakes. The first purpose of our education system must be to produce qualified citizens and leaders for the Islamic society. *Tarbiya*, real Islamic moral training, must be an integral part of it. This must be the *soul* of our education, not a ceremonial husk. All plans for improving our education will be totally useless unless they are based on a full understanding of this key fact. This requires revamping our curricula, rewriting our textbooks, retraining our teachers, and realizing that we must do all this ourselves. We do have a rich history of doing it. Are we finally willing to turn to our own in-house treasures to redo education the way it should always have been?

What is Wrong with Our Education System?

QUICK QUESTION: WHO discovered America? The almost guaranteed answer: why, Columbus, of course. The bright student may even know the famous story that Columbus thought he had reached India and therefore called the people he found Indians.

If providing sound knowledge and developing critical thinking are any goals of an education system, the answer highlights the miserable failure of the education system in the Muslim world today on both counts. For no one asks the obvious: how can anyone be credited with discovering a land that was already populated? Columbus may have been the first European to discover America, but he was certainly not the first man. Millions of other men and women had reached there before him and had been living for centuries. The assertion about Columbus reveals a Euro-centric mindset but the bias goes undetected and unquestioned.

This is not the only questionable fact that our schools and colleges and textbooks and teachers have been dispensing. In every field of study, they have been passing on "facts," ideas, values, assumptions, perspectives, explanations, "truths," and principles that are questionable, secular, and anti-Islamic. All while sincerely believing that they are providing a great service by promoting education.

Education is a wonderful thing. But, what are we really teaching?

In science, we are teaching our students to look at the universe from the viewpoint of a person who does not know God.

$$\text{وَكَأَيِّن مِّنْ ءَايَةٍ فِى ٱلسَّمَٰوَٰتِ وَٱلْأَرْضِ يَمُرُّونَ عَلَيْهَا وَهُمْ عَنْهَا مُعْرِضُونَ}$$

"And how many Signs in the Heavens and the Earth do they pass by? Yet they pay no attention to them." [Yusuf, 12:105]

A proper study of science would make one appreciate both the Power, Majesty, and Grandeur of Allah as shown in His creations and the humbleness and limitations of human knowledge and abilities. Today our science education, in its best form, gives exactly the opposite message. It also fails to enable students to separate scientist's opinions from their facts. Let's ask: In the wide Muslim world is there any Islamic school teaching science whose graduates can challenge Darwin's Theory of Evolution on scientific grounds? Are we teaching our children to put science in its proper place, to know its limitations? Are they fully aware of the cultural biases that science and technology bring with them? Can they filter them out before importing technology?

A medical doctor would not be considered competent if he did not know the limitations of the medicines and procedures he used. An engineer would be considered unqualified if he did not know the limitations of his tools. Why then our teaching of science does not include a discussion of its limitations? Because for the secular mindset science is the ultimate tool: the supreme arbiter of Truth and Falsehood. Without even realizing it, we have accepted the proposition and our science education reflects it.

The problem is not limited to science and technology. The best of our MBAs have learned that the goal of a business is to maximize profits, the goal of marketing is to create demand, and the proper way of making business decisions is through cost-benefit analysis. All of these are as solid in their eyes and as questionable in reality as the assertion about Columbus. The best of our journalism graduates do not have a different model for journalism than the one presented by the West. They do not have their own definition of the news, their purpose for gathering it, or their own moral standards that must regulate its dissemination. In economics we have been teaching that human beings are utility-maximizing animals governed by Maslow's hierarchy of needs. In our teaching of history, we see random events without a moral calculus driving them. We do not see Allah's laws that govern the rise and fall of nations. In psychology or sociology, medicine or engineering, civics or geography, it is the same story. In fact, our schools and colleges have been the main agency for secularization of Islamic societies. They have been effectively teaching that Islam is irrelevant to understanding this world or to solving its problems. Many of their graduates develop misunderstandings and doubts about their faith. But even when they are strong practicing Muslims, they have not been trained to challenge the secular dogmas that have been integrated into their curriculums.

For centuries our societies, culture, and education system were free of the secular/religious dichotomy. Our schools taught all subjects of importance using a *naturally unified* approach. As long as Muslims were the leaders in all the sciences subjects like medicine, astronomy, and chemistry had not developed their secular biases.

The dichotomy started in the West during its "Renaissance" as it threw away its religious dogmas—which had become a burden—and found a speedy path to material progress using a-religious or secular approaches. The Industrial Revolution gave it momentum. Colonialism brought secular ideology and the religion of secular humanism to the Muslim lands.

At this time, Muslims were at a low point on several fronts. They had surrendered intellectual leadership to the West and had failed to keep pace with scientific developments there. They found themselves in a no-win situation. If they accepted and taught the western sciences, they would also be teaching anti-Islamic dogmas. If they stayed isolated, they would be left behind in science and material progress.

In response, Muslims developed two approaches. Our darul-ulooms preserved Islamic knowledge and values by hermetically sealing themselves against western influences. It is due to this effort that Islamic knowledge is alive and well today. (Where they were lax in this matter—as in some Arab countries—the result was a compromise in their Islamic character without any advantage in the quality of education.) However, they are not equipped to provide leadership in most other areas of the society. This role has gone to the graduates of the western-style schools and colleges. Unfortunately, these schools and their curriculums nurture secular ways of looking at this world and solving its problems. The tensions created by the two diametrically opposed systems can be seen today in every Muslim country.

This dichotomy must end. We cannot move forward without revamping our education. We cannot fully establish Islam in our societies without producing educated citizens and leaders needed for an Islamic society. The time is now to develop integrated Islamic curriculums and remove secular biases from all of our education. Merely establishing more schools is not the answer. Developing educational institutions that can teach *every* subject in the wholesome Islamic context is. It is a monumental task. But without it we'll continue to spread ignorance in the name of education.

Unity

In this section:

- Muslim Unity
- Islamic Brotherhood
- Religious Wars
- Kosova: Where Were the Muslims?

Muslim Unity[68]

"I GAVE A LOT OF thought to the causes of the sorry state of the Ummah, during the years of my captivity in Malta," said *Sheikh-ul-Hind* Maulana Mahmood-ul-Hasan. It was 1920, and at 69, not only was he one of the most distinguished scholars of his time, he had also spent a lifetime in political struggle. His audience was a gathering of ulama, eager to hear the lessons of a lifetime of study, struggle, and reflection. His conclusion: "Our problems are caused by two factors; abandoning the Qur'an and our infighting." He spent the few remaining days of his life addressing these causes.

These reasons are as valid today as they were then. They are also related; the second being caused by the first. The Qur'an had declared us one brotherhood and had warned us against infighting. We have ignored those teachings and the billion-strong Ummah has turned into an ummah fragmented into a billion segments.

A very large number of our internal battles are the result of narrowly defined self-interests. Islam could have been the force that helped us overcome that. Unfortunately, instead of letting it fulfill that role, today we have made even religion

---

[68] Adapted from two talks of Mufti Muhammad Shafi, the late Mufti of Pakistan, given in 1963 and published in the booklet *Wahdat-e-Ummat*.

provide us with additional and irresolvable points of conflict. We fight over petty issues of *fiqh*. We fight over fine points of religious interpretation. We turn minor points of religious law into big battlegrounds while most important and fundamental teachings of religion are violated.

We do all this even as this religion has been under attack from all directions. Thousands of people become apostates every year in Pakistan. Qadianis (who declare Mirza Ghulam Ahmed of Qadian to be a prophet), and *munkareen-e-hadith* have been busy attracting our new generations to their falsehoods. *Haram* is being declared as *halal*. Our masses are ignorant of their religion and easily indulge in customs borrowed from polytheists. On top of all that is the western culture of hedonism, of shamelessness, of moral anarchy, that is invading our societies through film, television, radio, and obscene literature. [And we might add now the Internet. KB] Corruption of all sorts has permeated all layers of our society. Should not we be reflecting on this and asking ourselves what would the Prophet ﷺ expect of us, the heirs of the prophets? In the Hereafter shall we be able to give a sufficient answer by mentioning that we wrote a book on *rafa-yadain* (the issue of raising hands during certain movements in obligatory prayer)?

Once I saw Maulana Anwar Shah Kashmiri in a very sad mood. What is the matter, I asked. "I have wasted my whole life," he said. "You have spent your entire life in spreading Islamic teachings. Thousands of your disciples are themselves ulama who are serving the religion. If that is a waste, what hope can anyone else have?" I insisted. "Look, what has been the main thrust of all our efforts," he replied. "It has been to show why Hanafi school is better than others. Imam Abu Hanifa did not need this. His grandeur did not need our approval. Imam Shafi'i, Imam Malik, and Imam Ahmed ibn Hanbal could not care less about it. All that one can ever prove in these matters is that a certain position is right but has the probability of being wrong and the other position is wrong but has the probability of being right. Moreover, these issues will not be resolved even in the Hereafter. For Allah ﷻ will not humiliate Imam Shafi'i, Abu Hanifa, Malik, or Ahmed bin Hanbal by showing that they were in error." Then he added: "Today when the roots of Islam are under attack, we have been busy taking care of the leaves."

It is not that debates or disagreements in religious interpretation are themselves evil. Today many western educated Muslims, with scant understanding of their religion do think that way. Some even suggest that we should bury all *fiqhi* schools and create a new one. This is neither possible nor desirable. Differences of opinion are inevitable wherever people have both intellect and honesty. Complete consensus on every issue is possible only when everyone is dumb, so they cannot think of a different idea, or they are dishonest so they willingly agree with a position that they consider wrong. After all religious interpretations are not personal rights that can be sacrificed away.

The problem occurs when we overstate these differences. There were differences of opinion in *fiqh* among the Companions, the Successors, and great *mujtahideen*. But they did not turn these into fights. They disagreed but they maintained respect and love for each other. The brotherhood remained intact. They had tolerance for the other view.

How can we have tolerance for something we know is wrong? Of course we cannot have any tolerance for anything clearly established as wrong by the Qur'an or Hadith. We can never show accommodation for apostasy. We can never agree on changing the Shariah's established definitions of *halal* and *haram*. But beyond this there are issues about which the Qur'an and Sunnah are silent or are subject to more than one interpretation. Here the *mujtahideen* deduce the intent of the Qur'an and Sunnah based on their best ability. Here disagreements are possible. As long as those involved are qualified *mujtahideen* (like the four respected imams), their differing views have to be respected. We can follow only one opinion, and we should try and determine the one closest to the intent of the Shariah, but we cannot declare opposing views as evil. We exaggerate when we deal with people holding valid opposing views as if they were outside the bounds of Islam.

Overstatement (*ghuloo*) is the main cause of most fights involving our religious groups. It also happens with Islamic organizations. Most are doing useful work in the areas they chose based on their abilities and inclinations. Had they developed a spirit of cooperation and considered their differences as just a natural division of labor, together they could have become a formidable force. Unfortunately each one of them considers their work and methodology as the only methodology for Islamic work. If a person leaves one of these organizations to join another, he is treated as if he had recanted his faith. This is *ghuloo*. It produces the tribalism of *Jahiliya* (the pre-Islamic period of ignorance) among religious workers.

Pious people are not extinct today. What we sorely need are the reformers who can rise above their narrow perspectives and heed the universal and unifying call of Islam.

THE SHIP AND THE LIFEBOATS [69]

THE ABOVE comments of Mufti Muhammad Shafi regarding *ghuloo* (overstatement) and tribalism in Islamic workers need to be understood in light of Muslim experience with colonialism and its aftermath. Colonialism had hit them hard. It subjugated them physically, politically, economically, culturally, and mentally. It was like a big crash in which their ship was destroyed. In the immediate aftermath, survival was the main goal, and people came with whatever lifeboats they could. After the formal ending of direct colonial rule after decades of struggle, there was the time to pick up the pieces and build the ship again. The problem is they had been living

---

[69] This section contains the author's reflections on the above.

in the lifeboats for so long, they confused them with the ship. They still do.

The schools for secular education were one such lifeboat. They imparted some skills necessary for survival in a changed world, although they impoverished Muslim education and society tremendously in so many ways[70]. But today so many well-meaning people who get excited about spreading education in the Muslim world think of nothing more than establishing more of these same schools. Campaigns for "democracy," whatever it means, were another such lifeboat, aimed at returning control of Muslim affairs to them thereby seeking liberation. Today, democracy or no democracy, nowhere do Muslims have any control over their affairs, but this lifeboat has become a ship and *Khilafah*, the Islamic system of governance, remains a strange entity.

Most important, Islamic organizations were such a lifeboat, aimed at gathering like minded people so they could focus their resources and energies on some of the important things. Islamic teachings encompass our entire life and no private organization can handle all of them to the exclusion of others. Charity is a big part of Islam and it needs organized efforts. So does Islamic education. And calling to Islam. And *amr-bil-maroof-wa-nahi-anil-munkar*. And the struggle on the battlefield. And so on. Those engaged in media, political, charitable, or other struggles are all part of the jihad. In the absence of the *Khilafah*, these are all lifeboats. Yet each of them is considered to be the ship by its occupants and captains, thereby creating new lines of cleavage within the Ummah.

The claim that what an organization is doing is *the* task that needs to be done and the way it is doing it is the only Islamically legitimate way of doing it is as damaging as it is common. It helps recruitment for a particular organization but hurts the overall cause. It may make the riders of the lifeboat feel good, but it pushes further the day when we can

---

[70] See "What is Wrong with Our Education System?" which begins on page 315.

build the ship again. Little do we realize that one cannot live forever in the lifeboats.

The attitude also betrays lack of appreciation of the current situation of the Ummah. Since the formal end of colonialism we have been living with its legacies. One of them is an education system that we embraced as a ticket out of our miseries during that period of oppression; it compounded our problems by producing self-doubt and self-hate. It produced generations of perfect strangers within the house of Islam, who were then—for this "achievement"—given leadership roles in all areas of Muslim societies. They hated their languages, their culture, and their religion. It is such people who rule the Muslim world today.

Simultaneously, a whole gamut of institutions, from sophisticated research centers to slick media, is dedicated to the campaign to sow doubts, to spread confusion, and to denigrate Islam. In hot spot after hot spot around the world, the sword is busy prosecuting a war on Islam. The pen is busy in both conducting a war on Islam and in trying to foment a war within Islam.

With that armada arrayed against it, not only the ship is missing here, but the lifeboats cannot even make a fleet because of their illusion that each of them is not a lifeboat but *the* ship.

This is not to suggest that the situation is entirely hopeless. For these are also the times when people all over the world are coming to Islam in unprecedented numbers. At a time when Muslims have lost control of the sword and the pen, Islam is finding new followers everywhere everyday. (It is quite revealing that even as Islam continues to spread despite the sword, some people continue to insist that it spread by the sword.)

Within the Muslim world also there are signs of awakening. Muslims are coming back to Islam after having toyed with one false ideology after another. More women are choosing hijab and are becoming more assertive about it as a symbol of their Islamic identity. There is a greater interest in

Islamic knowledge. Qur'an lectures are attracting crowds that were not seen in the past. The nature of the questions people ask about Islam is also changing. There are more "how to" and "what to" questions than "why" questions coming from the secular educated groups. As a small indicator of the new trend, the Biswa Ijtimas (annual gatherings of Tablighi Jamaat in Bangladesh) lately have attracted around two million attendees. What is more, they come from widely varying segments of society. A parallel growth can be seen in Islamic activism. Politics, media, relief and charity, education, and community service are all attracting new workers and new organizations. There is a new enthusiasm, new energy, and new awareness.

Can we imagine how much speedier our recovery could be if we rose above our petty perspectives, pooled our resources, and recognized the difference between the lifeboats and the ship?

Islamic Brotherhood

إِنَّمَا ٱلْمُؤْمِنُونَ إِخْوَةٌ

"The Believers are but a single Brotherhood." [Al-Hujurat, 49:10]

الْمُسْلِمُ أَخُو الْمُسْلِمِ لَا يَظْلِمُهُ وَلَا يُسْلِمُهُ وَمَنْ كَانَ فِي حَاجَةِ أَخِيهِ كَانَ اللَّهُ فِي حَاجَتِهِ وَمَنْ فَرَّجَ عَنْ مُسْلِمٍ كُرْبَةً فَرَّجَ اللَّهُ عَنْهُ كُرْبَةً مِنْ كُرُبَاتِ يَوْمِ الْقِيَامَةِ وَمَنْ سَتَرَ مُسْلِمًا سَتَرَهُ اللَّهُ يَوْمَ الْقِيَامَةِ

"A Muslim is the brother of another Muslim. He does not oppress him, nor does he leave him at the mercy of others. And whoever becomes busy in taking care of the need of his brother, Allah will be taking care of his need. And whoever lifts a hardship from a Muslim, Allah will lift a hardship from him from among the hardships of the Day of Judgment. And whoever covers the faults of a Muslim, Allah will cover his faults on the Day of Judgment." [*Bukhari*, Hadith 2262]

THE ISLAMIC BROTHERHOOD is not based on economic interests, race, or color. It is based on something infinitely

Islamic Brotherhood

superior: rejection of falsehood and acceptance of the Truth as revealed by the One True God.

Not only is this brotherhood based on faith, it is also a part of that faith. The Prophet ﷺ said: "You cannot enter Paradise unless you become a total believer and you won't become a total believer unless you love each other."[71] Obviously, faith and community are inseparable in the faith community produced by Islam. Even a casual reader of the Qur'an would note that it almost always addresses the Believers and not the Believer. All acts of worship that are declared pillars of Islam have a collective form. The five daily salats are best performed in congregation, that being twenty-seven times more valuable than the individual prayer. The special Friday prayer cannot be offered individually at all. Zakat is obviously aimed at making the rich of the community take care of the needs of its poor. Fasting, an essentially individual act, has been given a collective form through unity in time. Hajj enforces unity in both time and place, bringing the believers together in the plains of Arafat in their remembrance of Allah ﷻ.

Those who join in the worship of Allah ﷻ produce a brotherhood that embodies the best moral values of the faith: mercy, compassion, fear of Allah ﷻ, piety, and justice. It is a Solid Cemented Structure[72], a tremendous force in the service of right and against wrong. Its members are to help each other in righteousness and piety but not in sin and rancor.[73] They are to be strong against unbelievers but compassionate amongst each other.[74] They do not do injustice to others nor do they tolerate any injustice to themselves. In their love and concern for each other, all members of this brotherhood are one body: when any part of the body suffers, the whole body feels the pain.[75]

---

[71] *Muslim*, Hadith 81
[72] As-Saff, 61:4
[73] Al-Ma'idah, 5:2
[74] Al-Fath, 48:29
[75] *Bukhari*, Hadith 5552

This brotherhood was established in the most unlikely place: Arabia, where before Islam internecine war was a way of life. On both social and political levels, this was one of the greatest achievements of Islam. On both levels, it remains one of Islam's greatest goals. We can imagine the sensitivity of the Shariah about it by reflecting on its teachings regarding the relations between believers. It is forbidden, for example, for two Muslims to start a whispering conversation in the presence of the third. This might offend the one left out and weaken the brotherhood. It is not permissible for a Muslim to sever relations with his brother for more than three days.

بِحَسْبِ امْرِئٍ مِنْ الشَّرِّ أَنْ يَحْقِرَ أَخَاهُ الْمُسْلِمَ كُلُّ الْمُسْلِمِ عَلَى الْمُسْلِمِ حَرَامٌ دَمُهُ وَمَالُهُ وَعِرْضُهُ

"It is sufficient evil for a Muslim that he should look down upon his brother. The life, wealth, and honor of a Muslim are inviolable by another Muslim." [*Muslim*, Hadith 4650]

The books of Hadith are full of such teachings.

This brotherhood was a force for good, a purveyor of peace and justice for everyone. It provided stability in a quarrelsome world. To the downtrodden and oppressed everywhere, it provided freedom. When it was powerful, it even saved the Jews and Christians in Palestine and Spain from each other.

Two unfortunate developments in this century have impaired this brotherhood. The first was the destruction of *Khilafah* and the emergence of independent nation-states in the Muslim world. This made it possible for "national interests" to be declared that are at cross-purposes to the interests of the brotherhood. Not only that, it destroyed the means for both defining and defending the brotherhood interests. The second development was the emergence of the United Nations Organization and the participation of individual Muslim nation-states in it, solely at its terms. The

UN was and remains an organization of unequal powers, designed to perpetuate that inequality. Its purpose was to establish hegemony of the western alliance over the rest of the world—not for any higher moral purpose but solely for economic exploitation. Its very structure (with real decision making in the hands of a few in the Security Council) guaranteed the disenfranchisement of the weak, and the entire Muslim world found itself in that category at the official ending of colonialism.

While the UN has failed miserably in its declared goals, it has been tremendously successful in the real ones. While it promised peace and justice, it has delivered death and destruction and exploitation and oppression. It provided legal cover for the first US-Iraq war in 1991. It facilitated the carnage in Bosnia by tying the hands of the victims. It perpetuated genocide in Iraq through the imposition of the most brutal economic sanctions in the history of the world, resulting in death of a million people through starvation and disease.

If any one country or group of countries had tried to commit such atrocities on their own, there would have been a tremendous reaction. But we have allowed ourselves to be deceived by the legal camouflage provided by the UN. And witness how low we have fallen with our own accord. Muslims are not allowed to kill the women and children of their enemies even in war. How could then they support the killing of their own women and children? A Muslim is not really a believer if he eats his full while ignoring the plight of a hungry neighbor. How could a believer then participate in economic sanctions designed to starve his own people to death?

When giving commands regarding the Islamic brotherhood, the Qur'an uses a beautiful style with a profound message. Instead of saying, "greet each other" it says, "greet yourself."[76] Instead of saying, "do not defame

---

[76] An-Nur, 24:61

each other," it says, "do not defame yourself."[77] Instead of saying, "do not kill each other," it says, "do not kill yourself."[78] The message is clear: Whatever is happening to others in the brotherhood is actually happening to yourself. Any aggression against any part of the brotherhood is an aggression against all of it.

We must free the brotherhood from the servitude to the ideology of nation-states and the unjust international organizations so we can stop killing ourselves.

---

[77] Al-Hujurat, 49:11
[78] An-Nisa, 4:29

Religious Wars

MAULANA YUSUF ISLAHI, a prominent scholar and author from India, narrates the following incident. Once, somewhere in southern India, argument developed between Hindus and Muslims over a procession of Muharram floats (*Tazias*), a practice rather common in the subcontinent to mark the mourning over the martyrdom of Sayyidna Husain ﷺ. Young Hindus were adamant not to let it pass through a certain intersection while Muslim youth were as determined to go through. To avert the impending clash, older people from the two groups got together and tried to workout a compromise. After much haggling, a suggestion was made that the floats could be allowed provided they met some height restriction. However a thoughtful Hindu elder asked: "How can we ask them to limit the size of the float. They would have to use the size as prescribed in the Qur'an."

This incident is not typical of the Hindu-Muslim clashes that take place routinely in India. The Maulana used it to highlight the pathetic work Muslims had done in introducing Islam to their fellow beings. But it also highlights another important fact: many of our religious wars are based on ignorance.

This is even truer in case of our internal wars, those between Wahhabis and non-Wahhabis, Barelvis and

Deobandis, Hanafis and Shafi'is, etc. We fight over issues that are peripheral as if they were central, or issues over which Shariah itself allows a diversity of opinions as if there can be no two ways about it. Or sometimes we have a legitimate concern but we present it in ways that are wrong and damaging. In all those cases we do harm while being sure that we are doing good.

Consider the differences between the four schools of *fiqh*. As a rule these differences occur on issues that are open to *ijtihad*; either the Qur'an and Sunnah provided no clear cut and direct prescription or they include injunctions that on the surface are contradictory. The leaders of the four schools of *fiqh* were qualified *mujtahids* who used their tremendous knowledge and understanding to resolve the apparent conflict or provide the missing answer. While the answers they come up with will be different, there is no answer that can be called a *munkar* (evil), as long as it comes from a qualified *mujtahid*. The Shar'iah does not permit us to wage a war against other interpretations because we can only wage war against evil.

Certainly, these are not petty issues. The attention that scholars have given to them and the academic arguments that have been developed around them are a testimony to the fact that the minutest details of our religious observances have to be guarded carefully so that—unlike all other religions—both their form and substance can be preserved until the end of time. Yet the same scholars have also shown us how not to over-emphasize them.

When Imam Shafi'i offered Fajr salat in the masjid next to Imam Abu Hanifa's grave, he omitted the *qunut* and the raising of hands at every movement, out of respect for the great Imam. Imam Tahtavi writes about the visit of Qadi Abu Asim, a Hanafi scholar to Imam Qaffal, a Shafi'i scholar. Imam Qaffal asked his guest to lead the prayers and asked his muezzin to call the *iqamah* the Hanafi way. Qadi Abu Asim, on the other hand, followed the Shafi'i way in leading the salat.

Such accommodation is possible when either practice is acceptable in both schools but they differ on which one is preferable. Many of the issues that divide us fall in this category. But even when such accommodation is not possible, we have to keep the differences in their proper place and never let them eclipse the common ground. Our religious wars are a result of ignorance or not following the religious teachings, and not a result of following them. Here are some of the often-ignored *Shar'iah* teachings in this matter.

Never lose sight of the big picture. Two persons who truly believe in Allah ﷻ, the last Prophet ﷺ, the Qur'an, and the Hereafter, will always be closer to each other than to any person who does not share these beliefs. One of the unfortunate events in the early history of Islam was the war between Sayyidna Amir Muawiah ؓ, and Sayyidna Ali ؓ. The news came that the Byzantine ruler was planning to invade Arabia to take advantage of this internal rift. Upon learning that, Sayyidna Amir Muawiah ؓ wrote a letter to the Byzantines: "If your forces head this way, I will be the first to join the army of Ali to stop you." This explains why early internal friction—unfortunate as it was—did not stop or even slow down the tide of Islam from reaching the four corners of the world.

Avoid heated arguments. The differences should be discussed in an academic and civilized manner, without being rude. It is difficult for most of us to see the light of truth in the heat of the argument. "Argumentation extinguishes the light of knowledge in the heart," says Imam Malik.

Have interest in closing the gap, not in widening it. It requires sincerity, humbleness, and understanding. During the British Raj, an English judge once confronted a prominent Muslim scholar with a difficult question. "These other religious leaders have declared you a *kafir* (non-believer) and according to the hadith when a Muslim declares another Muslim as *kafir*, one of them is right. So what do you say about them?" The judge was knowledgeable and clever but he had underestimated the wisdom of the Muslim scholar. "These people have given the opinion because of their misunderstanding that I do not respect the Prophet ﷺ. And it is true that anyone who disrespects the Prophet ﷺ is not a Muslim. So while they are wrong in applying it to me, I cannot call them a *kafir*."

Consider unilateral withdrawal. If the issue is not of religious doctrine or law, we should remember the hadith:

$$\text{أَنَا زَعِيمٌ بِبَيْتٍ فِي رَبَضِ الْجَنَّةِ لِمَنْ تَرَكَ الْمِرَاءَ وَإِنْ كَانَ مُحِقًّا}$$

"I guarantee a home in the suburbs of Paradise for the believer who walks away from a dispute despite being in the right." [*Abu Dawood*, Hadith 4167]

Kosova[79]: Where Were the Muslims?

JUST IMAGINE THE year is 2100 CE, long after we are all dead. A school child is studying Muslim history of the last century. He finds extremely disturbing events that took place toward the end of that century. An area that was home to two million people was turned into an almost empty wasteland in a matter of days. Murders, expulsions from homes, and dishonoring of Muslim women took place at an unprecedented rate. It was the continuation of a rampage that started in the neighboring Bosnia some years earlier. There, murder and mayhem continued for four long years, at the end of which big powers, posing as mediators, turned the area into their colony. The most disturbing fact is that it was not that Muslim armies fought and lost; these were simply one-sided battles with armies of murderers, rapists, and thugs victimizing innocent and helpless people.

---

[79] Kosova is the Albanian spelling of the name of the province where Muslims have faced atrocities by the Serbians for a long time. Serbs refer to it as Kosovo. By using that spelling, the mainstream media quietly lended support to the Serbian claim. That outside Muslims also have generally used this name is a reflection of their chronic faliure to question the mainstream media.

Where were the Muslims, he wonders. He finds that despite a successful effort by their adversaries to reduce their numbers through birth control, there were still 1.2 billion of them in the world. They were on all continents, in all countries. More than 50 countries in the world had majority Muslim populations and Muslim rulers. Did they have no armies or weapons? Actually, they had big armies and lot of weapons. One country was even a nuclear power and had successfully developed ballistic missiles that could hit faraway targets. Another Muslim country with a big army was just next to the troubled area. Some of the countries were very rich. Together, they had sufficient resources to stop the atrocities.

Maybe they did not get the news of the tragic events in time. Actually, they did have good communication equipment. Although they did not really control that equipment and those controlling it used to color and distort things a lot, yet Muslims everywhere were able to hear and see the horrors faced by their fellow brothers and sisters as they were taking place. They saw their plight, they heard their cries, but not a soldier moved from the Muslim world to help those whose lives, honors, and properties were being trampled simply because they were Muslims.

Maybe they had become totally indifferent to the plight of their fellows. Maybe they had lost their faith—no, lost their soul—so they just did not care. Actually, despite all their problems, individual Muslims all over the world were still deeply concerned about their fellows. They talked about them. They raised money for them. They prayed for them. They desperately petitioned whoever they thought could help.

Then what was happening? The student is perplexed. As he continues to dig through historical accounts, he finds something curious. As the massacres were continuing in Kosova, the big army of Turkey was busy attacking Kurd Muslims. Neither the Turks nor the Kurds thought that they should be fighting the Serbs, who were brutalizing the

Kosova: Where Were the Muslims?

Muslims in Bosnia and then in Kosova, instead of each other. Not long before that two big Muslim countries, Iran and Iraq, fought a decade-long war that killed and wounded millions and cost billions. Both declared Israel as their real enemy but fought each other instead.

Their enemies had certainly done their part in igniting the flames of those internecine wars, but they had tried that throughout history. The intriguing development that facilitated this fiasco was a strange new ideology that had gripped the Muslim world. The devastating ideology was that of the nation-state. According to it each Muslim country was an independent nation. And so they became. Each with its own national flag, national anthem, national days, and national interests. As Muslim governments took legitimacy from the concept of nation-state, they owed their allegiance to it also—when they did not owe their allegiance to their foreign masters. In the halls of power, the Ummah died. Muslim leaders did talk about the Ummah but only as a remote, ceremonial entity. The governments and armies were there to protect the national boundaries and national interests; nobody looked after the boundaries or interests of the Ummah.

The murders, arsons, and dishonoring of women in Kashmir was not the concern of anyone except Pakistan and that only because the area was a strategic source of Pakistan's water. If it were not for the "national interests," Pakistan would have nothing to do with them either. The brutalization of Muslims in Palestine was not the concern of anyone except the Palestinians themselves. Even Jerusalem and Al-Aqsa had become Palestinian problems. Bosnia and Kosova were responsibility of no one, because they did not exist at all on the new maps of national interests.

It was a bizarre ideology, exported by the colonial powers so their hold would remain strong even after they had formally given up the colonies. But in those strange days people normally had one of two reactions to most anything that came from their former colonial masters; they either

UNITY

welcomed it, thinking it would bring them progress and happiness, or they became resigned to it thinking it inevitable. However, the ideology of nation-states was exactly opposed to the Islamic idea of one Ummah and life was torn between the conflicting concepts. Hajj symbolized the dichotomy. It was the annual reminder that Muslims were one people, as believers from all over the world wore the same two-sheet dress, circumbulated the same Ka'ba, making the same commitment, "O Allah I am here." It had also been turned into a reminder of the most important belonging of a pilgrim: his passport. Without that certificate of belonging to a nation-state no one could perform Hajj or even move from one point to another in the sacred land.

The student finally understands the ideological trap that guaranteed the tragedies of Bosnia and Kosova. But he cannot figure out why Muslims of the period allowed themselves to be so trapped. Did they not remember the Qur'anic declaration,

$$إِنَّمَا ٱلْمُؤْمِنُونَ إِخْوَةٌ$$

"The Believers are but a Single Brotherhood." [Al-Hujurat, 49:10]

Did they not remember the Qur'anic command,

$$وَٱعْتَصِمُوا۟ بِحَبْلِ ٱللَّهِ جَمِيعًا وَلَا تَفَرَّقُوا۟$$

"And hold fast, all of you together, to the Rope of Allah (i.e. this Qur'an), and be not divided among yourselves." [Al-i-'Imran, 3:103]

Did they not remember the hadith,

$$الْمُسْلِمُونَ كَرَجُلٍ وَاحِدٍ إِنِ اشْتَكَى عَيْنُهُ اشْتَكَى كُلُّهُ وَإِنِ اشْتَكَى رَأْسُهُ اشْتَكَى كُلُّهُ$$

"The believers are like one body. If the eye suffers, the whole body suffers, and if the head suffers, the whole body suffers." [*Muslim*, Hadith 4687]

Did they not know that the devastating idea of nation-states was actually the idea of creating permanent divisions in the Ummah? Did they not even see that while they were suffering under the yoke of this imported ideology, Europe, which concocted it, was breaking the national barriers, and evolving into a European Union? What was going through their minds? Why did they allow themselves to be imprisoned in the cage of that stinking nationalism?

He gives up. History is so full of intrigues!

Staying the Course

In this section:

- Surviving the Melting Pot
- "Not Fearing the Blame…"
- Valentine Day, Birthdays, and Other Daze

Surviving the Melting Pot

MUSLIM IMMIGRANTS FIRST came to the western countries more than a century ago. In Australia they went as Afghan camel drivers. In the USA they went variously as Lebanese autoworkers and Punjabi farmers (not to mention African slaves). These earlier Muslims worked very hard to serve these lands. They built roads, opened access to mines, and performed grueling work to till the land or run the factories. Their great contributions and economic successes aside, they had one glaring failure: they failed to build Muslim communities that could last. Their descendants disappeared into the "melting pot." Today one cannot find the Muslim children of these earlier Muslims.

Another wave of Muslim immigration started after the Second World War and gained momentum two decades later. Will the children of these immigrants survive as Muslims in a land that has a history of assimilating people of all faiths? Or will they too meet the fate of the children of earlier immigrants? Today the "melting pot" is hotter than ever, the popular culture is stronger than ever, and the influence and reach of the media in promoting the popular culture is greater than it ever has been. What is the chance of survival for those being raised in the eye of the storm?

It can happen. But it won't happen without properly guided effort. Here is the advice from the scholars.

Religious Obligations

Salat (obligatory prayer) is the most important of a Muslim's obligations. It is impossible to build a wholesome life without this pillar. As the hadith says,

$$بَيْنَ الْعَبْدِ وَبَيْنَ الْكُفْرِ تَرْكُ الصَّلاةِ$$

"Between a person and disbelief there is only the giving up of salat." [*Tirmidhi*, Hadith 2544]

In the ex-Soviet Union and other communist countries, it was a "crime" to offer salat. Those who prayed did so secretly and at great personal risk. In the western countries, there is no such barrier. Those who fail to pray regularly have nothing but their own laziness or weakness of faith to blame.

We should be regular in performing other religious obligations as well. In addition we must allocate time for reading the Qur'an and good religious books in our daily schedule. To survive in a non-Muslim environment, says Maulana Yusuf Ludhianvi, "all these are as important as food and medicine."

Halal

A concern for *halal* and *haram* consumption is not only an important obligation; it is a prerequisite for building a wholesome Islamic life. The Qur'an says,

$$يَٰٓأَيُّهَا ٱلرُّسُلُ كُلُواْ مِنَ ٱلطَّيِّبَٰتِ وَٱعْمَلُواْ صَٰلِحًا$$

"O Messengers! Eat things good and pure and work righteousness." [Al-Muminun, 23:51]

At-Tayebat (good and pure) is a beautiful way to refer to *halal* as *haram* things are not good or pure. This verse teaches us a very important fact: physical actions have moral and spiritual consequences as well. Thus eating *halal* is necessary for leading a life of righteousness.

Science, by definition, cannot go beyond the physical world in its explorations. Those who are ignorant of the limitations of science and therefore seek guidance from it in areas where it is unable to provide any get easily confused on this issue. "Why is pork *haram*?" they might ask. Answer: because Allah ﷻ said so. And He said so because it is bad for our moral and spiritual health.

A glass of water may look clean, but if somebody tells us that it contains a poison or virus, we would not touch it. *Haram* is the same way, only more so. Whatever the Shariah has declared as *haram* is as unsafe as poison, although its poisonous consequences will be apparent in the Hereafter.

Materialism

Today the entire world is in the grip of rampant materialism. But it is more corrosive in its birthplace. In the Muslim world materialism is rampant but people are not (yet) presented as role models simply because of their wealth. Over here the life styles of the rich and famous are an object for adulation.

Additionally Maulana Yusuf Ludhianvi cautions: "Never allow yourself to be impressed by the great worldly possessions of a non-believer. If you realize the eternal doom that unbelief promises, you will feel pity rather than envy."

Religious Guidance

The tremendous interest in question and answer columns in newspapers, magazines, and on the Internet is a sign of the concern of Muslims for religious guidance and for doing what is right. The downside is that all sorts of "experts" have also sprung up to dispense legal opinion and religious guidance.

This state of affairs is a result of general ignorance of even basic religious teachings among today's "educated Muslims." Additionally, there is a commonly held opinion that the person giving a wrong *fatwa* is responsible for it, not the one that follows it.

Actually, we are responsible for searching for the authorities carefully before we put our trust in them. We do so in other realms of life. We do not accept medical advice simply because the giver appeared to be a doctor. We ascertain qualifications before we accept advice. Fortunately, that profession is generally regulated and we don't have to deal with unqualified practitioners very often. In case of religious guidance, it is up to us to exercise the same caution.

Conduct

Justice, honesty, integrity, kindness, sincerity, and truthfulness are important qualities of a good Muslim. He should be a man of principles, a source of good. According to one hadith, the believers are like rain, spreading their goodness wherever they go.

It was these qualities of Muslims that opened the hearts of millions of people in Asia and Africa to the truth of Islam. People knew the tree of Islam by the fruits of the good conduct it produced in its followers.

Children

The above are necessary for building a strong Muslim home. However, we need to do more to insure that our children do not step out from our tiny islands only to drown into an ocean of godlessness. Two of the greatest bad influences come in the name of entertainment and education. The first is television and we must protect our children from it. The second is the secular education system that forcefully promotes ideas that are totally anathema to Islam to those most impressionable and least able to question them. Muslims must develop their schools that teach all subjects in an Islamic context. On both of these issues we have shown scant progress.

"Not Fearing the Blame…"

WHAT WILL THE people say? Will they approve of it? Will they laugh at it? It seems that such concerns influence our actions—especially our public conduct—more than anything else. Social pressure is a powerful force. It works by appealing to our desire not to be insulted, ridiculed, or criticized. In a righteous society it could also be a force for good, as some people will avoid a bad name more than a bad action. But in the real world out there it mostly turns into an evil force, pressuring people into doing things they know are wrong or keeping them from doing what they know are right. The question of right and wrong is changed into a question of acceptable and unacceptable to this evil force.

In some cases we recognize it easily. Nearly every parent in the West today seems to be concerned about peer pressure, especially on the teenagers. There is hardly a sin that attracts teenagers—drugs, violence, lewdness, fornication, gangs— that does not have peer pressure as its main or major cause. Countless lives have been turned upside down or totally destroyed by it. While it attracts our attention because of the scale of destruction it causes, the general trend is not different in other segments of the society. In many cases the same Muslim parents who are genuinely worried about the teen peer pressure, themselves seem to be giving in to the pressures for conformance.

The phenomenon is not limited to the western world either. Unfortunately today most Muslim countries mostly seem to be putting their weight on the side of wrong. There, un-Islamic traditions, innovations (*bid'ah*), and outright evils flourish under social pressures. The most visible symbols of an Islamic life are generally also the favorite targets of this pressure. Thus we see that in many Muslim countries even such a simple act as growing a beard (or observing *hijab* for women) are treated as crimes punishable by public ridicule! (In a country like Egypt, the same act calls for investigation by secret agencies. But that is an altogether different story.) To go beyond that and challenge any of the established un-Islamic practices qualifies one to be labeled as a fanatic!

Actually there is nothing new in all of this. This psychological warfare is as old as the struggle between good and evil. The Qur'an tells us that all the Prophets were insulted and ridiculed by the very people they were trying to save from the eternal punishment. They were called liars and sorcerers; they were ridiculed for being "too pious"; they were laughed at for being "crazy."

The story of Prophet Noah, peace be upon him, is so telling. His final act of building the Ark was considered proof-positive by his people of he being out of his mind. Building a ship in an area nearly a thousand miles away from the sea! What could be crazier than that! The Qur'an mentions:

وَيَصْنَعُ ٱلْفُلْكَ وَكُلَّمَا مَرَّ عَلَيْهِ مَلَأٌ مِّن قَوْمِهِۦ سَخِرُوا۟ مِنْهُ ۚ قَالَ إِن تَسْخَرُوا۟ مِنَّا فَإِنَّا نَسْخَرُ مِنكُمْ كَمَا تَسْخَرُونَ

"And he was building the Ark and every time that the chieftains of his people passed by him, they threw ridicule at him. He said: 'If you ridicule us now, then we'll ridicule you just the way you are sneering.'" [Hud, 11:38]

They were having a great time, making fun of Prophet Noah. Little did they realize that soon the Flood would wash away all of their ignorant self-assurance. One can imagine their horror when the end finally came, for it must have been in proportion to their delusion until that point.

Such is the story of the struggle between Truth and Falsehood. Truth will eventually triumph. But Falsehood has great fun before that, ridiculing the Truth. That is why Truth attracts people with foresight, patience, courage, and determination. They have their eyes set on the final outcome. They are not deterred by the flood of insults and false propaganda that they are sure to face. That is why the Qur'an mentions that one of the qualities of the believers whom Allah ﷻ loves and who love Allah ﷻ is that

$$ وَلَا يَخَافُونَ لَوْمَةَ لَائِمٍ $$

"They fear not the blame of any blamer." [Al-Ma'idah, 5:54]

That must be so because we must realize that the most ridiculous thing would be for anyone to leave the Straight Path for fear of being ridiculed by those who are happily rushing on their path to eternal doom. The most laughable act is to trade Truth for Falsehood for fear of being laughed at. The craziest deed would be to knowingly disobey Allah ﷻ for fear of being called crazy!

The Qur'an assures us, and history confirms it, that it is not a reasonable goal for a believer that he or she should be able to go through life without ever being subjected to mockery and ridicule. Such expectations produce failure at the first instant, when the rubber meets the road, and apologists personify such failure. Unfortunately, but understandably, in the age of the mega propaganda machine we see too many of them.

"Not Fearing the Blame…"

When their laughter becomes too loud, we should remember that the chieftains of the people of Noah were also laughing at one time. But who had the last laugh?

$$\text{إِنَّ ٱلَّذِينَ أَجْرَمُوا۟ كَانُوا۟ مِنَ ٱلَّذِينَ ءَامَنُوا۟ يَضْحَكُونَ ۝ وَإِذَا مَرُّوا۟ بِهِمْ يَتَغَامَزُونَ ۝ وَإِذَا ٱنقَلَبُوٓا۟ إِلَىٰٓ أَهْلِهِمُ ٱنقَلَبُوا۟ فَكِهِينَ ۝ وَإِذَا رَأَوْهُمْ قَالُوٓا۟ إِنَّ هَٰٓؤُلَآءِ لَضَآلُّونَ ۝ وَمَآ أُرْسِلُوا۟ عَلَيْهِمْ حَٰفِظِينَ ۝ فَٱلْيَوْمَ ٱلَّذِينَ ءَامَنُوا۟ مِنَ ٱلْكُفَّارِ يَضْحَكُونَ ۝}$$

"The guilty used to laugh at those who believed. And whenever they passed by them, used to wink at each other in mockery. And when they returned to their own people, they returned jesting. And whenever they saw them they would say: 'They have gone astray.' But they had not been sent as keepers over them. But on this day the Believers will laugh at the Unbelievers." [Al-Mutaffifeen, 83:29-34]

Valentine Day, Birthdays, and Other Daze

THERE IS A GROUP of practices that we can consider as the twin sister of *bid'ah*. Like *bid'ah* they flourish on the twin foundations of ignorance and outside influence. Like *bid'ah* they entail rituals. But unlike *bid'ah* the rituals have not been given an Islamic face. They are followed because they are considered an acceptable cultural practice or the hottest imported "in" thing.

Most of those who indulge in them do not know what they are doing. They are just blind followers of their equally blind cultural leaders. Little do they realize that what they consider as innocent fun may in fact be rooted in paganism. That the symbols they embrace may be symbols of unbelief. That the ideas they borrow may be products of superstition. That all of these may be a negation of what Islam stands for.

Consider Valentine's Day, a day that after dying out a well deserved death in most of Europe (but surviving in Britain and the United States) has suddenly started to emerge across a good swath of Muslim countries. Who was

Valentine? Why is this day observed? Legends abound, as they do in all such cases, but this much is clear: Valentine's Day began as a pagan ritual started by Romans in the 4th century BCE to honor the god Lupercus. The main attraction of this ritual was a lottery held to distribute young women to young men for "entertainment and pleasure"—until the next year's lottery. Among other equally despicable practices associated with this day was the lashing of young women by two young men, clad only in a bit of goatskin and wielding goatskin thongs, who had been smeared with blood of sacrificial goats and dogs. A lash of the "sacred" thongs by these "holy men" was believed to make them better able to bear children.

As usual, Christianity tried, without success, to stop the evil celebration of Lupercalia. It first replaced the lottery of the names of women with a lottery of the names of the saints. The idea was that during the following year the young men would emulate the life of the saint whose name they had drawn[80].

The only success it had was in changing the name from Lupercalia to St. Valentine's Day. It was done in CE 496 by Pope Gelasius, in honor of some Saint Valentine. There are as many as 50 different Valentines in Christian legends. Two of them are more famous, although their lives and characters are also shrouded in mystery. According to one legend, and the one more in line with the true nature of this celebration, St. Valentine was a "lovers'" saint, who had himself fallen in love with his jailer's daughter.

Due to serious troubles that accompanied such lottery, French government banned the practice in 1776. In Italy, Austria, Hungry, and Germany also the ritual vanished over

---

[80] The idea that you can preserve the appearance of a popular evil and yet somehow turn it to serve the purpose of virtue, has survived. Look at all those people who are still trying, helplessly, to use the formats of popular television entertainments to promote good. They might learn something from this bit of history. It failed miserably. Christianity ended up doing in Rome, and elsewhere, as the Romans did.

355

the years. Earlier, it had been banned in England during the 17th century when the Puritans were strong. However in 1660 Charles II revived it. From there it also reached the New World, where enterprising Yankees spotted a good means of making money. The valentine industry has been booming ever since.

It is the same story with Halloween, which has otherwise normal human beings dressing like ghosts and goblins in a reenactment of an ancient pagan ritual of demon worship. Five star hotels in Muslim countries arrange Halloween parties so the rich can celebrate the superstitions of a distant period of ignorance that at one time even included the shameful practice of human sacrifice. The pagan name for that event was Samhain (pronounced sow-en). Just as in the case of Valentine's Day, Christianity changed its name, but not the pagan moorings.

Christmas is another story. Today Muslim shopkeepers sell and shoppers buy Christmas symbols in Islamabad or Dubai or Cairo. To engage in a known religious celebration of another religion is bad enough. What is worse is the fact that here is another pagan celebration (Saturnalia) that has been changed in name—and in little else—by Christianity.

Even the celebration considered most innocent might have pagan foundations. According to one account, in pagan cultures, people feared evil spirits—especially on their birthdays. It was a common belief that evil spirits were more dangerous to a person when he or she experienced a change in their daily life, such as turning a year older. So family and friends surrounded the person with laughter and joy on their birthdays in order to protect them from evil.

How can anyone in his right mind think that Islam would be indifferent to practices seeped in anti-Islamic ideas and beliefs? Islam came to destroy paganism in all its forms and it cannot tolerate any trace of it in the lives of its followers. Further, Islam is very sensitive about maintaining its purity and the unique identity of its followers. Islamic laws and teachings go to extra lengths to ensure it. Salat is forbidden at the precise times of sunrise, transition, and sunset to eliminate the possibility of confusion with the practice of sun worship. To the voluntary recommended fast on the tenth of Muharram, Muslims are required to add another day (9th or 11th) to differentiate it from the then prevalent Jewish practice. Muslims are forbidden to emulate the appearance of non-Muslims.

A Muslim is a Muslim for life. During joys and sorrows, during celebrations and sufferings, we must follow the one Straight Path—not many divergent paths. It is a great tragedy that under the constant barrage of commercial and cultural propaganda from the forces of globalization and the relentless media machine, Muslims have begun to embrace the Valentines, the Halloween ghost, and even the Santa Claus. Given our terrible and increasing surrender to paganism the only day we should be observing is a day of mourning. Better yet it should be a day of repentance that could liberate us from all these days. And all this daze.

History

In this section:

- Baghdad
- Jerusalem
- Christmas

Baghdad

TIME WAS WHEN IT was the most advanced city in the world. In science and technology, commerce and manufacturing, intellectual pursuits and dissemination of knowledge, and arts and literature, its achievements were unparalleled in the east or west. The catastrophe that made all of that a distant memory was equally unprecedented in the history of mankind.

It started in 1218 CE. The savage armies of Chengiz (Genghis) Khan invaded and destroyed most of Central Asia and Persia razing to ground such great cities as Bukhara, Samarkand, Herat, Nishapur, and Balkh. He did not attack Baghdad, but paved the way for that invasion by his grandson, Halaku (Hulagu) Khan. In 1258, Halaku sacked Baghdad, killing 1.6 million people in the city and ending forever the signs of the glory of the great city. It was a complete scorched earth policy. They came, they looted, they destroyed, they burned, they killed, they left. The Mongols, as the whole world knows, were savage people.

Chengiz and Halaku Khan still rule the world today. Their logic and principles are still driving real-politick. The scene is repeated endlessly in Bosnia and Kosova, Kashmir and Palestine, Iraq and Beirut, Afghanistan and Sudan. But in their latest reincarnation they look so civilized and benign.

HISTORY

It is amazing what the make-up artists and spin-doctors of world's finest propaganda machine can do. It looks pretty, but is no less deadly. This is the unvarnished truth about the world we live in today.

Was the Mongol invasion just an accident that happened because of a blunder by Khwarizm Shah? While a superficial reading of history may make one think that it was, reality is entirely different. Forces of evil have always been present in this world and will remain so, but they become dominant only when the forces of good become weak due to internal problems. We can see the big problems in the Muslim world of that time that were the real cause of the tragedy that followed. First was the infighting. Khwarizm Shah had spent most of his time and energies fighting with the Ghauris and other Muslim rulers in neighboring territories. The sons of the great Sultan Salahuddin fought among themselves. The governors of Makkah and Madinah were engaged in a battle between them. Alqami', the vizier of Musta'sim, the last Abbasid khalifah who was killed by Halaku, had conspired against the Khalifah.

Then there was this love of money and the worldly pleasures. Everyone was busy raising his standard of living. Corruption was common. People were given to music and entertainment, pomp and show, conspicuous consumption, and vain pursuits. Khalifah Musta'sim himself was more interested in hunting and entertainment than the affairs of the state. There is a telling report about Badruddin Lulu, the ruler of Mosul, who once received two requests. Khalifah Musta'sim had asked him to send musical instruments and singers. Halaku Khan asked for cannons and other weapons used for demolishing castles. And while all this was going on, some religious leaders were discussing who was superior: Ali ؓ or Muawwiya ؓ.

After taking Baghdad, Halaku marched toward Syria and Africa. Everyone who came in his way was routed. He seemed so invincible. But in 1260 CE at Ain-Jalut, in Galilee, the forces of Sultan Baibers handed him a terrible defeat. The inspiring force behind the Sultan was Sheikh Izzuddin, a great scholar and reformer who urged the Sultan to move on and turn back the Mongol tide, and who himself participated in the jihad. His inspiring sermons brought the Muslims back to Islam by the thousands. When a people turn to Allah ﷻ, Allah's help turns to them. Within two years all of Syria had been liberated from the Mongols. What is more, due to the great work of *dawa* carried out by the great scholars of that time, within forty years of Halaku's invasion of Baghdad, his descendants had accepted Islam.

Today the moral and political picture of most parts of the Muslim world does not look much different from the one in the Baghdad of 1250s. Our tragedy is the same. The way out of that tragedy is also the same.

Jerusalem

سُبْحَٰنَ ٱلَّذِىٓ أَسْرَىٰ بِعَبْدِهِۦ لَيْلًا مِّنَ ٱلْمَسْجِدِ ٱلْحَرَامِ إِلَى ٱلْمَسْجِدِ ٱلْأَقْصَا ٱلَّذِى بَٰرَكْنَا حَوْلَهُۥ لِنُرِيَهُۥ مِنْ ءَايَٰتِنَآ ۚ إِنَّهُۥ هُوَ ٱلسَّمِيعُ ٱلْبَصِيرُ ۝

"Glory to Allah Who did take His Servant for a Journey by night from the Masjid-al-Haraam to the al-Aqsa Masjid, whose precincts We did bless, in order that We might show him some of Our signs. For He is the One Who hears and sees all things." [Al-Israa, 17:1]

THIS VERY FAMOUS verse tells us why al-Aqsa is and will always remain one of the holiest places in Islam. It was the destination of the Prophetic journey called *Isra* and the spot from where *Mi'raj* into heavens took place.

This verse is immediately followed by seven others that talk about Jerusalem and the Jewish history. The Jews had a Covenant with God. They would get His blessings, including control of Jerusalem, as long as they lived up to the terms of that Covenant. Otherwise they would be severely punished. Two major punishments were promised. Both happened as promised as the Jews ignored the repeated warnings.

Soon after Prophet Sulaiman's ﷺ death, his kingdom was divided into two: northern Israel, and southern Judah, which included Jerusalem. Both fought among themselves and courted pagans. The history of Jerusalem is thus a history of an ongoing battle between pure monotheism and paganism.

Jeroboam I, the first king of Israel (10th century BC), introduced a golden calf in the temples. In the next century king Ahab built a temple for Baal, a pagan idol, in Samaria, the capital. Various Prophets were persecuted at the insistence of his pagan wife Jezebel. As always moral corruption accompanied the spiritual one. Then in Divine retribution pagan Assyrians overran Israel in 721 BC. We see a similar trend in Judah, although on a reduced scale. There are periods of repentance during a general trend of accommodating the Babylonian and Egyptian pagans. Finally the promised punishment came to Jerusalem also. As the *Britannica* notes: "In 586 BC the doom prophecies of Jeremiah and Ezekiel came true. Rebellious Jerusalem was reduced [to rubble] by Nebuchadrezzar; the temple was burnt." The remaining Jews were exiled into Babylon. This was the first punishment mentioned by the Qur'an.

As they repented, and mended their ways, the Jews were given a second chance. In 538 BC Persian emperor Cyrus defeated the Babylonians and Jews were allowed to return to Jerusalem. In 515 BC the Temple was rebuilt. The next century saw a revival under Prophet Ezra. But Alexander's conquest of Palestine in 332 BC started the process of hellenizing Jews. Canaanite paganism was now replaced by Greek paganism. Three centuries later Roman Pompey walked into Jerusalem.

Then we see Herod being appointed the client king for the Roman Empire. He built the Temple but destroyed the religion. The Temple was still being rebuilt when Jews joined with Roman paganism to persecute Prophet Jesus and his followers. John the Baptist (Prophet Yahya ﷺ) was beheaded by Herod Agrippa, the grandson of Herod. So in 70 CE the second punishment mentioned by the Qur'an came. The armies of Roman commander Titus moved into the city and burnt it to ground on the ninth day of the Hebrew month of Ab, the very month and day on which 657 years earlier the Babylonians had sacked the first Temple, built by Prophet Sulaiman ﷺ. The punishment had come at an appointed time!

Prophet Muhammad's ﷺ night journey in which he lead all the prophets in prayers at al-Aqsa also signified that the leadership role had been transferred from the Children of Israel to the Children of Ismail. Along with leadership came the responsibility. As long as they remained true to the Covenant with Allah ﷻ, they would be successful and Jerusalem will be theirs. When they betrayed the Covenant, they would get the punishment also.

So Sayyidna Umar ﷺ just walked into Jerusalem in 638 CE. The vastly advanced war machine of the Roman superpower could not stand in the way of the Muslim forces, the new standard bearers of monotheism. Muslims ruled with justice, compassion, and fear of God. A new era of peace, justice, and prosperity started under them.

With the exception of an 88-year period of ruthless crusader rule, the area remained under continuous Muslim rule until 1917. It was Muslim infighting and waywardness that had brought the crusaders in 1099 and it was their turning to Allah ﷻ under the pious and God-fearing leadership of Salahuddin Ayyubi that defeated them in 1187. Again it was infighting and transgression that were at the root of the dissolution of the *Khilafah* and the British occupation of Jerusalem in 1917. As Muslims did not learn from their mistakes in the beginning of the century, in time it would lead to the establishment of a Zionist state. The rest is recent history.

The events of this century would readily be apparent to be a continuation of the centuries past, if we realize two facts. First, Israel is ruled today by Zionism and not Judaism, which in any case, over the centuries, has been "reformed" beyond recognition as the original revealed religion. And Zionism is just a particularly poisonous form of western political nationalism. Second, western civilization, despite all the polishing and enlightenment, remains at heart a pagan civilization. Any doubts in this regard could be quickly dispelled by looking at the Halloween and Christmas observations alone.

So this is Jerusalem's history of thirty centuries. Sins and transgression, hellinicized Jews, westernized Muslims, client kings, puppet regimes, humiliation and destruction. Repentance, trust in Allah ﷻ, righteousness, and victory. In this eternal battleground between monotheism and paganism, the forces of monotheism would win as long as they remained true to it. When they betrayed their Covenant, they would be punished.

The world needs monotheism for it alone can provide peace and justice for all as it did in the past. The world is waiting for the forces of true monotheism to conquer Jerusalem once again.

Christmas

قُلْ يَٰٓأَهْلَ ٱلْكِتَٰبِ لَا تَغْلُوا۟ فِى دِينِكُمْ غَيْرَ ٱلْحَقِّ وَلَا تَتَّبِعُوٓا۟ أَهْوَآءَ قَوْمٍ قَدْ ضَلُّوا۟ مِن قَبْلُ وَأَضَلُّوا۟ كَثِيرًا وَضَلُّوا۟ عَن سَوَآءِ ٱلسَّبِيلِ ۝

"Say O People of the Book! Do not exaggerate in your religion beyond the Truth, nor follow the vein desires of a folk who have gone astray and misled many as they strayed (themselves) from the Level Path." [Al-Ma'idah, 5:77]

BOTH MUSLIMS AND serious Christians can learn a lot from Christmas, the annual reminder of the victory of paganism over the religion of Prophet Isa (Jesus Christ) ﷺ.

No one disputes that the event and all its symbols came from pagan religions; it has nothing to do with the birth or teachings of Jesus Christ, peace be upon him. For one thing, no one knows with certainty the date of birth of Jesus Christ. "In fact, dates in almost every month in the year were suggested by reputable scholars at one time or another," notes *The American Book of Days*. For another, the celebration of birthdays is itself a pagan idea, never promoted by any

Prophet or Book of God, including the Bible. Early Church leaders opposed it strongly. As late as 245 CE African church father and philosopher Origen wrote that it was sinful even to contemplate observing Jesus's birthday "as though he were a King Pharaoh."

But the pagan world did have prayers and celebrations during the winter season. Those who worshipped the sun god because of its apparent power used to become concerned about the fate of their god, in a world of many gods, as days became shorter. It looked like the sun was being defeated by the god of snow that brought death and misery with it. "...in Rome, the sun in its winter solstice was at its weakest on December 25 and had to be born anew with the help of bonfires, lights, processions and prayer."[81] The Roman pagan celebration was called Saturnalia. The Persians also had similar celebrations for Mithras, their sun god.

The evergreens, holly, ivy, and mistletoe plants, which remained green even during this wintertime, were similarly considered by the pagans to have magical powers. The Druids, whose Stonehenge temples can be seen in England, regarded mistletoe with reverence and used to burn it in sacrifice during the solstitial festivities. They also used to hang it in their houses. When you don't know the One True God, even leaves and plants can become god. They thought it brought good luck, fertility, and protection from witchcraft, and was an antidote to poison.

In 1822 a Dr. Clement Moore, professor of divinity, wrote a poem titled "The visit of St. Nicholas." The poem became popular and Santa Claus was born. The reason for popularity? "...the time was ripe. A myth was needed, and the recreation of 'old Christmas' was well in the wind."[82] Some decades later *The New York Sun* answered an 8 year old's question: is there a Santa Claus? The answer has become classic and is worth noting. "Nobody sees Santa Claus, but that is no sign that there is no Santa Claus. The most real

---

[81] *Reader's Digest Book of Christmas*. (Reader's Digest, 1992).
[82] William Sanson. *A Book of Christmas*. (McGraw-Hill, 1968).

things in the world are those that neither children nor men can see." So Santa Claus is divine, and judging from the Christmas celebrations, certainly more important than Jesus Christ himself.

Early church leaders wanted to Christianize the pagan festivities, but their operating principle became: when you can't beat them, join them. For as Pope Gregory declared in 601 CE, "...from obdurate minds it is impossible to cut off everything at once." It was a license for another pearl of "wisdom": when in Rome, do as the Romans do.

And so they did. First slowly and then rapidly. The Son of God replaced the sun god. Saturnalia was replaced by the ceremony for Christ or Christ Mass, which later became Christmas. For several centuries it was solely a church anniversary, observed by religious services. "At Christmas, men and women were not, repeat not, to dress up or mime; there were not to be auguries, such as superstitions about fire; houses were not to be decorated, no presents given, no well-laden tables, and a strict watch was to be kept on drink." But false religion drives out true religion. Consider Christmas gifts, a carryover from the Roman practice of giving dolls as gift in lieu of their earlier barbaric custom of offering human sacrifices. "The early Church frowned on gift giving as a pagan custom. But the people enjoyed it too much to abandon it, and so finally the Church accepted the idea and sanctioned it."[83] Evergreens? "The early church forbade the use of them, but here again the custom was too deeply rooted and the ban was ignored. Finally the church accepted the use of evergreens for decoration." And on and on. Now consider this portrait of Saturnalia and contrast it with the original don'ts mentioned above: "...a fortnight of near riot, of drunkenness, noise and games, naked slaves singing, men dressing up as animals and behaving with less dignity, sex, often with perversion."[84] Anyone can see which picture represents today's Christmas more closely.

---

[83] Barbara Rinkoff, *The Family Christmas Book* (Doubleday, 1969).
[84] *Reader's Digest Book of Christmas*. (Reader's Digest, 1992).

With the advent of capitalism, the old pagans got a new supporter in the form of the adman. George Bernard Shaw observed: "Christmas is forced on a reluctant...nation by...shopkeepers and the press." This is how they could serve God, and make money at the same time.

This defeat of Christianity at the hands of paganism must be contrasted with Islam's resounding victory over it. Before Islam, Arabia was a pagan country—big time. But none of the pagan customs survived after Islam. None whatsoever. There was no such thing as "the people wanted it very much so the church allowed it." Islam completely eradicated not only the beliefs but also the practices and the symbols of paganism. This in itself is a miracle that serious students of comparative religions must reflect upon. Here is a living proof of the authenticity of the last Messenger ﷺ.

The success continued throughout the centuries. The secret of this great success lies in what Stuart Brown (author of *The Nearest in Affection*), deplores as Muslim "antipathy to innovation." The first khalifah Abu Bakr ؓ had declared in his first address as the new ruler, that he was a follower not an innovator, thereby setting the tone for all Successors.

Throughout Islamic history there have been attempts to introduce *bid'ah* (innovation) as innocent good practices, but unlike Christianity, there have always been rightly guided ulama that fought them strongly. The struggle continues today. Yes, Muslims can learn from Christmas. Those of us who may be wondering what is wrong with *Milad-un-Nabi* celebrations may do well to realize that Christmas also started as *Milad* for Jesus Christ, peace be upon him.

A Second Look

In this section:

- The News Protocol - Toward an Islamic Framework
- Islamic Ummah vs the Nation-State
- Beyond Elected Government. Just Government
- Secularism in France
- The Fundraising Dinner
- The Myth of Population Crisis
- Islamic Renaissance?

The News Protocol - Toward an Islamic Framework

"We mortals hear only the news and know nothing at all." - Homer, The Iliad.

SEVERAL YEARS AGO an Indian reporter for *Time* magazine approached Maulana Waheeduddin Khan, a prominent scholar and author in India, and interviewed him regarding the status of women in Islam. She raised the commonly asked questions and recorded each answer. A few weeks later she returned with more "follow-up" questions, which were twists on the original questions and went over his previous answers. Then a third time. When Maulana Waheeduddin wondered about the purpose of this exercise, the reporter boasted: "Because we cannot afford to be wrong."

The Maulana was so impressed by this answer that he narrated the story to Muslims as an example to be followed for seeking the truth and pursuing impeccable professional standards. Of course, when the article regarding women in Islam was finally published, it had all the usual accusations regarding Islam's treatment of women; it did not contain any of the answers that the *Time* reporter had painstakingly obtained from the Muslim scholar.

Time magazine may have been simply following a rule of propaganda: first get all the facts; then you can distort them as much as you like!

There is something very peculiar, very interesting about all this. *Time* is one of the most successful magazines in the world today. Although it routinely engages in anti-Islamic propaganda, it is considered reliable even in Muslim countries. Muslims may have a quarrel with a paragraph here, an article there, but they still consider the magazine as the model for what journalism is all about.

What is going on?

For answers we may have to look deeper into the evolution of journalism in the Industrial society. Modern journalism began as a result of two technological developments: the printing press and the telegraph. Together they made it possible to move and publish bits of information over vast distances at incredible speed. The first event took place in Germany, the other in the USA. As Neil Postman describes in *Amusing Ourselves to Death* (1985), it was the American development (1844), which made it possible to publish the large circulation daily newspaper by moving decontextualized information from all over the world and thereby created what is called "The News of the Day." Postman argues that the "telegraph gave a form of legitimacy to the idea of context-free information; that is, to the idea that the value of information need not be tied to any function that it might serve in social and political decision-making and action, but may attach merely to its novelty, interest, and curiosity."

The telegraph was developed and was first put to use in a society that did not put a premium on information-action ratio and did not have any built-in restraints against gossip, vain talk, scandals, and backbiting. Rather there was a huge market for these commodities waiting to be exploited. The telegraph simply facilitated what the society wanted to do any way. This market was exploited by the pioneers. One of them was Joseph Pulitzer. The Pulitzer Prize is the most prestigious prize for a journalist in the USA today. Pulitzer raised the circulation of *New York World* from 15,000 to 250,000 in three years, the highest in the world at the time.

How did he do it? "With a series of stunts and campaigns, Pulitzer revitalized the established formulas of sensationalism and idealism," says the *Britannica*. William Hearst was another pioneer and a very successful one at that. According to the *Britannica*, he was "interested in circulation-building sensation at any price, even if it meant dressing up complete fabrication as news." The *Penny Press* and the tabloids used the same formulas to achieve unprecedented commercial success.

Thus was born the modern media machine with its built in tendencies for sensationalism and entertainment and its disregard for acquiring information for the sake of action. Postman writes, "...most of our daily news is inert, consisting of information that gives us something to talk about but cannot lead to any meaningful action."

Technology has a way of forcing its social and cultural agenda. Just like the airhostess that came with the aircraft and was allowed in the Muslim world without any question, the newspaper was also greeted by blind and willing followers.

Paisa Akhbar and Beyond

The *Penny Press* inspired the *Paisa Akhbar* in British India. Throughout the Muslim world, Muslims obtained not just the printing press and wire service, (and other electronic technologies as they developed), but also the names and outlooks for their newspapers from the West. What is more, they received their definition of "news" from the West. The West, it may be added, did not have much of a definition to offer beyond novelty ("man bites dog") or curiosity ("what we know today that we did not yesterday").

A SECOND LOOK

To verify these assertions one needs to take just one look at the newspapers and news magazines in the Muslim world today. Of course we find some religious articles and some political commentary added to satisfy their Muslimness. But, one only needs to consider the deeper questions about purpose and philosophy to realize the near total absence of an Islamic framework. Like, what is the soul of this institution? What makes it tick? What is the goal? What place does it have in Islamic scheme of things? What is the purpose of writing and publishing? What determines what is news? What objective criteria decide what is fit to print? What are the rights and responsibilities of journalists in a Muslim society? What about freedom of press? Etc. etc.

More than fifty years ago, Mufti Muhammad Shafi, Mufti of Pakistan, wrote an article titled "Adab-ul-Akhbar" (The News Protocol). This was a rare effort to develop an Islamic framework for journalism. Commenting on the sensationalism in the Muslim press of his time he noted that there are those who "consider it *haram* (forbidden) to worry about *halal* and *haram*" in this profession.

THE ISLAMIC BASIS

For those who do worry about these things, his article did provide some guidelines and a basis on which to build an Islamic framework for this powerful profession. Mufti Muhammad Shafi quoted two ahadith that could form the basis for journalism in Islam. The first one, an excerpt from a long hadith in *Tirmidhi* collection describes the daily routine of Prophet Muhammad ﷺ. "I asked what was the Prophet's behavior like when he came outside the house. Hind bin Hala answered that it was his practice to keep quiet unless he had something useful and necessary to say…And he used to inquire about the well being of his Companions, and used to ask about the common occurrences among the people. Then he used to comment on these reports telling what was good and what was bad."[85]

The second hadith was reported by Anas ﷺ who said:

كَانَ إِذَا فَقَدَ الرَّجُلُ مِنْ إِخْوَانِهِ ثَلَاثَةَ أَيَّامٍ سَأَلَ عَنْهُ، فَإِنْ كَانَ غَائِبًا دَعَا لَهُ، وَإِنْ كَانَ شَاهِدًا زَارَهُ، وَإِنْ كَانَ مَرِيْضًا عَادَهُ

"When the Prophet ﷺ did not see a Companion for three days, he used to inquire about him. Then if the Companion had been away on a journey, the Prophet ﷺ used to pray for him; if he had been in town the Prophet ﷺ used to go and visit him; if the person had been sick the Prophet ﷺ asked about his health." [*Kanzul Ummal*, Hadith 18483]

It follows, says Mufti Shafi, that being constantly aware of the condition of the Ummah is a Sunnah. These days the press is the means for doing that. In addition, the press can be used for communicating the grievances of the common people to the government, demanding the rights of Muslims, and spreading the message of Islam. The most important thing to realize here is that the "news" here is sought for—in fact derives its meaning from—the possibilities of action. The objective is to be able to bring justice to a victim, help the weak and the needy, visit the sick. If nothing else is possible, at least one could pray for those who are in some difficulty. But there is an information-action ratio—close to one. In contrast, in the modern media world the ratio is close to zero. But in part due to its glitter and dazzle of new technologies, we hardly pay attention to the crucial difference.

FUNDAMENTAL RULE

Mufti Shafi also described a fundamental Islamic rule that should govern all discussion regarding journalism: The written word is subject to the same laws that govern the

---

[85] *Shamail Tirmidhi*

spoken word. And generally both are subject to the same injunctions whether they come from a journalist or a non-journalist. If something is a pious act, so is writing and publishing it. If it is *haram* in one case, it is so in the other as well. In fact the written word has a longer life and broader reach and so it stands to produce greater good or greater evil, and so bring proportionately greater reward or punishment.

Anyhow, in Islamic Shariah there are few exemptions for a journalist from the normal rules of conduct that apply to everybody else. For example, it is not that backbiting is prohibited for a common man, but is somehow permissible for a journalist. It is to be remembered that Shariah describes in detail the rules that should govern all discourse by a Muslim. The Qur'an, for example, forbids making fun of other people.

$$\text{يَٰٓأَيُّهَا ٱلَّذِينَ ءَامَنُوا۟ لَا يَسْخَرْ قَوْمٌ مِّن قَوْمٍ عَسَىٰٓ أَن يَكُونُوا۟ خَيْرًا مِّنْهُمْ وَلَا نِسَآءٌ مِّن نِّسَآءٍ عَسَىٰٓ أَن يَكُنَّ خَيْرًا مِّنْهُنَّ وَلَا تَلْمِزُوٓا۟ أَنفُسَكُمْ وَلَا تَنَابَزُوا۟ بِٱلْأَلْقَٰبِ}$$

"You who believe, let not some men among you laugh at others: It maybe that the latter are better than the former. Nor let some women laugh at other: it may be that the latter are better than the former. Nor defame nor be sarcastic to each other. Nor call each other by offensive nicknames." [Al-Hujarat, 49:11]

This is a general requirement and it is not lifted just because the person doing it is a columnist and can display his skills in front of a much larger audience and with more polish.

Furthermore the right to privacy is a sacred human right that nobody (including the journalist) can violate. The laws of God apply to everybody whether he is a prince or a pauper, for the Qur'an tells us,

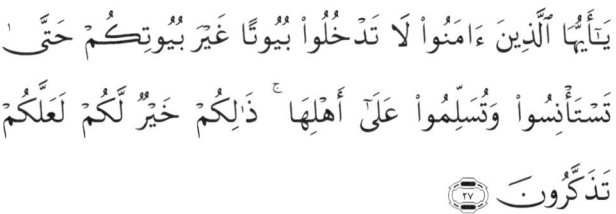

"O ye who believe! Enter not the homes other than your own, until you have asked permission and saluted those in them: that is best for you, in order that you may heed." [An-Nur, 24:27]

Similarly making a false allegation is a sin for a common man as well as for the writer. The requirement to cover up the sins of others applies as strongly to the reporter as to any other Muslim. This is generally ignored today although it has been greatly emphasized in the Shariah. One hadith says,

يَا مَعْشَرَ مَنْ آمَنَ بِلِسَانِهِ وَلَمْ يَدْخُلْ الإِيمَانُ قَلْبُهُ لاَ تَغْتَابُوا الْمُسْلِمِينَ وَلاَ تَتَّبِعُوا عَوْرَاتِهِمْ فَإِنَّهُ مَنْ اتَّبَعَ عَوْرَاتِهِمْ يَتَّبِعُ اللَّهُ عَوْرَتَهُ وَمَنْ يَتَّبِعْ اللَّهُ عَوْرَتَهُ يَفْضَحْهُ فِي بَيْتِهِ

"O community of people who have declared belief by their tongues but for whom belief has not entered their hearts, do not backbite Muslims and do not search for their faults, for if anyone searches for their faults, Allah will search for his fault, and if Allah searches for the fault of anyone, He disgraces him in his house." [*Abu Dawood*, Hadith 4236]

This one hadith destroys the basis for the entire tabloid press. The exception is when a person's wrong behavior will cause harm to others. In those cases alerting others to protect them is not only permissible, it may even be required.

OTHER GUIDELINES

There are other guidelines in *Adab-ul-Akhbar*. It is not allowed to unjustly accuse anyone—Muslim or non-Muslim, period. A victim, however, has the right to publicize his grievance and accuse the aggressor. This is explicitly allowed by the Qur'an. It says:

$$\text{لَا يُحِبُّ ٱللَّهُ ٱلْجَهْرَ بِٱلسُّوٓءِ مِنَ ٱلْقَوْلِ إِلَّا مَن ظُلِمَ ۚ وَكَانَ ٱللَّهُ سَمِيعًا عَلِيمًا}$$

"Allah loves not the shouting of evil words in public speech, except by one who has been wronged, for Allah is He who hears and knows all things." [An-Nisa, 4:148]

Thus airing grievances is permissible and if it can help the victim, it is an important job for the newspaper. A report, even if correct, should not be published if it is found that publishing it would hurt the interests of the society. No advertisement of any product or service should be published if the item in question is forbidden by the Shariah.

Regarding crime reports, which form the juiciest part of today's newspapers, Mufti Shafi declares elsewhere that such reports are simply not permissible in their current form. The details of crime promote an interest in crimes. A crime report should be published with the explicit purpose of protecting the society and discouraging crimes.

AN ISLAMIC CENTER FOR JOURNALISM

The love-hate relationship of Muslims to *Time* or other western media may be explained by the simple fact that it is the best example of journalism as defined by the West. Muslims feel the pain when they are hurt, but they don't have their own framework for journalism, their own definition of news, their own criteria on which to judge a news publication. They have borrowed all these from the West.

They feel that something is wrong somewhere but cannot pinpoint it because all the borrowed criteria they use suggest otherwise.

In this respect it is part of the larger problem of the contemporary Muslim society and seeking solutions requires collaborative efforts between religious scholars and professionals. Perhaps someone can establish a center for Islamic journalism that will bring together the 'ulama and the journalists who are serious about Islam. That way a framework for Islamic journalism can evolve through positive interaction between the scholars and the practitioners. Until that happens Muslims will keep on publishing newspapers and magazines. But they won't have an Islamic media. And the entire world will be the loser for that.

Islamic Ummah vs the Nation-State

IT IS EASY AND customary to blame the current Muslim rulers for the sorry situation obtaining in the Muslim world today. Their complicity is beyond a shadow of doubt. If the Muslim rulers had had their act together the slaughters in Afghanistan, Bosnia, Kosova, Kashmir, Chechnya, Iraq, and Palestine would not have been possible. But was it only because the Muslim rulers happened to be immoral, coward, and unscrupulous characters? Is the 1.2 billion strong Ummah suffering only because there are fifty-seven bad persons who are ruling it?

These rulers do not carry out all their plans personally. They have armies of compliant soldiers, bureaucrats, and other staffers at every level of government that do the dirty work. Further, the societies at large produce, nurture, and sustain the corrupt machinery of the corrupt governments. As we continue our investigation, we find that our problem is corruption; not only of the rulers but also of the ruled. Today we have strayed from the Shariah in our personal lives; we lie, cheat, steal at a higher rate than ever before; we exploit and oppress in our small spheres. In short, our problems are caused by our moral corruption.

But there is something more. And it gets scant attention in the Muslim discourse. Islam teaches us the correctness of belief is even more important than correctness of deeds. There is an implied message here: the corruption of ideas is far more devastating than the corruption of deeds. This may be applicable here as well. We complain about the particular tribal leaders that happen to be there today but forget about the tribalism that sits at the root of all this. This is the tribalism of the nation-states and it has been enshrined into the constitutions, legal structures, bureaucracies, and the entire apparatus of government in every Muslim country. Its language and thinking, though anathema to Islam, have gained widespread acceptance. While we condemn its outcome, we do not sufficiently examine or challenge the system itself.

We constantly talk about the Muslim brotherhood and the need for Muslim unity. We assert that Muslims are one Ummah. Simultaneously—and without much thought—we embrace the symbols, ideas, and dictates of its exact opposite. We have lived under our nation-states, celebrated our national days, and sang our national anthems all our lives. As a result the realization that the gap between the idea of the nation-state and that of one Ummah is wider than can be patched with good leaders of individual nation-states does not occur easily. We do not realize that we may be trying to simultaneously ride two different boats going in opposite directions.

So let us consider some real-life situations. In Pakistan, the provinces of Sind and Punjab share the Indus River. The available water is less than their combined needs. Quite naturally, there is constant bickering over the distribution of water. The conflict is resolved by the presence of a central government and by the realization that both provinces belong to the same country. Now imagine that the two provinces had been transformed into two separate countries. We can be certain that the small issue that nobody in the world knows about or cares about today would become a big international conflict. And it may matter little whether they were called Islamic Republic of Punjab and the Islamic Republic of Sind! The logic of a sovereign country is very different and once you embrace that there are consequences that good intentions and good people alone cannot overcome.

To understand that let us move from the Indus basin to the Furat-Dijla (Euphrates-Tigris) basin. What is presented as a hypothetical situation in the former has been turned into an unfortunate reality in the latter. Both Dijla and Furat originate in Turkey, pass through Syria, and end up in Iraq where they join to form the Shat-al Arab that then discharges into the Persian Gulf. Mesopotamia means the land between the two rivers, the two rivers having been the source of civilization since the ancient times. Add the artificial international borders between Turkey, Syria, and Iraq, and the same life giving water turns into an explosive that could rock the area. In 1974 there was a near war between Syria and Iraq as Syria began to fill the reservoir that has become Lake Asad, decreasing the flow of the river to Iraq to as little as 25 percent of the normal rate. Armies were moved and threats were exchanged, though finally diplomatic activity by the Soviet Union and Saudi Arabia defused the situation. In 1990 tensions ran high as Turkey stopped all flow in Furat for one complete month as it started to fill the Ataturk Dam.

Today Turkey's Southeast Anatolia Project, (GAP in Turkey) is promising a much more serious conflict in the days to come. The multi-billion dollar GAP includes more than 20 dams and 17 electric power plants, which will reduce water supply to Syria by 50% and to Iraq by 90% when it is completed in another twenty years. Even more bizarre is the plan Turkey has for part of the water that it denies to Syria and Iraq seriously endangering their agriculture and economies; it will sell it to Israel through the so-called Peace Pipeline that will run through the Mediterranean. The agreement with Israel was signed in 2001. "We have declared that we can sell water to whichever country needs water, regardless of its language or flag," said Cumhur Ersumer,

Turkey's energy minister at that time. "It looks like Israel will be the first country to buy Turkey's water." That is the logic of the nation-state as articulated by Suleyman Demirel: "Neither Syria or Iraq can lay claim to Turkey's rivers any more than Ankara could claim their oil. This is a matter of sovereignty."

We can be sure that accountants in Turkey can show that Turkey will benefit economically by doing what it plans to do. And even a so-called Islamist party in Turkey will be driven by those calculations pledging, as it does, allegiance to "Turkish national interests." A comparable situation would be Punjab denying water to Sind and then selling it to India. No matter how corrupt leaders in Pakistan become (if they have not already reached the limit) it is just impossible to imagine that outcome. And yet the same situation is not only possible, it is there in the other case. Such are the wonders of the corrupt ideology of nation-state!

Conflicts of interest between any two entities are normal and natural. What is crucial is the mechanism and structure for resolving them. Islamic laws of inheritance highlight this fact. Conflicts could develop even among close relatives over distribution of inheritance. Since Islam values very smooth relations and does not like even the slightest bickering there, the Shariah has provided the detailed rules for this distribution. Neither the people involved, nor the government can override this distribution. Thus a solid mechanism has been provided for resolution of these conflicts.

In case of two provinces of the same country, the mechanism for the resolution of their conflicts remains in the form of the central government as well as a firm realization on the part of everyone that they are riding the same boat. However when they turn into independent countries, both of these are lost.

The definition of self-interest can change with a change in the frame of reference. When the United States gave the Pakistani ruler the choice of either joining the invader or joining the target he did not hesitate for a minute to choose the first option. He justified it by espousing a philosophy of 'Pakistan First,' which is another way of saying, "Forget the Ummah." But the sad fact remains that under the frame of reference under which Pakistan and all Muslim countries operate today, that was an option.

The 1991 War on Iraq also drew legitimacy solely from this. If you don't believe this, try legitimizing that war after dropping the assumption that the border between any two Muslim countries is sacred and inviolable! The imposition of embargo on Afghanistan and Iraq is another example of the clash between Islam and the nation-state. Islam teaches that it is not a believer who eats while his neighbor goes to bed hungry. The system of the UN on the other hand, ordered its member-states not to supply any food or medicine to those dying of hunger and disease in Iraq. Again, the fact that Muslim countries complied with the latter without any consternation or serious opposition is a reminder of our subconscious acceptance of the nationalist ideology. The Qur'an warned us not to engage in disputes and infighting or we would become weak and powerless. But we have not only done exactly what was prohibited, we have given a permanent structure and legal cover to the arrangement for that infighting in the current political organization of the Muslim domain.

This exposition of the ideology of nation-state invariably leads to mental blocks. First, that this is anachronistic. Under the tide of globalization the nation-state is being swept away, anyway. Well, the campaign for globalization wants to relax some borders and erect and reinforce others. It just happens that the unity of the Ummah also requires the same but its lists of what is to be relaxed and what is to be strengthened are exactly the opposite.

The second mental block is that all this is impossible. We had a *Khilafah* centuries ago. Since then we have had a checkered history of nominal khalifahs with independent sultans running their own kingdoms. Today we have fifty-seven states and there is no way we can change that in our life times. Yes and no. While we had more then one centers of political power for centuries, the Muslim world was much more integrated then than we realize. It was one social, cultural, religious, and economic domain. Its language, system of education, currency, and laws were the same. There were no restrictions on travel, or movement of capital or goods. A Muslim could take up residence and start a business or get a job anywhere. Ibn Battuta traveled from Tunisia to Hijaz, East Africa, India, Malaya, and China, covering 75000 miles without traveling the same road twice. During the twenty-five year journey he took up residence where he wanted to. He even got government assignments as *qadi* and as ambassador in China for the sultan in India. If that was possible then, it should be easier now because of the huge advances in the communication and transportation technologies alone.

Certainly we cannot dismantle the fifty-seven Muslim governments overnight and replace them with a *Khilafah*. But we can gradually breakdown the barriers between them in travel, trade, and all exchanges at personal levels. With free flow of people, goods, capital, and ideas throughout the Muslim domain, a quiet revolution can begin. We could realize that this domain is much more self-sufficient and strong then we have ever realized. That its various parts complement each other's needs and strengthen each other. That it is the artificial borders between Muslim lands drawn by colonial powers that have terribly weakened it!

While the barriers to that vision are real and very serious, the most serious barriers are mental and psychological. We must break through the mental straitjacket and realize that another world is possible. Only then we will begin to see how to get there.

Beyond Elected Government. Just Government

إِنَّ ٱللَّهَ يَأْمُرُكُمْ أَن تُؤَدُّواْ ٱلْأَمَٰنَٰتِ إِلَىٰٓ أَهْلِهَا وَإِذَا حَكَمْتُم بَيْنَ ٱلنَّاسِ أَن تَحْكُمُواْ بِٱلْعَدْلِ

"Surely, Allah commands you to fulfill trust obligations toward those entitled to them and that when you judge between people, judge with fairness." [An-Nisa, 4:58]

THIS IS AN ESSENTIAL verse of the Qur'an to be consulted by anyone who wants to understand Islam's teachings about governance and government. While it talks about discharging trust obligations and being just in all situations, it has special implications for staffing and running public office.

Amanah (discharging one's trust obligations) and *adl* (justice) are highly stressed attributes of believers. Sayyidna Anas ؓ says:

مَا خَطَبَنَا نَبِيُّ اللَّهِ صَلَّى اللَّهُ عَلَيْهِ وَسَلَّمَ إِلاَّ قَالَ لاَ إِيمَانَ لِمَنْ لاَ أَمَانَةَ لَهُ وَلاَ دِينَ لِمَنْ لاَ عَهْدَ لَهُ

"The Prophet ﷺ did never deliver a khutbah in which he did not say the following words: 'One who has no *amanah* has no *iman* (faith) and one who breaks promises has no religion.'" [*Musnad Ahmed*, Hadith 11935]

Yet these all-important qualities become even more so when a person is occupying a position from where he can affect other people's lives. Thus, ulama explain that this verse specifies that all positions of authority are a trust to be given to those who are qualified for them. Further it specifies that whenever a Muslim is in a position to adjudicate a case between any two parties, he must do so with justice and fairness.

The conduct of the Prophet ﷺ in this regard and his numerous sayings on the subject further highlight the importance of this command. According to one hadith, if a person who has been charged with some responsibilities relating to the general body of Muslims gives an office to someone simply on the basis of friendship or connection of some sort without regard to the capability or merit of that person, the curse of Allah ﷻ falls on him. None of his acts of worship are accepted, whether mandatory (*fard*) or voluntary (*nafl*).[86]

We can discern some very important principles from the above. First, the selection of people for positions of authority, and their behavior once in office, is a religious matter. Islam does not recognize the separation of religion and state. Second, these positions are not a right of the people but a trust from Allah ﷻ to be discharged according to His commands with utmost concern for justice for all. Third, the people so chosen must be good, for the good of the society depends on that.

---

[86] *Jama-ul-Fawaid*

From this we can begin to see the difference between Islam and that immensely advertised political system called democracy. Democracy is concerned with the mechanism for selecting people for government. Islam is concerned with the outcome of that selection. Democracy makes a huge virtue of its mechanism—the electoral process. But, mechanisms can and do change with time and circumstances. The two leading models of democratic government, England and the United States, have different systems for electing the head of the government and the legislators, and their systems have also changed over time.

What matters most is what sort of rulers and managers of public life result from the process. Yet democracy is silent about it. It wants an elected government. Islam goes much further. It wants a just government.

What if corrupt people get elected through fair elections? Democracy offers no serious answer to this question. Early American leaders, like James Madison, claimed: "People will have the virtue and intelligence to select men of virtue and wisdom." But more than two centuries of history have made nonsense of this proposition. Just a casual look at the list of past US presidents will make one laugh at the suggestion about the "men of virtue."

What if democracies turn into tyrannies and the elected people commit atrocities against mankind? It is sufficient to glance at the historic record of this past century. The only use of atom bombs was made not by a rogue dictatorship but the leading democracy in the world. The atrocities committed by European powers against each other in the two world wars were mostly the works of democratic governments. Not long ago we saw with horror what happened in Bosnia and Kosova. Yet the Serb leader had been an elected one. In Kashmir, where Indian atrocities are no less serious but are much less publicized, the democratic world is quite happy that India is a democracy. We are constantly reminded that Israel—a country built on stolen land and sustained through constant oppression, torture, and treachery against the people whose land was stolen—is the only democracy in the Middle East. Well, then, what does that say about the system of government called democracy?

Democracy's record on the home front is equally unenviable. It is no secret that in the United States real power lies with big corporations and wealthy people. Manufactured consent replaces informed public opinion and provides the façade for the "government by the people." One result: pockets of abject poverty in the richest nation in the world. In a country that grows so much food that it does not know what to do with all of it, there are thousands of people who go hungry or eat off the trash. What is more, nobody thinks the system of government has anything to do with it. Nobody loses sleep over it, not the least the elected rulers. Now contrast this with the Islamic *Khilafah*, where Sayyidna Umar ﷺ worries: "If a dog dies of thirst at the bank of Euphrates, how shall I answer for that to Allah."

The widespread popularity of democracy indicates the yearning people have for justice, righteousness, and fairness that democracy promised but did not deliver. Democratic movements had started out with the noble intentions of ending the tyranny of autocratic rulers. However, as with all other efforts aimed at reforming human society that were free from divine guidance, they could not reach their goal. The world needs to know that it will find it in Islam. But before that the billion Muslims living in the world today also need to discover that fact. Unfortunately, our preoccupation with the vocabulary of democracy has shifted our focus to the electoral process and away from the requirement for establishing a just government. The sooner we realize our mistake, the better.

Secularism in France

IMAGINE THE FRENCH president snatching the headscarf from a little Muslim girl, then declaring that he was fighting aggression. Imagine a lineup of reporters and commentators nodding their heads in agreement and applauding the assault. Then imagine him making the pronouncement that he was doing it to uphold religious freedom and protect women's rights. Not to mention national security, the French Republic, secularism, liberalism, and the entire Western civilization. (Poor Muslim girl! Did she ever know that her hijab could destroy all of these?)

Welcome to another episode of the clash of civilizations. Here is another crusade, another "just war" based on principles. The most important—in fact the most sacred, noble, and inviolable—of these principles is, of course, secularism and the doctrine of separation of church and state. An AFP report about Muslim protest at the beginning of the recent campaign[87] stated: "The decision, *intended to reflect France's strict separation of religion and state*, has set off a storm of protest by Muslim leaders around the world." (Emphasis added.) A month later reporting on the vote in the French parliament, the *New York Times* (February 10, 2004) added: "The issue goes to the heart of France's self-image as a

---

[87] This article was written in March 2004.

secular state that keeps faith out of state schools and services to ensure no religion dominates or suffers discrimination." In the same paper Elaine Sciolino informed the readers that "France Has a State Religion: Secularism." (February 8, 2004). The *USA Today* assured its readers, "The French protect their secular tradition so fiercely because their ancestors suffered through religious conflicts, mainly between Protestants and Catholics." (February 4, 2004). This line, endlessly repeated by all mainstream agencies and media outlets, provided a justification and made the oppressive anti-Islamic stand look more principled.

MANY FACES OF SECULARISM

Secularism is a fascinating subject, not the least because of the richness of its meaning. For it means widely different things at different times and in different circumstances. Upon a cursory examination of French record on the subject, three flavors stand out: extra sweet, regular and bitter. In the extra sweet version it means support of church by state. In the regular version it means separation, i.e. mutual non-interference, of church and state. And in the bitter version it means the suppression of religion by state.

For a glimpse of Secularism-Extra Sweet, we can turn to Afghanistan of some years ago. In August 2001, the then Taliban government arrested some missionaries in Afghanistan who were working in the guise of relief workers. Among their "relief supplies" were thousands of CDs, videos, audiotapes, and bibles in local languages. They knew they were violating the law, which prohibited exploiting the sufferings of the people and evangelizing in the name of aid work. That is why upon their arrest they claimed that the literature was for their own personal use; they must have had plans to learn Farsi and Dari languages so they could understand Christianity better. But the Taliban were not buying that. Rather they planned trial in a court of law.

Among the governments that rushed to the aid of these missionaries (called "aid workers" by the media machine that knows the power of consensus lying) was the "fiercely and rigidly secular" French government. France expressed its deep concern over difficulties of "aid workers" in Afghanistan and called on the Taliban to stop hindering the actions of the agencies and humanitarian NGOs (September 7, 2001). "The trial in Kabul of several Afghan and foreign members of the NGO Shelter Now International (SNI) reflects the increasingly difficult climate in which the NGOs are forced to work in Afghanistan," a statement by the French Embassy in Islamabad quoted French Foreign Ministry spokesman as saying. The missionary nature of their work, which had been hidden by the media while they were in custody, was revealed once they were out. Two of them went on a yearlong speaking tour, "hoping to encourage others to go into missionary work."

What makes it even more fascinating (and extra-extra sweet) is the fact that there were no French citizens among the arrested missionaries!

For Secularism-Regular we can look at the France of the past century since 1905. After a power tussle, both church and state decided on peaceful co-existence. The church and state have defined boundaries and they generally remain within them. It is a case of live and let live. That is why the Jewish skullcaps and Christian crosses were not discovered to be violating "secular principles" and "fiercely guarded secular traditions" (labels used by the propaganda machine to justify Secularism-Bitter we are witnessing now) until hijab appeared on the scene. (It should be noted that crosses and skullcaps were included purely as a window dressing to create the illusion that the rule was causing equal misery to all three religions. The crosses are not even a religious obligation; the hijab is. Witness the non-protest by French Jews and Christians against the hardships supposedly imposed on them.)

Somewhere between Secularism-Sweet and Secularism-Regular lies the relationship between the French government and the Catholic schools. Nearly 20% of French students go to Catholic schools. So many can go there because they are affordable. And they are affordable because they are highly subsidized by the "fiercely secular" French government! Of course such inconvenient facts were carefully left out from the media coverage so as not to spoil a good story.

The Secularism-Bitter has been reserved to fix the problem of the undeserving "infidels" who refuse to learn how to behave as good colonial subjects. When the French were a minority in Muslim Algeria they imposed their culture on the majority. When Muslims became a minority in France the same French are not willing to give the minority even the right to follow their religion. So they have concocted this special brew of Secularism-Bitter which says that it is okay to be a Muslim in France but it is not okay to pray five times a day, observe fasts in Ramadan, insist on halal food, wear hijab if you are a female or a beard if you are a male, or take any other of your religious obligations seriously and sincerely. A report by a government body, the *Institut National d'Etudes Démographiques* (INED), declared assimilation of Muslims as a desirable goal, and then effectively defined an assimilated Muslim as one who did not pray regularly, did not fast, and made fewer visits to the country of origin. The policy has been in effect for decades. Each year the French government refuses about one-third of the applicants for naturalization, and some of those refusals are of candidates who meet the formal conditions for naturalization, but fail the "assimilation test" as defined here.

Secularism-Bitter flourishes in the other less-known France. The world knows of the France of Freedom, Equality, and Brotherhood. But there is another France too, that of Islamophobia and hate. Among its many bitter fruits have been the banning of Islamic publications, arbitrary arrests of Muslim leaders (especially during the time of Charles Pasqua, former interior minister), roadside identity checks for Muslims, restrictions on halal slaughter, and creative prohibitions on masjid building. For the six million French

Muslims, for example, there are only five purpose-built masajid.

Banning Hijab in Egypt

Actually this Secularism-Bitter, reserved for the Muslims, knows no boundaries. To catch a glimpse of it we can visit Egypt. The place is Champollion School in the Egyptian city of Alexandria. The school is run by a French NGO following a cultural agreement between Egypt and France in 1968. In October 2000, when 12-years-old Azzah Muhammad Zaki decided to wear hijab to this school, she was not allowed to enter. When her family questioned the decision, she and her three brothers were expelled. In the ensuing crisis, the French Consulate in Alexandria first denied that it had any relation with the school's administration or anything to do with its curriculum. But when the family brought a lawsuit against the school, the consulate submitted a plea to intervene with the court on behalf of the school and the parents' association. Further, sensing that their action was not defensible, it asked the court to consider two school officials as "diplomats" who could not be tried under Egyptian law. Too bad, Chief Judge Husain Al-Gabri rejected this saying that the international law did not grant diplomatic immunity to bureaucrats and awarded 600,000 Egyptian pounds (US$160,000) to the family.

Probably this was another case of the French government taking a "principled" stand, trying to help "national cohesion" and integration in Egypt!

Democratic Islamophobia

The media accounts repeatedly reminded their audiences that about 70% of the French public was in favor of the hijab ban and other anti-Islamic steps that were being legislated. This was used as a legitimizing statement so the readers could rest assured that it must be both right and good. For the goddess of democracy had blessed it.

What had been left out was the fact that both the French government and its media had worked long and hard on generating this Islamophobia. It "is not a recent phenomenon but was already clearly established as early as the First World War," says Neil MacMaster.[88] European colonial elites in Algeria and their supporters in France ran a well-organized lobby towards this goal. "A highly racialized stereotype of Algerians as criminals, primitive savages, rapists, transmitters of venereal disease and tuberculosis, was widely diffused through the press." To this day the French media routinely carries inflammatory anti-Islamic articles, headlines, and pictures. Hijab has been a major target of this long and vicious media campaign.

The French had gone to Algeria for good, or so they thought, declaring it a department of France. So the Algerian War of Independence (1954-1962) was traumatic and France is still bitter over its defeat. Toward the end of that war (1961-1962), France sowed the seeds of large-scale immigration from Algeria by systematically uprooting over three million peasants and sabotaging Algerian economic infrastructure. This immigration was considered necessary at that time because France badly needed manpower for rebuilding the country after the Second World War.

In the 1970s and 1980s these immigrants began to bring their families and slowly started to settle in the new land. Naturally, they began to demand basic rights to create an Islamic space to live in (masajid, schools, cemeteries, halal food, time and space for prayers, etc.). As they did, the campaign of demonization increased in scope and intensity.

---

[88] MacMaster, "Islamophobias in France and the 'Algerian Problem'," in *The New Crusades: Constructing the Muslim Enemy,* Emran Qureshi and Michael A Sells, eds., (New York: Columbia University Press, 2003), 291.

Islamic Threat

The increased visibility of Muslims was used by the extremists to generate fear. Muslims were not only bad people to be hated, they were also dangerous people to be feared because they were there to takeover the country. The Machiavellian propaganda campaign is showcased by one example. In 1981-1982 an anonymous forged letter was widely circulated in Dreux where the extremist National Front would score a decisive electoral victory a year later. The forged letter was supposedly written by an Algerian to a friend in Algeria. It said:

> "My Dear Mustapha. By the grace of the all-powerful Allah we have become lords and masters of Paris...Come quickly, we expect you in large numbers, since Mitterand has promised that we shall soon get the right to vote. We kicked the French out of Algeria; why shouldn't we do the same here?"[89]

Human Rights and Conventions

Another very important aspect of the hijab ban is that it violates the French constitution as well as a number of international treaties to which France is a signatory. Yet no media report bothered to even mention it.

Article 1 of the French constitution still says (The constitution was last modified on 17 March 2003): "France shall be an indivisible, secular, democratic and social Republic. It shall ensure the equality of all citizens before the law, without distinction of origin, race or religion. It shall respect all beliefs."

And Principle VII of the Helsinki Accords, of which all European countries are signatories, states: "The participating States will respect human rights and fundamental freedoms, including the freedom of thought, conscience, religion or belief...They will promote and encourage the effective

---

[89] Ibid, 298.

exercise of civil, political, economic, social, cultural and other rights and freedoms all of which derive from the inherent dignity of the human person and are essential for his free and full development...the participating States will recognize and respect the freedom of the individual to profess and practice, alone or in community with others, religion or belief acting in accordance with the dictates of his own conscience."

Nice words. But French Muslims have heard other nice words like democracy, tolerance, and civil rights before. As for democracy, for the six million Muslims in France, there is not a single Muslim member of parliament. And now the bans on hijab, on opting out of obscene sex classes, and on refusing treatment from a doctor of the opposite sex are the latest in a series of concerted efforts by successive governments to dispense "tolerance" and "civil rights" to Muslims in France.

Of course we can count on the media machine to act as the cheerleaders as France moves down the path of (in)equality, (in)tolerance, and Islamophobia.

The Fundraising Dinner

FUNDRAISING IS NECESSARY for the establishment and survival of Muslim institutions and supporting noble causes. The fundraising dinner thus has become a very common occurrence in the Muslim communities in the West. The event is typically organized in a big hotel. People buy a ticket for the entry and during the program professional speakers use a variety of techniques to encourage more donations. The purpose may be helping victims in the latest hotspot or building a masjid; the technique remains roughly the same.

This is one practice that Muslims living in the West have borrowed from their host countries, and so it requires a close examination of its historic development and underlying philosophy. The charitable fund raising methods of the West have to be examined in the light of the West's ideas regarding wealth, poverty, and charity.

In the West, the rich believed that they were better because they had more money. But it was good to believe that they got more money because they were better in the first place. There are academics that made a career out of proving the latter. One of them was Herbert Spencer (1820-1903). It was he who produced the phrase "survival of the fittest" as he applied Darwin's ideas to the world of economic life. "Partly by weeding out those of lowest development and partly by subjecting those who remain to the never ceasing discipline of experience, nature secures the growth of a race who shall both understand the conditions of existence and be able to act up to them," wrote Spencer. "It is impossible in any degree to suspend this discipline by stepping in between ignorance and its consequences, without to a corresponding degree, suspending the progress."

Spencer was immensely successful in the United States where his books were "very little less than divine revelation," notes John Kenneth Galbraith. He was further helped by William Graham Sumner, whose was "perhaps the most influential single voice on economic matters in the United States in the second half of the last century." These were the high priests of world capitalism. Sumner's creed: "The millionaires are a product of natural selection."

They were naturally superior and they had the money to prove it. But to be fully enjoyed, this superiority had to be advertised. Hence the need for, what Thorstein Veblen (1857-1929) called, the Conspicuous Consumption, the consumption designed to impress with the cost involved. This advertisement, though always there, has been easier in the age of television with its ability to turn the "Life Styles of Rich and Famous" into popular entertainment.

In the case of charity, the West faced a dilemma. Capitalist doctrines would suggest that charity was immoral, because it interfered with the "wholesome" weeding out process through which the society progresses. But then there was also the Bible and it had different ideas on the subject. The then US Vice President Nelson Rockefeller said in 1975: "One of the problems of this country is that we have this Judeo-Christian heritage of wanting to help those in need." But Rockefeller was unduly concerned. The West had already found a solution to this problem. It was that charity would be allowed because it was good for the ennoblement of the rich. Along with Conspicuous Consumption, Conspicuous

Charity could serve the needs of the rich just fine by affirming their superiority. Hence all the mechanisms for advertising the generosity. This should explain both what goes on around the world with the aid agencies and what goes on in the benefit concerts and fund raising dinners at home.

These ideas, like all other ideas of *Jahiliya* (pre-Islamic dark ages), were hardly new, though. Thousands of years ago *Qarun* (Korah in the Bible) made the same assertion. Referring to his immense wealth, he said: "These riches have been given to me on account of the knowledge I possess."[90].

Similarly the Conspicuous Charity. The pre-Islam Arabs had a tradition of a benefit game. They would slaughter a camel, then hold a draw to distribute meat portions to the participants. The person who did not win any would pay for the camel. The meat would all be distributed to the poor. The event was well advertised and those who refused to participate were ridiculed for being stingy.

Islam, which had complete success in eradicating both social as well as the economic consequences of poverty in a miraculously short period of time, banned the practice. Charity was a duty, performing it for showing off was a sin at par with *shirk*, the sin of associating others with Allah ﷻ. Spending in the path of God was an act of worship, just like prayers and fasting. One's state of affluence or poverty was a test. Spending on worthy projects beyond mandatory requirements was a great act of piety.

At the same time what a person earned through permissible means, was his or hers, and could not be taken away without his free will. On this last point Islamic Shariah is so sensitive that Muslim jurists have declared that if money was obtained for a masjid or other Islamic cause under even subtle pressure, then it must be returned. It is forbidden to use such money.

---

[90] Al-Qasas, 28:78

The Fundraising Dinner

The concept of obligation is also central to Islam's teachings in this matter. Zakat is one obligation, as all Muslims know. It is not the only one. If there is need for a masjid in a neighborhood, it becomes an obligation on all Muslims in that area to raise funds for it. If there is no Islamic school in an area, it is a religious obligation for all the Muslims in that community to establish one. 'The difference between zakat and these obligations," says Mufti Muhammad Shafi, the late Mufti of Pakistan, "is only in that the former has a fixed rate and collection period, while the others are based on need."

The typical Muslim fundraising dinner in North America today does not seem to be informed by these ideas. There is a delicate difference between inspiring others and showing off. This difference normally gets ignored. There is also the element of pressure. Social pressure is used in selling the tickets to the events as well as during the event. In purely economic terms, the whole enterprise is a costly one, with a part of the entry fee going toward the hotel bills.

The normal justification for the practice is that it works. But this may also be a self-fulfilling prophecy. When people have been conditioned to high pressure fundraising techniques, it is possible they will not respond to other requests for donations.

The fundraising dinner has become a two-edged sword. It provides needed funds for many worthwhile projects. Yet it is also distorting our ideas of charity and spending in the path of Allah. We need to take a hard look at it and reform it as it is not a good idea to break one thing while fixing others.

The Myth of Population Crisis

WHEN A HIPPOPOTAMUS gave birth some years ago, the "world famous" San Diego Zoo in California celebrated the arrival for weeks. At the zoo, it is always a joyous occasion at the birth of a panda, a kangaroo, an elephant, or what have you. You are assured that each arrival has enriched the world!

Now contrast this with the birth of a child in, say, Pakistan or Egypt. An unbelievable assortment of "experts" would immediately tell you that it is a moment of great sorrow. That the world is somehow impoverished by the birth of each child.

It is a strange world in which the arrival of a hippo is a blessing but that of a human child is a burden. But it is even stranger that the argument given is economic. A hippo needs 100 pounds of food everyday, compared with a few pounds for human beings. Further it does not produce any of the food it consumes. No animal ever does. Only human beings produce their own food. Lions eat goats and so do human beings. But lions do not breed goats; human beings do. Jay-hawks eat chickens, as do human beings. But jay-hawks do not breed chickens, human beings do. If there were an economic argument against overpopulation, you would think that it would apply to all animals except human beings.

Yet an extremely powerful propaganda machinery has been busy for more than a century in spreading the nonsense that the world faces a human "overpopulation problem." While at the micro-level, the idea had been there in many ancient *Jahiliyah* societies, where people even killed their children so they won't have to feed them, its introduction at the macro-level is recent. It was Reverend Thomas Robert Malthus (1766-1834) who forcefully presented the idea that the human population would always exceed our ability to produce food by some natural law. He opined that population grows in a geometric progression (2, 4, 6, ...) while production of food grows in arithmetic progression (2, 3, 4, ...). Even if there is plenty of food for everyone at the beginning, in two generations there will be more people than the means to feed them. Hence the "population problem."

Malthus based his theory on very limited observations in American colonies and even more limiting assumptions about the progress of agriculture technology. The result is a theory that is totally contradicted by facts. World population has not been growing as fast as his theory suggests; African population is smaller today than it was before the European-led slave trade played havoc with it. The increase in food production, on the other hand, has been much greater than Malthus allowed. World population has more than doubled since 1950, but food supplies have more than tripled. Further, experts believe that if technology continues to improve at today's rate, it will be possible to feed ten billion people on roughly the same amount of land currently devoted to agriculture. As a result of improving crop yields, the area that is used to grow crops—about three billion acres globally—has increased little in the last two decades. Other estimates suggest that the world can support 33 billion people.

While as a work of science Malthus's theory was worthless, it was received enthusiastically for political reasons.

The Industrial Revolution—and capitalism that accompanied it—did not deliver what they had promised. It was expected that as it became easier and cheaper to produce goods, everyone would share in the resulting prosperity; the rising tide would lift all boats. It did not. Capitalism produced a small class of very rich people and a large mass at barely subsisting levels. This made many people to start questioning the system. Karl Marx's was one extreme and misguided reaction to the very real injustices. Other critics differed in their prescriptions but agreed that the issue was political and social justice. Malthus's *An Essay on the Principle of Population* (1798) was avowedly a reply to William Godwin's *Inquiry Concerning Political Justice* (1793), a work asserting the principle of human equality. And its purpose was to justify existing inequality by shifting the responsibility for it from human institutions to the laws of the Creator. As Galbraith would say, his work provided a satisfactory formula for the rich to suffer the misfortunes of the poor. Malthus was a priest in the service of the East India Company and taught generations of its staffers who would then go out and plunder the colonies with the satisfaction that the plight of their victims was the result of "natural laws."

After World War II, when European powers found it difficult to maintain direct control of their colonies, they were concerned that the newly liberated colonies would develop and become economically independent and politically powerful if left to grow on their own. The current population control mafia is born of these concerns. While Malthus's original theory remains discredited, the neo-Malthusians have tried to resuscitate it with "concerns for the environment." Add to it the UN charlatans who are never short of fancy phrases like "reproductive rights." And you get the Population Control Bomb that has been devastating the world.

It did not have to be like this. The clear Qur'anic teachings destroy the basic assumptions of the population control campaign.

The Myth of Population Crisis

$$\text{وَٱلْأَرْضَ مَدَدْنَـٰهَا وَأَلْقَيْنَا فِيهَا رَوَٰسِىَ وَأَنۢبَتْنَا فِيهَا مِن كُلِّ شَىْءٍ مَّوْزُونٍ ۝ وَجَعَلْنَا لَكُمْ فِيهَا مَعَـٰيِشَ وَمَن لَّسْتُمْ لَهُۥ بِرَٰزِقِينَ ۝}$$

"And the earth We have spread out (like a carpet); set thereon mountains firm and immovable; and produced therein all kinds of things in due balance. And We have provided therein means of subsistence, for you and for those for whose sustenance you are not responsible." [Al-Hijr, 15:19-20]

$$\text{وَإِن مِّن شَىْءٍ إِلَّا عِندَنَا خَزَآئِنُهُۥ وَمَا نُنَزِّلُهُۥٓ إِلَّا بِقَدَرٍ مَّعْلُومٍ ۝}$$

"And there is not a thing but its (sources and) treasures (inexhaustible) are with Us; but We only send down thereof in due and ascertainable measures." [Al-Hijr, 15:21]

$$\text{وَمَا مِن دَآبَّةٍ فِى ٱلْأَرْضِ إِلَّا عَلَى ٱللَّهِ رِزْقُهَا وَيَعْلَمُ مُسْتَقَرَّهَا وَمُسْتَوْدَعَهَا ۚ كُلٌّ فِى كِتَـٰبٍ مُّبِينٍ ۝}$$

"There is no moving creature on earth but its sustenance depends on Allah: He knows the time and place of its definite abode and its temporary deposit: all is in a clear Record." [Hud, 11:6]

These verses clearly demolish any basis for use of birth control as a tool of economic policy. How can anyone who believes in the One Creator, Master, and Nourisher of the universe, entertain the idea for a moment, of limiting the number of children for fear of want? Our job is to use the resources wisely and distribute them justly. And Allah ﷻ will provide for all human beings as He has promised and as only He can provide. Muslims are bound by their faith to work to dismantle the obscene birth control establishment in their lands and devote their energies to solving the problems caused by capitalism, imperialism, and neo-colonialism.

Islamic Renaissance?

A CAUSE VERY DEAR to a large number of well-meaning Muslims today is the bringing about of an Islamic renaissance. There are organizations, publications, and web sites devoted to the cherished goal. The discussion is passionate and intense. But is it possible that we are using the wrong label and asking the wrong question? It is essential that we define our goal clearly before we hope to achieve it. Therefore it is worth pondering over the intrusion of the French word *renaissance* in the Islamic discourse. What is meant by "Islamic renaissance"?

Renaissance means revival, and there can be no disagreement about the need to bring about an Islamic revival in the Ummah. But this word also refers to a distinct historic event that took place between the 14th and the 16th centuries CE in Europe. It was a major transformation that subsequently led to Reformation, Industrial Revolution, colonialism, and domination of European powers in the world. The phrase Italian Renaissance and later the European Renaissance was used in the 19th century to refer to this historic period. While some later historians also suggested using the term in a generic sense and talked about other renaissances, it is this specific period of history that most people have in mind when they use the word.

There is a common romantic perception that this produced a new and improved Europe, one that became a beacon of light for the humanity. The reality may be slightly different. So it is important to revisit what was going on then.

During what was later called as the European Dark Ages, the church had developed into a strong oppressive monopoly that demanded blind following. Common people could not read or write, have access to the scriptures, or even understand the liturgies used in church services. It was all Greek to them. Their job was to have faith in the church leaders, to obey them, and to keep on paying them. Needless to say, this usurpation of power did not help the morals of the church leaders many of whom were of less than noble character.

It was a tyranny and it called for a revolt. That came under the banner of humanism. The label is misleading, though. It was not about being more humane; some of the worst crimes against humanity were committed or began during this period—witch hunting, mass slaughter, exploitation at an unprecedented scale, slavery of the worst kind. Humanism meant turning attention away from God to man; from spirituality and morality to physical pleasures; and from the Hereafter to this world.

Breaking away from the crippling grip of the church had its advantages. People could begin to learn how to read and write. They could access the tremendous knowledge stores in sciences developed by the Muslims. Their newly released energy was devoted to the betterment of physical provisions in this world, and there is no denying what it achieved there.

But there was a cost. Corrupt and distorted religious teachings were replaced by corrupt teachings of philosophers and humanist thinkers. Ancient Greek and Latin writings and artifacts of all kinds were dug up and received with the zeal and devotion as if they had been sent by God. It was a rebirth no doubt. But of what? Of pagan antiquity. As a first sign of this paganism interest in the occult, magic, and astrology grew. While some of these practices later ended, superstition remains alive and well today.

As preoccupation with here and now replaced the belief in the Hereafter, the desire for immortality resulted in the interest in paintings and sculptures. These were celebrated and worshipped as works of art. Some years ago when there was a row over the destruction of statues in Afghanistan, it was simply a cry from the angry followers of this pagan religion.

That we find a large number of the renaissance paintings and statues to be nude also reflects on the morality of this "cherished" period. It is the same story in literature and performing arts. In 1599 the Original Globe Playhouse—the place where Shakespeare's plays were staged—was built in London. A Privy Council report about it complained about "Lurid tales… sex and violence, wanton gestures, and bawdy speeches." Sounds familiar? Four centuries later technology has helped spread that cesspool of immorality around the world and in the process the stench has increased a thousand-fold.

The first great political philosopher of the Renaissance was Nicolo Machiavelli (1469-1527). He forcefully advocated that for the prince (i.e. the ruler) any moral consideration should be secondary to getting, increasing, and maintaining power. "It's good to be true to your word, but you should lie whenever it advances your power or security—not only that, it's necessary." Also the prince should know how to be deceitful when it suits his purpose, though, he must not appear that way. Machiavelli was criticized loudly and followed widely—which may have been just fine with him. To this day he is being followed enthusiastically by the political leaders in the West. Anyone wondering why this president or that prime minister did this or that need only read *The Prince* to understand their guiding philosophy.

This then is the true legacy of Renaissance. Writing in the *Washington Report on Middle East Affairs*, Greg Noakes declared: "For a number of modern thinkers, both Muslim and non-Muslim, Islamic society, too, is badly in need of a reformation, or better yet a renaissance, to break religious shackles that keep the Muslim world backward and ignorant. If Muslims are to develop, the secularists argue, Islam must be relegated to the private sphere and rational humanism allowed to guide society."[91] This is the authentic pagan call for an Islamic renaissance, though Noakes, who has been a Muslim since 1989, does not question these assertions.

Our choice of words colors our thinking. No wonder many who are talking about the Islamic renaissance are also trying to get the European experience to guide their efforts. We need to realize that contrary to conventional historiography what happened in Europe beginning in the 14th century was that a dark age ended—and another one began. We are still living under it.

Islam calls for *islah* and *tajdid*—self-reform and renewal. The dictionary may tell us that renaissance can be translated as *tajdid*. But history tells us otherwise. When we talk about *tajdid* and *islah*, we think of the likes of Sayyidna Umar bin Abdul Aziz, Hasan Basri, Imam Ghazali, Shah Waliullah, and Maulana Ashraf Ali Thanvi. When we talk about the Renaissance, the names that come to mind are Plato, Petrarch, Leonardo da Vinci, the Medici, and Machiavelli. And the difference between the two lists is like that between day and night.

---

[91] Greg Noakes, "Secularism and the Islamist Challenge," *Washington Report on Middle East Affairs* September/October 1993, 57

Index

'Aad, 54
"an eye for an eye", 123
"Keep your fingers crossed.", 13
"Knock on wood.", 13
"time is money", 213, 214
"Whose Islam?", 141
18th Amendment, 119
Abbasid, 131
Abdul Rahman ibn Abi Lailah, 69
Abdullah bin Hasn, 216
Abdullah Chakralawi, 40
Abdullah ibn Amr ibn al-'As, 43
Abdullah ibn Maslamah Qa'nawi, 196
Abdullah ibn Mubarak, 172, 173
Abdullah ibn Umar, 180
Abdur Rahman ibn abi Na'um, 217
Abu Abdullah Al-Qurtubi, 307
Abu Bakr, 65, 285
Abu Hurairah, 44, 283
Abu Sufyan, 78
Abul Hasan Ali Nadwi, Maulana, 1, 96
adaab, 209
Adab-ul-Akhbar, 378
adhan, 92, 118, 132
Adler, Alfred, 212
Afghanistan, 361, 388, 413
Ahle-Qur'an. See munkareen-e-hadith
Ain-Jalut, 362
Aisha, 285
akhlaq, 209
Al-Aqiq, 60
alcoholism, 119
Alexander the Great, 365
Algeria, 399
Ali ibn Abi Talib, 172, 335
Al-Jami of Mu'ammar ibn Rashid, 44
Alqami', 362

altruism, 146, 164
Americana, 14
Amr ibn al-A'as, 253
amr-bil-maroof, 243, 245
Anas ibn Malik, 44
Anwar Shah Kashmiri, Maulana, 322
Arafat, 88, 104, 106, 230, 329
arrogance, 209, 211
Ascension to the Heavens. See Mi'raj
Ashraf Ali Thanvi, Maulana, 1, 163, 164, 192, 216, 240, 246, 414
astrologers, 14
ayatul-kursi, 19
Baal temple, 365
Badr, 74, 77, 108, 124
Baghdad, 361
Bahishti Zewar, 216
Bahlool, 219
Balkh, 361
Barelwi, 140
Batani, 11
baya, 248
Bible, 59, 138, 369
bid'ah, 230, 231, 232, 245, 351, 354, 371
birth control, 409
birthday of Prophet Muhammad. See milad
birthdays, 356
Biswa Ijtima, 327
blasphemy, 87
blasphemy laws, 80
Bosnia, 146, 339
Brazelton, Dr. T. Berry, 257
bringing up our children, 279
Britannica, 14, 199, 377
Brown, Stuart, 371
Bucaille, Maurice, 47
Buddhism, 199

Index

Bukhara, 361
Buthan, 60
Cave Hira, 55
charity, 100
Chengiz (Genghis) Khan, 361
Christian Healing Ministry, 86
Christianity, 136, 138, 199
Christmas, 368
Clinton, Bill, 264, 270
Clinton, Hillary, 257
CNN, 227
colonialism, 286, 318, 324, 411
Columbus, 315
confession (Christianity), 175
conspicuous charity, 404
conspicuous consumption, 403
Convention on the Elimination of All Forms of Discrimination Against Women, 294
Coptic calendar, 253
Copts, 253
cost-benefit analysis, 317
Covenant of al Ridwan, 69
crimes of honor, 292
Crossley, John P., 114
Cyrus, 365
darul-iftas, 182
darul-ulooms, 318
death, 217, 220
Dehalvi, Ismail Shaheed, 163
democracy, 325, 392
Deoband, 163
Deobandi, 140
Dershowitz, Alan, 270
dhikr, 206
dhimmi, 124, 130, 131
discipline, 282
Dr. Hamidullah, 34, 44, 46, 59
Dr. Mustafa Azami, 44
Druid, 255, 369
du'a, 107, 108, 109
earthquake in Turkey, 221
East India Company, 408
education, 311, 326
education system, 60
education, secular, 325
Egypt, 398

Einstein, 19
emancipation of women, 258, 259, 264
Empty Quarter of Arabia, 54
Encounter, 23
European Dark Ages, 412
European Renaissance, 286
European Union, 341
extremism, 134, 137
Ezra, 365
family, 193, 276
Farewell Hajj, 88, 105, 229, 230
feminism, 287
feminist movement, 264
fiqh, 246, 307, 309, 323
folklore, 14
France, 399
freedom of choice, 147, 150
fundraising dinner, 168, 169, 402
Gabriel. *See* Jibreel
Galbraith, John Kenneth, 403
Gamal Abdul Nasir, 57
gambling, 226
gender equality, 301
Ghulam Ahmed Pervaiz, 40
ghuloo, 324
Godwin, William, 408
Gorbachev, Mikhail, 271
Gospels, 46
Habib-ur-Rahman Azami, 34
Hadith, 34, 40, 42
Hadith rejecters. *See* munkareen-e-hadith
Hadith scholars, 71
hadith-e-qudsi, 206
Hadith-Jibreel, 191
Hajj, 103, 104, 340
Halaku (Hulagu) Khan, 361
halal earning, 225
Halloween, 255, 356
Haroon-ur-Rashid, 219
Hart, Michael, 171
Hasan Basri, 414
haya, 183, 184, 185, 186, 195, 196, 197, 198, 249, 291
healing prayer, 86
Hearst, William, 377
Heaven, 152, 276

Index

Hell, 152, 156, 163, 238, 274, 276
Helsinki Accords, 400
Herat, 361
Hereafter, 35, 37
Herod Agrippa, 365
hijab, 197, 289, 296, 303, 351
Hinduism, 138, 199
Hoover, Herbert, 14
horoscopes, 14, 15
Hudaybiyah, 69
Hudhayfa ibn Yaman, 124
human rights, 400
human sacrifice, 254, 356
humanism, 318, 412, 414
humbleness, 210, 212
humility, 249
Husain Al-Gabri, 398
husband, responsibility of, 259, 267
I'tikaf, 97
ibada, 96, 97, 107, 108
Ibn Abi Layla, 180
Ibn Battuta, 254, 389
Ibn Jareej, 180
Ibn Taghri Berdi, 254
Ibrahim, Prophet, 11, 12, 104
ifraat, 135
Ihram, 104
ihsan, 191
ijtihad, 114, 181, 295, 334
Imam Abu Hanifa, 202, 334
Imam Ghazali, 414
Imam Malik, 90, 179, 322, 335
Imam Qaffal, 334
Imam Shafi'i, 334
Imam Tahtavi, 334
iman, 95, 191, 193, 196, 197, 244, 391
IMF, 102, 227
indecency in cyberspace, 264
Industrial Revolution, 214, 255, 263, 264, 286, 318, 408
inferiority complex, 212
information age, 190
inhibition, 196
Institute for Qur'anic Research, Munich, 60
intentions, 161, 162, 166, 169, 386, 393
International Community, 110, 132, 146
Iqbal, 286
Iran, 339
Iraq, 146, 339
islah, 414
Islamic awakening, 326
Islamic brotherhood, 328
Islamic education, 182
Islamic feminism, 288
Islamic journalism, 383
Islamic renaissance, 411
Islamic Socialism, 287
Islamophobia, 397, 398, 399, 401
Isra, 175, 364
istighfar, 174, 175, 176, 177
Istikharah, 16
Jabir ibn Sulaym, 236
Jacobs, Louis, 37
Jahiliya, 123, 154, 197, 404
Jane Dixon, 15
Jareer ibn Abdullah, 75
Jerusalem, 175, 339, 364, 365, 367
Jesus, 14, 24, 25, 26, 27, 30, 46, 255, 365, 370, 371
Jewish law, 136
Jews of Arabia, 55, 210
Jibreel, 62, 147
Jihad, 22, 101, 103, 108, 167, 171, 188, 260, 272, 308, 363
John the Baptist, 365
journalism, 317, 378
Judaism, 136, 138
justice, 121
Juvenile Crime Bill, 271
Ka'ab bin Ashraf, 81
Ka'ab bin Ujrah, 69
Kafa'a, 290
karamat (miracles), 248
Kashmir, 146, 339
Kenosis, 2, 24, 26
KGB, 58
khalifah, 124
Khilafah, 325, 388, 389

417

Index

Khilafah, dissolution of, 330, 366
Khubaib ibn Adi, 77
Khwarizm Shah, 362
kibr, 209, 210
kindness to animals, 128
King Faisal Chair in Islamic and Arabic Studies, 114
kinship, 283
knowledge, 308
Knox, John, 24, 25
Kosova, 146, 339
Kurd, 338
Lipset, Seymour, 9
liquor, 226
London Bridge, 254
Los Angeles Times, 113, 114, 257, 264
Lupercalia, 355
Lut, Prophet, 202
Luther, Martin, 175, 263
Machiavelli, Nicolo, 413
Madison, James, 392
Magna-Carta, 105
Maldive, 254
Malik bin Anas, 179
Malthus, Thomas Robert, 407
man, nature of, 145
manners, 209
Manzoor Naumani, Maulana, 1, 32, 87, 169
marital bliss, 266, 269
marriage, 266
Marx, Karl, 408
masajid, 53
Maslow's hierarchy of needs, 317
MBAs, 317
media, 345
media machine, 185, 190, 261, 262, 357
media, reforming the, 140
melting pot, 345
mercy, 127
Messiah, 38
Mi'raj, 91, 147, 364
milad, 73, 76
Mill, John Staurt, 263
miser, 99
Mistah, 285

Mithras, 369
moderation, 135
modernization, 117, 118
modesty, 196
monasticism, 97
money, love of, 99
monotheism, 367
moral training, 313
morals, 209
mosque, 53
Muadh ibn Jabal, 187, 188
Muawiah, 335
muezzin, 118, 119
Mufti Muhammad Shafi, 324, 378
Muhammad ibn Salma, 81
Mujaddid Alf Thani, 95
mujahideen, 22
mujtahideen, 323
munkareen-e-hadith, 40, 322
muraqaba-maut, 248
mureed (disciple), 248
Mus'ab ibn Umayr, 73
musalsal, 126
musalsal bil awwalia, 126
musalsal bil masafaha, 126
music videos, 152
Muslim domain, 389
Muslim Personal Law, 132
Musnad Ahmed, 44
Mussanaf of Abd al-Razzaq, 44
Musta'sim, 362
Mustafa Kamal Pasha, 297
muttaqeen, 200
nadhir, 35
national anthem, 339
National Front (France), 400
nationalism, 341
nation-state, 104, 330, 332, 339, 385, 387, 388
natural disasters, 221, 222
Nebuchadrezzar, 365
Newsweek, 9, 86
NGO, 398
Nishapur, 361
Noah, 351, 352
Noakes, Greg, 413
Nostradamus, 15

Index

Obaidullah Hasan Qirwani, 11
omens, 15
opium cultivation, 119
Orientalists, 71
Owais Qarni, 170
paganism, 106, 256, 354, 368
pagans of Arabia, 55, 86
paintings (Renaissance), 413
Paisa Akhbar, 377
Pakistan, 80
Palestine, 146, 339
Palestinian refuge camps, 149
palm-readers, 14
Paradise, 156, 239
parental authority, 276
parental control, 282
parents, 274
pbuh, 71
peer pressure, 350
Penny Press, 377
Perestroika, 271
Pharaoh, 220
Pickthall, Marmaduke, 132
plague, 224
Plato, 414
pledge (to a *Shaikh*), 248
Pledge of Aqaba, 104
Pope Gregory, 370
population control, 406
pork, 12, 347
pornography, 226, 302
Postman, Neil, 376
Powell, Colin, 270
prayer, 86
Prohibition, 119
prophets, 31, 32, 136
Pulitzer, Joseph, 377
punishment, 36
Puritans, 356
Qadi Abu Asim, 334
Qadi Ibn Abi Lailah, 202
Qadianis, 322
qadis, 124, 303
Qara, 77
Qardawi, Shaikh Yusuf, 62
Qari Abdul Basit, 57
Qarun (Korah), 404
Queen Surraiya, 297

Qur'an, 53, 54, 55, 56, 58, 60,
  61, 62, 63, 64, 114, 115
Qur'an, interpreting the, 63, 64
Qur'an, style of, 55
Qur'anists. *See* munkareen-e-
  hadith
Quraish, 69, 210
racism, 106
Ramadan, 94, 95, 97
reason, 10, 11, 12
reformed churches, 113
reformed synagogues, 113
Renaissance, 317, 373, 411, 413
repentance, 243
Resurrection, 38
Revelation, 11, 12, 148
riba, 140, 226
Rockefeller, Nelson, 403
Rockfeller Foundation, 296
Roosevelt, Franklin, 14
Sa'd ibn Mu'az, 74
Saeed bin Al-Musayeb, 65
Sagan, Carl, 86
Sahifa Hammam ibn Munabbah,
  44
Sahifa Sadiqa, 44
Sahih Muslim, 44
Salahuddin Ayyubi, 366
salat, 90, 92, 93
salat, Hadith rejecters, 45
salat-alan-nabi, 70, 71
Sall-Allahu alayhi wa sallam, 71
Samarkand, 361
Samuelson, Robert, 9
Santa Claus, 357, 370
Satanic Verses, 113
Saturnalia, 255, 369
sawaa-as-sabil, 134
schools of fiqh, 140
Science, 10, 14, 21, 54, 86, 140,
  207, 234, 266, 316, 347
sculptures (Renaissance), 413
self-righteousness, 202, 203
separation of Church and State,
  139
September 2001, 132
Shah Riza Pahlvi, 297
Shah Waliullah, 126, 414

Index

Shaikh (spiritual mentor), 248
Shaikh Ahmed Farooqi, 95
Shaikh, qualities of, 247
Shakespeare, 413
Shariah, 139, 246, 277
Sheikh Izzuddin, 363
Sheikh-ul-Hind Maulana Mahmood-ul-Hasan, 163, 321
shirk, 71, 162, 404
Shu'bah ibn Hajjaj, 195
Siddiqi, Abdul-Hameed, 191
Sihah Sitta, 196
silatur-rahim, 284
sin, 243
Society of Jesus, 23
son of God, 136
Soviet Union, 61, 287, 346, 386
Soviet Union, Qur'an in, 58
Spencer, Herbert, 402
Stonehenge, 369
Suffa, 60
Sufis, 246
Sulaiman, 365, 366
Sultan Baibers, 362
Sumner, William Graham, 403
Sunnah, 39, 81, 102, 106, 114, 139, 159, 229, 230, 231, 235, 245, 246, 323, 334, 379
superstition, 14, 15, 17, 253, 356, 370
survival of the fittest, 402
Tablighi Jamaat, 327
Tabuk, 308
tafreet, 135
tafsir, 65, 288, 309
Taha Hussein, 40
Tahajjud, 193
tahzeebe akhlaq, 249
Taif, 88
tajdid, 414
Taliban, 119
taqwa, 64, 105, 199, 200, 201, 202, 266
Taraweeh, 53, 96
tarbiya, 313
tarot-card readers, 14
tasawwuf, 246

tauba, 99, 100, 101, 174, 175, 200, 243, 307
Tauheed, 103, 108
taxation, 227
taxes, 227
Tazias, 333
television, 60, 152, 198, 280, 286, 322, 348, 355, 403
The Prince (Machiavelli), 413
Third World, 117, 118
thirteen, fear of. *See* Triskaidekaphobia
Thomasius, Gottfried, 24
time, 213, 214
Time, 375
tithe, 101
Titus, 366
tolerance, 114, 131
Trinity, 24
Triskaidekaphobia, 14
Troll, Christian, 23, 24, 26
Turkey, 338
Uhud, 74, 273
Umar bin Abdul Aziz, 414
Umar ibn Khattab, 90, 130, 204, 229, 253, 303, 366, 393
Umayyads, 131
ummah, 15, 60, 72, 89, 103, 104, 105, 127, 129, 134, 150, 179, 230, 242, 245, 321, 339, 340, 341, 379, 388
ummatan wasatan, 134
UN, 259, 388
UN Social Action Program, 152
Universal Declaration of Human Rights, 105, 114
University of Southern California, 113
Urwah ibn Mas'ud al Thaqafi, 69, 78
US Declaration of Independence, 105
USC. *See* University of Southern California
Uthman ibn Affan, 69, 197
Uthul, 77
Valentine's Day, 354
Veblen, Thorstein, 403

Index

vivisection, 128
Waheeduddin Khan, Maulana, 57, 375
wealth, 98
wealth, disparity of, 117
Webster, Daniel, 25
West, 117
western civilization, 255
westernization, 118
wife, responsibility of, 259, 267, 268
Winthrop, John, 139
Wollstonecroft, Mary, 263
women's rights, 133, 300

Woodsmall, Ruth Frances, 296
words, 187, 188, 189
World Bank, 102, 227
WTO, 227
Yahya, 365
Yazid bin Yazid, 65
Yusuf Ludhianvi, Maulana, 346, 347
Zaid ibn Adathna, 77
zakat, 100, 101, 102, 246
Zia Gokalp, 40
Zionism, 106
Zionist, 366